GW00746000

Book 2

OFFICE PRACTICE

Fourth Edition

by SHEILA T STANWELL MInstAM FSCT

Adviser on Commercial and Secretarial Education,
Ministry of Education, Jordan;
formerly with
International Labour Organisation
and United Nations Development Programme

Illustrated by Rosel Woods

EDWARD ARNOLD

© SHEILA T. STANWELL 1976

First published 1964
by Edward Arnold (Publishers) Limited,
25 Hill Street, London, W1X 8LL

Reprinted 1964, 1965, 1966, 1967, 1968
Second Edition 1970
Reprinted 1970
Third Edition 1973
Reprinted 1974 (twice)
Fourth Edition 1976

ISBN: 0 7131 0067 2

The full Course comprises:
    Commerce (4th Edition)
    Office Practice (4th Edition)
    English in the Office Book 1
    Clerical Duties (3rd Edition)
    The Structure of Business
    1001 Answers
    1001 Exercises
    Office Practice Assignments
    Spirit Master Documents

The following Supplements are also available:
    S2 Law and Business: Recent Legislation
    S3 Understanding the Financial Section of Your Newspaper (2E)
    S4 Government Departments, Local Authorities and their Functions(2E)
    S5 Commerce and the State (2E)

Printed in Great Britain by
Butler & Tanner Ltd, London and Frome

Preface to the Third Edition

INCREASING numbers of young people start their working lives in offices. In order to carry out intelligently the duties assigned to them, they should know something about the structure of a firm, the methods and machines in general use, and the information which a junior clerical employee may reasonably be expected to possess.

The results of recent surveys of office methods and procedures have revealed very little consistency in practice, and no standardised methods of handling correspondence or keeping records even amongst firms of similar size in comparable industries. We should like to have omitted, for example, any reference to the registration of incoming and outgoing mail, but from the information available it would appear that many firms still maintain such records. The situation can be described only in general terms, and the frequent use of such loose phrases as 'in some offices' has been unavoidable.

When the first edition of this book was published in 1964 Office Practice could not be numbered amongst the most popular school or examination subjects. In the past ten years, however, as more and more young people have prepared to start their working lives in offices, the subject has increased in popularity to such an extent that it is now offered by almost all the regional examination boards for the Certificate of Secondary Education.

It could be said that Office Practice as a subject achieved academic recognition when an examination for the Teacher's Certificate in Office Practice was established by the Royal Society of Arts a few years ago. One of the newest Office Practice examinations is the Section 3 paper of the Junior Secretary's Certificate which was introduced by the London Chamber of Commerce Commercial Education Scheme in 1972.

As Office Practice examinations have increased in number, so have the syllabuses widened to include a more extensive knowledge of office methods and procedures. At the same time, despite attempts at simplification, office work itself has become more diverse and young people preparing to enter the business world today have considerably more to study than their counterparts who started their careers fifteen or twenty years ago.

In preparing this third edition of OFFICE PRACTICE, the authors have attempted to cater for both these developments. As a guide to those familiar with the first and second editions and to give new readers an idea of the level and scope of the text, it has been thought convenient to itemise here those sections which are new or markedly different from previous editions.

1. In Chapter 1, *Large Organisations and Small Firms*, the work of those divisions which usually involve all new entrants to a firm, such as the Personnel, Salaries and Wages, and Postal or Mail departments, has been described in greater detail; and a section on O & M has been added. The diagram showing the departmental structure of a typical company has been updated.
2. There is a new Chapter 2, *Reception*.
3. Bearing in mind the entry of Britain into the European Economic Community and the hopes of the Metrication Board that all branches of British industry will have adopted the metric system of weights and measures by 1972, the authors spent some time looking at the present and into the probable future position regarding *typewriters* and *paper sizes*. The information which came to light— such as the fact that 'ten spaces to the inch' has been internationally adopted as the formula for computer print-out and OCR*, and the reports from leading paper manufacturers and stationers regarding the continuing popularity of the quarto and foolscap paper sizes—indicates that the time has not yet come for the complete metrication of typewriting display calculations. The simplification which it was hoped the introduction of the A series of paper sizes would bring about has developed instead into a period when there is less standardisation than ever before. Traditional British sizes and the A series exist side by side, typewriters from British firms are now offered in pitch ratios of 11 and 16 in addition to the former 10 and 12 in order

* OCR—Optical Character Recognition.

to gain acceptance in Europe, and European typewriter manufacturers are standardising two pitch sizes 2·1 mm and 2·54 mm (the metric equivalents of 10 and 12 spaces to the inch) so that their machines will be acceptable in the computer industry, an industry dominated by America, which is a non-metric country. The authors have, therefore, listed in Chapter 3 the traditional British and the A series of paper sizes (including the new $\frac{2}{3}$A4 size), as well as the most usual type sizes; and they have included certain recommendations for display typists who may have to work on one of many paper sizes in a machine of inch-based or millimetre-based pitch.

4. The *photocopying* section has been revised to give prominence to electrostatic copiers (both direct and indirect) as they gradually take over from the older processes and as the thermal copiers become more widely used for making stencil and spirit masters.

5. Chapter 4, *The Post Office*, has been decimalised and the information given accords with the most recent Post Office Guide issued in August 1972. Section (b) MONETARY SERVICES has been moved into a new chapter METHODS OF PAYMENT to which has been added a section on cheques and the various payment facilities offered by banks.

6. Chapter 5, *Communications*. The main changes in this chapter concern the recommended layouts for business and official letters. A simplified layout was recommended by the Civil Service Department in August 1969 and this has been adopted by most ministries and government departments. At the same time, as far as business letters are concerned, it seems that a style has evolved which combines the efficiency and modern appearance of left-axis designs and open punctuation with the need for the date to be conspicuous on the right-hand side of the page when handling carbon copies or looking through files. The telephone section has been enlarged to describe transcopiers (the new office machines which create photocopies of documents between one telephone subscriber and another), and to indicate the newest uses for telephone answering machines other than their original and obvious purpose of answering the telephone and recording a message when the subscriber is not there to answer the telephone personally. A section

has been added on the Datel Services of the Post Office which provide facilities for the rapid transmission of computer data.

7. The section on *Commercial Documents* has been enlarged into a separate chapter. Both our shopkeeper, Margaret Mansfield, and her supplier, the Yorkshire Knitting Wool Co Ltd, have had 'face-lifts' to keep up with the times and this is reflected in the new design of their letterheads.

8. The chapter on *Record-keeping* has been enlarged to include sections on stock records, wages records, credit and payment records, VAT records, and visual aids.

9. The Appendix on Decimalisation has been withdrawn and replaced by one on Metrication, which describes the International System of Units and gives examples of the most common metric units, conversion factors, symbols and definitions.

10. A new Appendix includes the examination syllabuses of the regional examinations boards and leading examining bodies; and a new range of examination papers replaces the former Secretarial Duties papers by up-to-date papers in Office Practice.

The book is intended as a guide for pupils preparing for the Royal Society of Arts examination in Office Practice, the London Chamber of Commerce Junior Secretary's Certificate, Section 3, Office Practice, and the Office Practice papers of the regional examination boards for the Certificate of Secondary Education. The contents also cover many items in the Commerce and Secretarial Duties syllabuses of the main examining bodies and will be found useful for the Certificate in Office Studies.

London 1972   Sheila T. Stanwell

PREFACE TO THE FOURTH EDITION

Generally speaking textbooks are revised every five years or so; thus in the normal course of events and bearing in mind the very considerable amount of new and revised material which was included in the third edition, the fourth edition of OFFICE PRACTICE would have been scheduled for publication in 1978.

However, educational publishers and authors are keenly aware not only of the importance of keeping their textbooks up to date, but also of their reputation amongst teachers and students as producers of accurate and reliable teaching material, and of their obligation in this respect to all who read and use their publications.

During the last three years there have been several important innovations such as the introduction of flexible working hours, the metrication of the postal services and new legislation regarding health and safety in offices. It has therefore been decided to produce a revised fourth edition of OFFICE PRACTICE, rather than a reprint, in order that these developments can be included. The main revisions and additions are as follows:

1. In Chapter 1 a section on the law relating to office workers has been added, including the new *Health and Safety at Work Etc. Act, 1974* (HASAWA). HASAWA has been described as "the most important statute for industry and commerce ever to have been passed through Parliament". Directors, secretaries, officers and managers are now personally responsible and liable for prosecution if the Act is contravened as a result of their neglect, and maximum penalties on conviction are a fine not exceeding £400 and/or a term of imprisonment not exceeding two years.

2. In the *Personnel* section of Chapter 1 and in the *Wages Records* section of Chapter 9, the National Insurance sections have been rewritten in accordance with the provisions of the Social Security Act 1973. Under this Act, which came into force on 6 April 1975, the former National Insurance Scheme, including the Graduated Pensions Scheme, was replaced by a Basic Scheme under which National Insurance contributions are calculated as a percentage of gross salary and collected together with PAYE deductions.

3. Chapter 4, *The Post Office*, has been revised in accordance with regulations for metrication of postal services which came into effect on 29 September 1975. All weights are now in grammes and kilogrammes, instead of ounces and pounds, and size limits are in millimetres and metres instead of inches and feet.

4. The commercial documents have been updated in accordance with the reduction of the standard VAT rate to eight per cent, most business communications have been updated and some material has been reset in imitation typescript where this will make it more meaningful to the reader, e.g. examples of addressing envelopes.

5. Appendix II, BRITISH COUNTIES AND THEIR COUNTY TOWNS, has been revised in accordance with the Local Government Act 1972 which was based on the findings of Redcliffe-Maud Report 1971.

6. Appendix III, PRINCIPAL COUNTRIES OF THE WORLD—THEIR CAPITALS AND CURRENCY has been enlarged and Appendix IV, EXAMINATION PAPERS, has been updated.

For the convenience of readers the *Preface to the Third Edition* has been retained as it lists most of the important developments that took place in the few years prior to 1972.

It is pleasing to record that OFFICE PRACTICE is used in schools and colleges in many countries where office staff need to know how to work in English. Both the publishers and myself are always interested to receive comments and suggestions for future editions from readers, both at home and overseas.

Amman, January 1976   Sheila T Stanwell

Contents

x

Introduction

WHAT kind of office do you want to work in when you leave school or college? Do you want to work in a commercial office? In a professional office? In a large firm? In a small office? Do you know the advantages and disadvantages of working in a large organisation? Why do some people prefer working in very small offices? Could you write down a list of twenty or so different kinds of offices?

You may never have seen an office, but if you were asked to describe one, you would certainly mention a typewriter and a telephone. What other machines are to be found in offices? Many people working in offices never touch a typewriter; what kind of work do they do? Does a shorthand-typist spend all

1

her time taking down letters in shorthand and transcribing them? What else does she need to know?

One purpose of this book is to teach you the answers to these questions, so that when you leave your school or college you will have some idea of the work you will be expected to do, and the type of office in which you would like to do it.

Chapter I

Large Organisations and Small Firms

(a) LARGE ORGANISATIONS

If you work in a large organisation, you will find that there is a number of departments each responsible for some function of the firm. In each department information will be received, sorted, acted upon, filed and passed on. This is called 'the clerical function', and it is the responsibility of the head of each department to see that the work is carried out satisfactorily. He will probably be assisted by a deputy or assistant head of the department, and a number of clerks who may be specialists in various aspects of the work.

In addition there will be a typist, shorthand-typist or audio-typist (possibly five or six in a large department) whose duties will be primarily concerned with the passing on of information, mainly in the form of letters, memoranda or reports: in some firms the typewriting for the whole firm is centralised in one department called the Typing Pool. A supervisor is in charge of the Typing Pool, and she will allocate to the typists the work required by the various departments.

In most large organisations new employees spend the first week learning about the different departments of the firm. This is called an Induction Course and enables new employees to understand how the work of the department to which they are eventually assigned fits in with the main function of the firm. A typical Induction Course will include information on the products made by the firm, welfare facilities, arrangements for further education (either in the firm's training school or on a part-time day release system at a college of further education) and sometimes a visit to other branches of the firm or the factory where the products are manufactured.

THE DEPARTMENTAL STRUCTURE OF A FIRM

The following plan shows most of the departmental heads and departments to be found in firms dealing either with production,

3

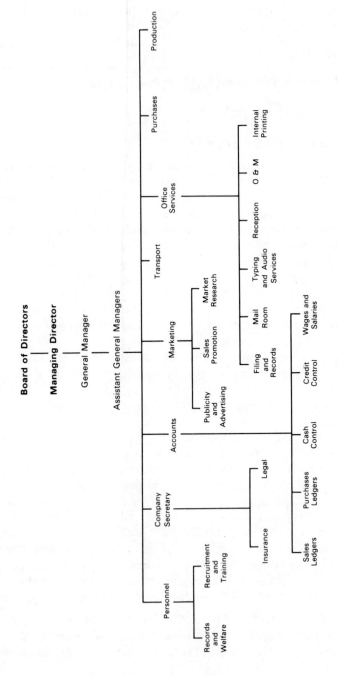

sales or service on a large scale. The names of the departments and their managers will, of course, differ greatly from firm to firm, and according to the nature of the business, but there will in all probability be some of the administrative departments shown on the plan, and all businesses must have departments or people whose responsibility it is to buy, or sell, or to keep records.

We shall discuss some of these departments in more detail, particularly those you will probably be directly concerned with if you are appointed to a junior position straight from school or college, while the work of others is made clear in the consideration of equipment, and in the titles COMMERCE and CLERICAL DUTIES in this Series.

THE PERSONNEL DEPARTMENT (sometimes called the Staff Department) is responsible for the employment of new staff and the head is usually called the Personnel Officer. His work includes: the insertion of advertisements for staff in newspapers and trade journals; contact with employment agencies; liaison with careers masters and mistresses in schools and colleges; interviewing, testing and selection of new applicants; salary scales; promotion; staff records; staff welfare and medical facilities; resignations and dismissals.

When you apply for a post, you will probably be asked to report to the Personnel Department and the Personnel Officer or one of his staff will interview you. If you have not already filled in an application form, you may be asked to complete one as soon as you arrive at the company's offices before the actual interview.

On page 7 you will see an example of a typical application form. Look through it to see the sort of information you are asked to give. Before you start to complete a form, note carefully any special instructions such as USE BLOCK CAPITALS. Now you are at the beginning of your course but by the time you are ready to apply for a post you will probably have taken some examinations. Notice the amount of blank space under EXAMINATIONS PASSED and make up your mind that when the time comes you will not have to leave that space empty. If you are awaiting the results of some examinations, it is quite in order to list the examinations you have taken and write against

5

them 'Awaiting results'. In the Previous Employment sections you may list any Saturday or holiday jobs you have done.

Pay especial attention to the section headed *Referees 1.....* *2..... 3.....* In this context a referee is a person to whom your prospective employer can write asking for his opinion of your ability and character. Before you give a person's name as a referee you should ask for his or her permission; make sure you know the spelling of the names of your referees, complete with any academic qualifications, and their titles and addresses. The communication a referee sends to a prospective employer is called a reference; a reference is a confidential document and not intended to be seen by the person about whom it is written. A testimonial, on the other hand, is a letter, sometimes addressed *To whom it may concern* which a person is usually given, if he asks for it, by an employer or authorised academic official. Generally speaking, a testimonial testifies to a person's attendance, ability, and the way he has carried out his duties whilst working under the authority or supervision of the official who signs the testimonial. During the course of your working life you may accumulate a number of testimonials. Look after them carefully and never send the original documents through the post.

When you go for an interview for a job, take with you your last school report, the result slips of any public examinations you have passed, and any testimonials you may have. At the interview you will be told the work you will be expected to do and in which department or section of the firm you will start. If you are applying for a clerical post you may be given a test in arithmetic, English and general or commercial knowledge. If you are applying for a clerk-typist's, audio-typist's or shorthand-typist's post you will most likely have to do a short typewriting or transcription test, so be prepared for this by taking a pen, pencil, notebook and eraser with you. At some point during the interview you will be invited to ask questions. This is an opportunity for you to show your interest in the firm and in the work which you hope to do.

When the interview is over you should know (*a*) the sort of work you will be expected to do, (*b*) the conditions of service, (*c*) whether you have been offered the job, and if so, (*d*) whether you have accepted it and the date upon which you should report for work. Sometimes the person who is interviewing you may

6

say something like, 'Before making an appointment I've some other applicants to see, so I'll write to you within a few days'. On the other hand, if you are offered the job then and there and you are not sure whether you want it, it is quite in order for you to say, 'Thank you very much, would you mind if I thought about it for a little while and talked it over with my family (or teachers) and let you know definitely tomorrow morning?'

INSTRUCTIONS Please answer each question clearly and completely. Type or print in black ink.	LONGLY GLOBAL PRODUCTIONS Application for employment as				Do not write in this space
Surname	Other names (Mr/Mrs/Miss)				Date of Birth

Education

NAME AND ADDRESS OF SCHOOL OR COLLEGE	FROM	TO	EXAMINATIONS PASSED OR CERTIFICATES OR DIPLOMAS	MAIN COURSE OF STUDY

Previous employment

NAME AND ADDRESS OF EMPLOYER	FROM	TO	POSITION

Knowledge of languages		MOTHER TONGUE				HOBBIES
Other Languages	Very good	Good	Average	Poor		

References: List three persons not related to you, who are familiar with your character and qualifications

	FULL NAME	FULL ADDRESS	BUSINESS OR OCCUPATION
1.			
2.			
3.			

I certify that the statements made by me in answer to the foregoing questions are true, complete and correct to the best of my knowledge and belief.

DATE _____   SIGNATURE _____

For use by Personnel Department only		
MEDICAL REPORT	SCHOOL REPORT REFERENCES	
DATE APPOINTED	DEPARTMENT	POSITION

Most prospective employers will think none the less of you for this, but make sure you keep your word and either telephone or write within the time you have mentioned.

THE TRAINING DEPARTMENT may be part of the Personnel Department, but very large firms appoint a Training and Education Officer who has his own staff to assist with the work of preparing training schemes at various levels throughout the firm. A technical firm may have an Apprentice Scheme for boys who wish to become qualified engineers. Banks and insurance companies have schemes to assist their employees to obtain their professional qualifications. Some firms also have clerical training schemes, through which commercial apprenticeships are offered to boys and girls who wish to study for the National Certificate in Business Studies, and girls are often allowed to attend classes to increase their shorthand and typewriting speeds and to improve their general education.

THE SALARIES AND WAGES DEPARTMENT is responsible for the payment of salaries and wages to all employees of the firm. The word 'salary' is usually used for payment which is made monthly, and the word 'wages' is used for payment made weekly. Monthly salaries are usually paid by cheque or straight into an employee's bank account. Wages may also be paid by cheque, but weekly paid employees more often receive each Friday a pay packet containing their wages in cash. The staff of the Salaries and Wages Department have to understand the Pay as You Earn (PAYE) tax tables, and the National Insurance Contribution Tables so that they can make the necessary deductions from each employee's pay.

The deductions for income tax under the PAYE scheme are made each time an employee is paid. The employee is allowed a certain amount of tax free pay each year and the rest of his salary or wages is liable for tax. The amount of tax free pay depends on the employee's code number which is allocated by the Inland Revenue.

When you start work for the first time your employer will inform the office for his tax district. The tax office will send you an Income Tax Return which you must fill in with information about your personal circumstances, such as dependants and payments for life insurance or mortgage. The form must

8

be returned to the tax office and your code number will be set according to the personal allowances permitted for your circumstances.

Deductions for National Insurance formerly varied according to age and sex, but since 6 April 1975 (when the Social Security Act 1973 came into force) National Insurance contributions have been calculated on a percentage basis related to earnings. For the 1975/76 tax year the standard rate contribution for employees was 5·5 per cent. National Insurance contributions are now collected with income tax under the PAYE procedure.

All employed earners in Great Britain are liable to pay National Insurance contributions. The Department of Health and Society Security issues National Insurance numbers to all contributors so that accurate records can be kept of their contributions. National Insurance numbers consist of two letters followed by six figures and a suffix letter, e.g. AB 123456A. You will probably be issued with a National Insurance number card shortly before you reach school-leaving age. The number on the card will be your National Insurance number and when you start work your employer will need you to tell him what your number is.

Further information about the way employees are paid, the deductions from pay and the documents used in wages records are in Chapter 9, Section (*d*).

THE ACCOUNTS DEPARTMENT is one of the most important in the firm.   The head of the department (the Chief Accountant) and his assistants will probably all be qualified accountants, and it is their responsibility to see that the bills sent to the firm by suppliers are paid promptly and that invoices are sent out to customers who have bought the firm's products.   Much of this work is now done by machines, and we shall learn more about these in the section on Calculating Machinery, Punched-card Accounting and Computers.   At the end of the financial year the records kept by the Accounts Department will be audited and, in the case of registered companies, a copy of the audited accounts and balance sheet for the year will be sent to the shareholders, who will naturally wish to see what profit has been made during the year.

THE SALES DEPARTMENT under the direction of the Sales Manager is responsible for selling the products manufactured by the firm. It will probably be divided into two main sections: one will supervise sales to the home market and the other sales to overseas buyers (called the export market). A large number of salesmen will be attached to the department, and they will spend most of their time travelling in the territory allotted to them, selling further supplies to old customers and trying to get as many new customers as possible. In a technical firm there is frequently a Service Section within the Sales Department, which provides a repair and maintenance service to purchasers of the firm's products.

THE PURCHASING OR MERCHANDISING DEPARTMENT is responsible for purchasing the raw materials and machinery used in the manufacture of the firm's products. Arrangements for the purchase of office equipment, stationery and possibly food for the canteen will also be made by the Purchasing Department. Salesmen from other firms may visit the Head of the Department, who will use his experience to guide him in spending as wisely as possible the money allocated to 'Purchasing' by the Management (i.e. buying the best quality materials at the most favourable prices). The invoices from suppliers are sent to the Purchasing Department where they are checked and often franked with an 'Approved for Payment' stamp after satisfactory delivery of the goods. The franked invoices are then passed to the Accounts Department for payment.

THE ADVERTISING DEPARTMENT arranges the advertising programme for the firm whereby its products are brought to the attention of the public. The Advertising Manager decides how the amount of money allocated to advertising shall be allotted amongst the various advertising media—newspapers, magazines, television, films, coupons and free offers, point of sale displays, hoardings, etc. He must know the advertisement rates charged at any given time and for any given periodical, and the space must be bought and the advertisement designed. He will be assisted in this work by copy-writers and commercial artists. If he decides to advertise on television, he will have to engage the services of script-writers, producers and the large number of people who work together to produce a TV commercial. Many firms employ the services of an advertising agency to do some of this work for them.

THE TRANSPORT DEPARTMENT arranges for the firm's products to be delivered to the customers who have ordered them. Goods may be transported by rail, road, sea or air, and the Transport Manager must choose the safest and most economical means of transport for the various consignments of goods. He will be in touch with the Freight Departments of leading shipping and air companies and know the current freight rates. Some firms own their own fleets of vans, and these will be operated under the supervision of the Transport Manager.

THE LEGAL DEPARTMENT. The legal aspect of the company's business may be looked after by the Company Solicitor or the Company Secretary, depending upon the size of the firm. Some firms, however (such as retail furniture stores or radio and television suppliers), have a Legal Department which not only looks after agreements and guarantees but takes the necessary steps when customers fail to pay. Other legal problems arise in connection with patents, insurance, employees' compensation and motor accidents.

THE POSTAL DEPARTMENT. In a large firm all the mail received is usually opened and sorted in the Postal Department, and distributed throughout the firm by messengers. The messengers also collect the mail from each department and take it to the Post Room where letters are stamped for posting and internal communications are sorted and taken to the addressees. In some organisations the Postal Department is called the Mail Room or Registry. As part of an induction or training course new employees sometimes spend a week or so working in the Registry so that when they start work in the departments to which they have been assigned they will know how the incoming mail has been processed and how the outgoing mail will be handled. As correspondence forms a large part of the work of typists and audio- and shorthand-typists, it is important for them to be familiar with Mail Room procedures.

The person responsible for opening the mail must make sure that any envelopes marked PERSONAL are put on one side, unopened, and sent direct to the addressees, and that 'classified'

11

mail (that is, mail marked SECRET or PRIVATE or CONFIDENTIAL) is correctly handled according to company rules. When the remaining envelopes have been 'tapped' to make sure that the contents fall to the bottom and cannot be inadvertently sliced by the paper knife or opening machine, the envelopes can be slit and the contents removed. Any letters mentioning enclosures must be checked to make sure that the enclosures have been enclosed. A missing enclosure should be noted on the covering letter. Money, cheques and postal remittances must be carefully noted and processed according to company practice. It is usual to stamp incoming mail with the date of receipt; some date stamps also include the time of day. Some organisations keep a record of Incoming Mail. A typical Incoming Letter Book ruling is shown on p. 304. A large work surface is needed for incoming mail. When all the letters have been opened (or otherwise dealt with) and stamped they have to be sorted in pigeon holes, or trays, or folders, for the individual departments or officials.

Another large work surface is needed for outgoing mail. Some firms also record all outgoing mail; a specimen ruling for this is shown on p. 305. Much of the work in the Postal Department is now mechanised. There are machines for opening and sealing letters, and machines for printing stamps on the envelopes—*franking machines* (see Chapter 3, OFFICE MACHINERY, section (*e*) Mail-handling equipment). In spite of these mechanical aids, the staff of the department still need to have a thorough knowledge of postal rates and regulations for sending telegrams and cables, letters and packages to all parts of the world; and the work of the Mail Room is more efficient if the furniture and machines are arranged in a logical sequence to suit the flow of work.

Letters and parcels are usually despatched by one of the services operated by the Post Office (Chapter 4). Urgent parcels can be sent by one of the Post Office Express services or by the Red Star service which is operated by British Rail. The Red Star service is available from Monday to Friday, and Saturdays too by certain services. The parcel, clearly marked with the sender's name and address, the *name only* of the consignee and the name of the destination station, is taken to the Parcels Office of the nearest British Rail station. The consignor nominates the train on which the parcel must travel and pays the parcel fee

When all the letters have been opened (or otherwise dealt with in the case of 'classified' or PERSONAL mail) and stamped, they have to be sorted into pigeon holes, or trays or folders for the individual departments or officials.

plus the Red Star charge. The consignor then telephones the consignee and tells him the arrival time of the train so that the consignee can collect the parcel as soon as it arrives at the destination station.

British Rail also operate a *TCF* ('to call for') parcels service and a *C & D* (collection and delivery) parcels service. TCF packages, which are distinguished by a yellow label, can be collected or the consignor can take them to the British Rail

13

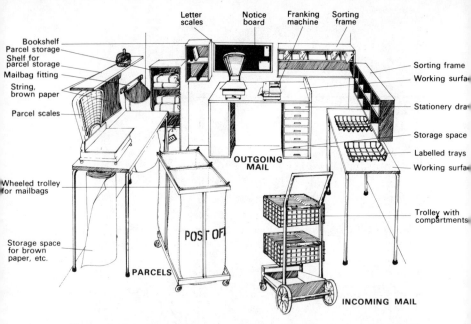

The work of the Mail Room is more efficient if the furniture and machines are arranged in a logical sequence to suit the flow of work.

Sending a parcel by British Rail's Red Star Service

parcels office himself. The package should be addressed to only one person; no postal address should be shown. The package will be held at the destination station until it is collected.

The C & D service covers the whole country. The average journey time is about three days.

CENTRAL FILING DEPARTMENT. Some large firms keep all the files in one Central Filing Department so that the records may be available to any member of the firm. In addition to this some departments may store some of the current paper-work in the department, to be handed over to the Central Filing Department at the end of the year. In other firms each department is responsible for its own filing, and this usually becomes part of the duties of the shorthand-typist. Whichever system (central or localised) is used, one or more of the principal methods of filing will be applied, and we shall study these further in the chapter on filing.

INTERNAL PRINTING DEPARTMENT. Most large firms keep in one department all equipment for reproducing copies of a document. The stencils or master copies prepared by the typists are sent to the duplicating room to be 'run off'. All this equipment will be studied in greater detail in Chapter 3, as many offices have their own duplicating and office printing machines, and shorthand-typists are expected to know how to operate them.

ORGANISATION AND METHODS DEPARTMENT. In the Organisation and Methods Department, called O and M for short, specialists study the way work is done in a firm and suggest any changes for greater efficiency. Such changes may include the replanning of an office to allow easier access to machines or files or the re-designing of documents, such as stock cards, to make the recording and retrieval of information simpler. In factories the O and M Department is often called the Work Study or Time and Motion Department. All these titles indicate that O and M is concerned with the saving of the employees' time and the firm's money.

Each member of staff can practise O and M in his or her own work. Even the most straightforward types of work can be done in a more or less efficient way. When copy-typing, for

15

example, the typist can be more efficient in several ways: by putting the paper to be copied in the most convenient position; by having erasing materials near at hand; by having an adequate supply of paper, flimsy and carbons neatly arranged at her desk; by having her dictionary handy. At times when she is not busy, she can check that all pencils are sharpened, that her desk is orderly and that her typewriter is clean and her ribbon still usable. If O and M is practised by all members of staff continuously, an office can run smoothly and the wasting of time and effort will be avoided.

Many firms that are too small to have a separate O and M Department employ the services of a consultant in organisation and methods. One or more specialists from the O and M consultant come into the firm and study the workings of each department over a period of time. From their observations they make suggestions to the firm about improving its efficiency.

One of the most recent ways in which businesses have sought

An open-plan office. At the Birmingham offices of Flowstream International Ltd, Dexion Office Landscaping has resulted in a 20 per cent increase in productivity.

to improve their efficiency is the adoption of *office landscaping*. In a 'landscaped' office the floorspace is not divided into a number of small rooms or offices; instead, a vast open area is laid out with desks, furniture and equipment. Although the furniture and office machines may appear to be set out in no clear pattern, they are in fact arranged into groups by the skilful use of portable acoustic screens, curtains and tub plants. The groupings are determined by the work-flow of the department. It is claimed that open-plan offices are considerably more efficient than the older type of small partitioned rooms.

Another way in which firms have tried to increase output and efficiency is by the introduction of flexible working hours. This arrangement, which has become known as *flexitime*, permits staff to choose their own working hours within certain limits.

The fixed periods of the day during which all members of staff must be present are known as *core time*. In addition to the core time, every member of staff must work a certain number of additional hours each day or week. These additional hours are flexible and can be varied daily to suit each individual's personal requirements, providing each employee works the total number of daily or weekly hours stipulated by the management.

Example

Total number of weekly hours (5-day week)—35 hours

Core time: 10.00 am to 12.30 pm
            2.00 pm to 4.00 pm

Between 12.30 pm and 2.00 pm, a lunch break of 30 minutes (minimum) is compulsory. Additional hours may be worked from 8.00 am to 10.00 am or 4.00 pm to 6.00 pm.

Thus a person could work as follows:

Monday	8.00 am to 12.30 pm	4½ hours
	1.00 pm to 4.30 pm	3½ "
Tuesday	9.00 am to 1.00 pm	4 "
	2.00 pm to 5.00 pm	3 "
Wednesday	9.30 am to 1.30 pm	4 "
	2.00 pm to 6.00 pm	4 "

Thursday	9.00 am to 12.30 pm	3½	"
	1.00 pm to 5.00 pm	4	"
Friday	10.00 am to 12.30 pm	2½	"
	2.00 pm to 4.00 pm	2	"

Flexitime was originally introduced to ease rush-hour travel by staggering working hours, and to enable married women workers to vary their hours to fit in with their family responsibilities and children's school hours.

However, in addition to these advantages, flexitime has brought about two changes in the behaviour and attitudes of office workers: firstly, employees tend to avoid taking "time off" for medical appointments, preferring to fit in such personal items outside working hours; and secondly, white-collar workers who have traditionally rejected attempts to make them record their arrival and departure times (either by signing a time book, using a time clock or completing a personal time sheet) are now willing to keep records of their hours of attendance.

Some firms also permit employees to accrue time by working sufficient additional daily hours to enable them to take a half day's or a full day's holiday subject to certain limits, such as not more than four half days or two full days per month.

(b) SMALL OFFICES

If you work in a small office, you will find that all the functions carried out by the departments of a large organisation may be performed by very few people (sometimes a dozen or more, sometimes only two or three); in all offices letters are received and answered and filed, information is received, acted upon and recorded, goods are purchased, bills must be paid, money collected from customers and clients, the service provided by the firm or the goods made by it must be brought to the attention of the public and sold, staff must be employed, salaries and wages paid, and the object of all these activities is for the firm to make a profit at the end of the year.

In a small office such as an estate agent's, a builder's, a local newspaper, or the office attached to a small factory, such as a factory making belts or clothing accessories, the owner of the firm will engage staff himself and pay the wages. He will probably employ a bookkeeper or accountant to keep the books and handle some of the firm's financial affairs. There may be one or two clerks between whom will be divided the remainder of the clerical work. The owner may 'get the business' himself or he may employ one or two salesmen. He will certainly employ a shorthand-typist or an audio-typist. A senior shorthand-typist will probably act as secretary to the owner, whilst a junior will take the letters from the remainder of the staff and assist with the routine clerical work.

The following table summarises the comparisons between large and small firms.

LARGE ORGANISATION	SMALL FIRM
1. Employee has very little contact with the management.	1. Employee has direct contact with the owner or manager and some knowledge of the firm's business.
2. Pension scheme for all employees (sometimes non-contributory).	2. Private pension schemes sometimes available for senior employees only, sometimes non-existent.
3. Filing, duplicating, typing and postal services tend to be centralised.	3. Typist types, files and uses duplicator. She opens post in the morning, takes and transcribes letters, keeps postage book and takes mail each evening for posting.
4. Facilities for further education provided.	4. Employees who wish to obtain further qualifications must attend evening classes.
5. Sports clubs and welfare facilities.	5. None provided.
6. Canteen meals at subsidised prices. Morning coffee and afternoon tea provided and sometimes brought to the office.	6. No canteen facilities. Luncheon vouchers sometimes given. Tea usually made by office junior.
7. Fixed pay scale (sometimes tied to age).	7. Salary increase granted according to either (a) progress of employee, or (b) increase in firm's business, or (c) whim of owner; or a combination of any two or all three factors.

19

8. Good opportunities for pro-motion within the firm.	8. Few channels of promotion. Indeed in a very small firm, a junior may 'start at the top'.

A Committee of Inquiry on Small Firms under the chairmanship of Mr. J. E. Bolton was appointed by the then President of the Board of Trade in July 1969. According to the Report of the Committee* known as the Bolton Report, there are $1\frac{1}{4}$ million small firms in the United Kingdom, employing 25 per cent of the working population and accounting for nearly 20 per cent of the gross national product. In farming, financial and professional services, small firms represent approximately 40 per cent of all firms' net output. In addition to this economic importance, small firms also encourage closer personal and human relationships, and the goods they produce bear the marks of better workmanship and craftsmanship than those produced by the mass-production methods of larger firms.

Bearing in mind the social and economic importance of small firms and their gradual decrease in recent years (during the first half of the 1960's approximately 50 000 small shops disappeared), the Bolton Report makes 60 recommendations to assist small firms to develop. The Government's initial response to the recommendations has been (1) to announce a Minister and a Department in the Department of Trade and Industry to look after small firms, (2) to propose amendments to the Companies Act 1967 to exempt small companies from certain legal obligations, and (3) to consider the establishment of Advisory Bureaux for small firms.

(c) OFFICE WORKERS AND THE LAW

During the nineteenth century several Acts of Parliament were passed to provide regulations concerning the working conditions of young people in factories and the government appointed inspectors to make sure that employers complied with the regulations.

Since that time successive governments have felt it necessary to pass laws to safeguard the rights of employees in offices and shops, as well as in railway premises and factories, and today the duties of employers concerning these rights are

* HMSO, Cmnd 4811.

laid down in a number of Acts of Parliament. Legally, it is the responsibility of the Company Secretary or the owner of the business to make sure that the firm complies with its statutory obligations towards its employees, although in practice in medium- and large-sized organisations the actual work of seeing that the conditions are fulfilled (such as those relating to ventilation, toilet facilities, salaries and wages) may be the responsibility of the Personnel Department or the Office Manager.

The Offices, Shops and Railway Premises Act 1963 sets out minimum standards of working conditions for the health, safety and convenience of workers. All employers must register with their local authorities and obtain a fire certificate where more than twenty people are employed, or more than ten are working above ground level. The main provisions of the Act cover a number of points concerning

— the cleanliness of floors, stairs and passages

— lighting, heating and ventilations (the temperature must reach 16°C/60°F within one hour of starting work)

— the entitlement of each person to forty square feet of floor space

— the provision of a certain number of lavatories and basins with running hot water, and the provision of fresh drinking water, chairs, cloakroom facilities and first-aid boxes.

The Industrial Training Act 1964 was formulated to improve industrial training and to spread the cost of training more evenly amongst firms by establishing a levy and grant system. Although the Act does not give employees the right to demand training, it implies that employers have a duty to provide some form of staff training. The Secretary of State for Employment was given power to establish Industrial Training Boards (ITB's) for sections of industry and commerce. The government also has a retraining programme to teach new skills to people whose jobs have become obsolete owing to the increasing use of machines.

The Redundancy Payments Act 1965 requires all employers to pay a lump sum, called a *redundancy payment,* to all employees who are dismissed because they are redundant, subject to certain exceptions such as employees who work less than 21 hours a week. Redundancy pay is calculated on the number of years of continuous service; for example, one week's pay is given for each complete year of service between the ages of 22 and 40, and one-and-a-half week's pay for each complete year of service between the ages of 41 and 65.

The Equal Pay Act 1970 came into force on 29 December 1975 and aimed at eliminating discrimination between men and women in their pay and conditions of employment.

The Contracts of Employment Act 1972 made provisions in three areas

— employers and employees have rights to minimum periods of notice to terminate employment
— employers must give employees written particulars of their main terms of employment
— employers must inform employees of their statutory rights.

The Health and Safety at Work Act 1974 (HASAWA) sets out employers' responsibilities concerning the health, safety and welfare of all employees, particularly including the provision and maintenance of safe machinery and equipment, the provisions of necessary instruction, training and supervision, and the provision of a safe and healthy working environment. Every firm must prepare a written statement of its health and welfare policies and provide details of the organisation and arrangements for carrying out this policy. The document must be brought to the notice of employees and should state the arrangements that are being made, the name of the boss, the particular arrangements which are being made for such hazards as fire-fighting, and the relationships with the local inspectorate. The document should also give information on the employee's role in the new arrangements including details of joint consultation.

The Act also states that every employee has a duty while at work to take reasonable care for the health and safety of himself and others.

22

Under the provisions of the Act, the *Health and Safety Commission* was established on 1 October 1974, and the *Health and Safety Executive* on 1 January 1975. The Health and Safety Commission is responsible for the development and implementation of national policy on health and safety at work. The Commission is appointed by the Secretary of State for Employment; it carries out his directions and keeps him informed of its work. The Commission has powers to approve and issue codes of practice. The Health and Safety Executive is directly responsible to the Commission, and together with the Inspectorate will advise industry and Government and enforce the law. The *Inspectorate* unifies all previous specialist inspectorates, such as those for factories, mines, quarries and explosives. It is responsible for enforcing the requirements of the Act.

The penalty for any person not complying with the regulations or requirements of the Act is a fine not exceeding £400 and/or a term of imprisonment not exceeding two years. Further reading: "The Employer's Guide to Health, Safety and Welfare at Work", by Ewan Mitchell published by Better Books Ltd.

The Employment Medical Advisory Service which was set up by the Employment Medical Advisory Service Act 1972 (EMAS) will continue to function, but the 1972 EMAS Act will be absorbed into the new Health and Safety at Work Act. The Employment Medical Advisory Service is now part of the Health and Safety Executive and gives advice and information on medical problems connected with employment. The Service employs medical advisers who have the right to enter factory premises in the course of their duties; they may also carry out a medical examination of any employee whose health may be in danger because of his work, subject to the consent of the employee.

The Law of Master and Servant is the name given to the body of Common Law affecting employees' rights. Under Common Law an employee (servant) is entitled to a safe place of work, safe access to that place, safe tools with which to perform his tasks and safe work fellows. He is under an obligation to give his employer (master) regular attendance

23

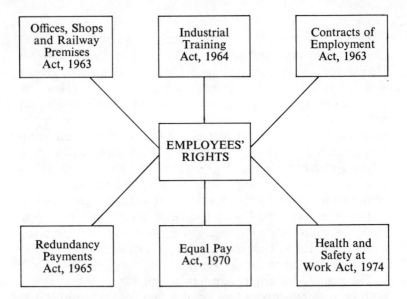

RECENT GOVERNMENT LEGISLATION AFFECTING EMPLOYEES' RIGHTS.
Employees also have rights under Common Law. These rights cannot be affected by Statute and are frequently fallen back upon when statutory protection proves insufficient. The body of Common Law affecting employees' rights is known as The Law of Master and Servant.

according to agreed hours, performance of his work to the best of his ability, and loyalty, e.g. he should not reveal the trade secrets of his master. These Common Law rights and duties cannot be affected by Statute and are frequently fallen back upon when statutory protection proves insufficient, as for example in the case of persons employed as domestic servants in private households who are not covered by the provisions of the Health and Safety at Work Act.

EXERCISES

1. Explain the following words and expressions:
   - (*a*) the clerical function
   - (*b*) an induction course
   - (*c*) part-time day release
   - (*d*) welfare facilities
   - (*e*) a personnel officer
   - (*f*) salary
   - (*g*) PAYE
   - (*m*) advertising media
   - (*n*) point of sale display
   - (*o*) freight
   - (*p*) an audio-typist
   - (*q*) subsidised prices
   - (*r*) referee
   - (*s*) reference

(*h*) an apprentice scheme	(*t*) testimonial
(*i*) audit	(*u*) classified mail
(*j*) the export market	(*v*) office landscaping
(*k*) maintenance service	(*w*) O and M
(*l*) franking	

2. Describe the kind of office in which you would like to work, and give reasons for your choice.

3. Make a list of offices under three headings—Commercial, Industrial and Professional.

4. Study the application form illustrated on p. 7. Write down how you hope to complete the form:
   (*a*) at the end of your present course,
   (*b*) in five years' time,
   (*c*) in ten years' time.
   If you have the facilities to do so, make three copies of the form and complete each one as you have indicated in (*a*), (*b*) and (*c*).

5. You attended an interview yesterday afternoon, were offered the job and have now decided you would like to accept it. Write the letter of acceptance (supply suitable names and addresses).

6. Part of your office duties are to deal with your employer's mail. Whilst you are on holiday the switchboard operator has been asked to take on this part of your work. List your hand-over instructions for her under two headings *Incoming Mail* and *Outgoing Mail*.

7. On p. 6 in the section on THE PERSONNEL DEPARTMENT is the sentence 'When the interview is over, you should know ... (*b*) the conditions of service ....' What is meant by 'conditions of service'?

8.

> JUNIOR SHORTHAND OR AUDIO-TYPIST for TV producer's office. Write for application form and further particulars to: Personnel Officer, Medway Television, Rochester, Kent.

Write a letter asking for an application form and further particulars.

9. Weekly National Insurance and State Graduated Pension

25

deductions may be made from every employee's salary by the employer. Find out:
- (a) the current amount of deductions for each class of person,
- (b) the address of your nearest Department of Health and Social Security Office.

10. The company for which you work wishes to adopt a standard form of application which would be used by all applicants for employment in its offices. Draft a suitable application form.

11. List the services provided by the O & M department of an organisation. Indicate how these services can be of benefit to that organisation. (RSA, OP, II)

12. Describe the steps you would take in wrapping and despatching a parcel from an office. Assume you have use of a franking machine. (RSA, OP, I)

13. Explain the office services which are provided to a business organisation by the following divisions:
- (a) Sales;
- (b) Accounts;
- (c) Planning and Research;
- (d) O & M. (RSA, OP, II)

14. Draw a typical organisation chart for a limited liability company engaged in manufacturing. Describe briefly the duties performed by the senior staff mentioned in your chart. (RSA, OP, II)

15. Explain the importance of each of the following items in handling incoming mail in an office:
- (a) letter opener;
- (b) date stamp;
- (c) enclosure;
- (d) stapler;
- (e) money. (RSA, OP, I)

Chapter 2

Reception

IF you visit the offices of a big organisation, as soon as you walk through the main entrance you will probably see the receptionist. Large firms and public corporations usually have a full-time receptionist whose major job is greeting visitors.

Some firms have a lavishly decorated reception area by the main door rather like the entrance to a smart hotel.

The receptionist and the reception area give a visitor his or her first impression of a firm. Some firms have a lavishly decorated area by the main door rather like the foyer of a smart hotel with occasional tables, comfortable chairs, and magazines, newspapers and company literature displayed for waiting callers.

In many firms the reception duties are handled by the switchboard operator who sits in the reception area.

In many firms the reception duties are handled by the switchboard operator who sits in the reception area.

Smaller firms may not have a specific room for reception. A caller walks straight into the general office where he is greeted by one of the office staff. Sometimes there is a counter with a sign ENQUIRIES.

RECEIVING VISITORS

All firms, large or small, expect their receptionist or the member of staff handling reception duties to be efficient and courteous. As soon as a visitor arrives, he may give his name, his company and the name of the person whom he wishes to see to the receptionist. She should make sure she has heard all of this clearly and can repeat any difficult names. If she is in doubt about pronunciation, she should ask and confirm immediately, then she should quickly note down the caller's name and particulars. A visitor may hand the receptionist his business card which is printed with his name, his company's name and address, sometimes the position which the person holds in the company and sometimes the card also lists the goods the firm sells or manufactures. If a visitor does not give the receptionist his name and the name of his company, he should be asked politely. The visitor should then be asked if he has an appointment, if he has not already said so. Many visitors only call by appointment as it would be a waste of time if they arrived to see someone who was away or at a meeting.

A business card.

In some firms the receptionist is supplied with a list of appointments for each department or each official every day, or she may have been told to put the appointments in a desk diary or appointments book. If this is the case, the receptionist can check her list. If the visitor is expected, the receptionist should telephone the person concerned or his secretary. When a visitor arrives without an appointment, the receptionist should telephone the person concerned to see if he can arrange time to see the caller.

If the person telephoned says he will come down or send someone immediately, the receptionist should inform the visitor and ask him if he would like to sit down, as 'immediately' sometimes means a few minutes. If the person is on the telephone or engaged, she must tell the visitor and offer him a seat, 'Mr. Smith is on the telephone but he should be able to see you in a few minutes. Would you like to take a seat?' Most people do not get too impatient if they are kept informed of the reason for the delay. There may be some company literature or the morning papers in the reception area which the receptionist can offer to the visitor. When there is a long wait, the receptionist could offer the visitor a cup of coffee, if this is company practice.

29

TIME	Management	Personnel	Accounts	Marketing	Transport	O/Services	Purchases	Production
9.00								
9.15								
9.30								
9.45								
10.00								
10.15								
10.30								
10.45								
11.00								
11.15								
11.30								
11.45								
12.00								
12.15								
12.30								
12.45								
1.00								
1.15								
1.30								
1.45								
2.00								
2.15								
2.30								
2.45								

This is a page from an appointments book such as a large organisation might have pre-printed for use in Reception. The receptionist dates the pages chronologically and uses one page for each day. The headings across the top of the columns refer to the departments. When she is told of the appointments, she writes the name of the caller in the column of the department he is visiting; she may also write the name of the official who is expecting the visitor. From this type of diary, the receptionist can see how many visitors are expected at any given time on any day. As each visitor arrives she may put a tick against the name and enter the name and time of arrival in the Reception Register or Visitors' Book.

If the person wanted is out of his office, the receptionist may be able to ask someone to look for him or there may be an intercom system for *paging* people.

'To page' a person means to search for him by calling out his name. The term dates from the time when boys known as 'pages' were employed to run errands; in those days 'to page' meant to summon a person by means of a page who walked round the premises calling out the person's name until he was found. Nowadays paging may be done by electronic radio equipment.

In one system, the receptionist or telephone operator has a microphone through which she can broadcast the name of the person who is being paged. The broadcast is relayed through

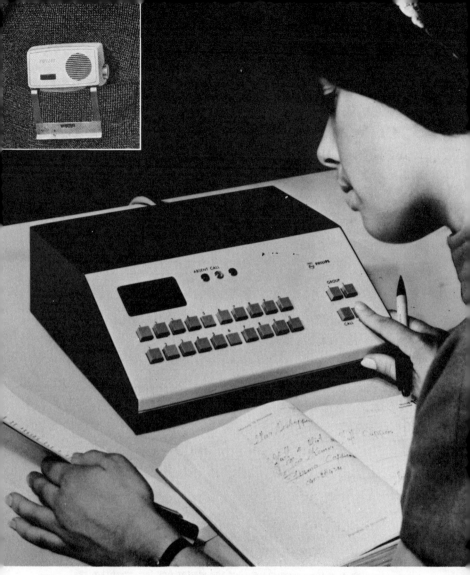

This receptionist is using a Philips IP 90 Inductive Paging System, through which she can contact up to 88 people individually—inset photograph shows a receiver ('bleep') in a breast pocket

loudspeakers installed in suitable places throughout the building. As soon as the person being paged hears his name, he should go to the nearest telephone and contact the operator.

Another method avoids everyone in the building being distracted by the telephonist's paging announcements. With this method each person within the system carries a small receiver with him, usually in his pocket.   A number is allocated to each person and his receiver makes a sound signal, a 'bleep' noise, when the receptionist pages him by pressing the appropriate buttons for his code number on the control panel, and then depressing the 'Call' button.   When the person called hears the sound signal, he presses a button on his receiver and listens to the message which the receptionist is broadcasting to him.

RECEPTION REGISTER						
Date	Name	Firm	Address	Time of arrival	Referred to	Time of departure

A typical ruling for a Reception Register or Visitor's Book.   The receptionist is not always required to enter the time a visitor departs; but in factories or buildings where top secret work is going on it is normally a rule that the official responsible for the visitor conducts him to the main door and then reports to the receptionist that the visitor has left the premises.

In any event, the receptionist should make every effort to find someone to deal with the visitor as soon as possible.   Neglected callers tend to become annoyed and impatient.   The receptionist should always treat a caller the way she would like to be treated if she were visiting a firm.

It is always a good idea for the receptionist to keep a register of the appointments every day.   This visitors' book or reception register is a record of the date, time, name of the visitor, his company, its address and possibly its telephone number too. This could be useful to other members of the firm and helpful to the receptionist herself if the visitor comes again. It is usual to have an additional column in the reception register where the name of the official or department whom the visitor has called to see is entered. Sometimes the times of arrival and departure are also noted.

Smaller firms may not have a specific room for reception.

In firms where visitors walk directly into the general office, there is usually one person who has responsibility for the reception duties, but if she is out of the office or on the telephone someone else must handle callers. If you were working in such an office and you looked up and noticed someone standing by

33

the door waiting for assistance, it would be both bad manners and bad office practice to leave him there unattended. You should greet the visitor as if you were a full-time receptionist. Make a note of his name, company, and the time, and leave this for the receptionist to put in her visitors' book.

In many small and medium-sized firms the receptionist will ask a visitor to find his own way to the office he wants. If a visitor is told 'first door on the left', it does not prevent him from walking into the first door on the right. When a 'lost' visitor wanders into the office, ask politely whom he wishes to see and his name and company. It is good practice to take a visitor who has lost his way to the proper destination, if you can spare a few minutes, and introduce him to the secretary in the correct office.

When a caller arrives at the department he is visiting, he must be greeted and taken to the person he wishes to see. As he has already given his name to the receptionist, the person who receives him should appear to be expecting his arrival and greet him by name, and not waste time by asking for his name and particulars all over again. Depending upon the practice in the department or firm, the visitor may be taken directly to the person expecting him with an introduction, or the member of staff who has greeted him may go ahead to announce his arrival.

RECEIVING GOODS

In firms where there is no reception area, goods and messages are often delivered to the General Office. If the person who handles reception duties is engaged or absent, you may be called upon to take her place. Messages or letters delivered by hand must be sent promptly to the person concerned. You may have to take them yourself or there may be an internal messenger. You should make a note of the arrival and despatch of messages for the usual receptionist.

When goods arrive they may be accompanied by a delivery note which gives a description of the quantity and type of goods sent. A delivery note is used when the goods are delivered by the supplying firm's own transport. When goods are sent by outside transport, they are usually accompanied by a consignment note. This is a document provided by the transport contractor and gives details of the goods being sent (consigned), the name and address of the sender (the consignor), the date of

34

A good appearance helps with the impression you make not only on visitors but also upon all the other people you come across in your business life; and the knowledge that you are 'looking the part' will give you poise and confidence. All the characters in the above illustration have paid attention to their appearance, but do they all 'look the part' against an office background?

despatch, and the name and address of the firm to which they are to be delivered (the consignee).

When you take delivery of goods you will probably be asked to sign for them. If not, ask for the delivery note or the consignment note. Then make sure that the goods really have been ordered by your firm by checking the official order number or the name of the person who has ordered the goods (in the case of goods ordered by telephone). If these details are not shown on the delivery or consignment note, you will have to check with the Purchasing Department if you are working in a large firm. In smaller firms it will be necessary to find the right individual; for example, envelopes are usually ordered by the person in charge of stationery. When you have confirmed that the order is genuine, check the goods against the information on the delivery or consignment note. Mistakes in packing can occur and these are more difficult to rectify when someone has signed for the wrong goods. If the delivery note says, '2 doz. white window envelopes', open the package and check that it does contain 24 white window envelopes. When the quantity and type of the goods match the information on the delivery note, you can sign for them. (If the delivery is a very large one and it would be impractical and too time-consuming to check and examine each item, you may qualify your signature with the words 'Not examined'.) Make sure that the goods are sent to the right department as soon as possible. If the wrong type or quantity has been sent, inform the person who ordered the goods and ask for instructions.

Some offices keep a Goods Received Book in which is entered details of all goods delivered. If this is the practice in your firm, you should enter the delivery in the Goods Received Book or complete a Goods Received Note as soon as you have accepted the goods and before you have them sent to the department or person who ordered them. More information about receiving goods will be found in Chapter 9, (c) Stock Records.

APPEARANCE

The full-time receptionist will pay special attention to her personal appearance. As she is the first person seen by visitors to the firm, her personal appearance forms part of their first impressions of the firm.

When you start work, remember that you too will meet visitors even if reception duties are not part of your official responsibilities, so it is important that you pay attention to your appearance. A good appearance helps with the impression you make not only on visitors but also upon all the other people you come across in your business life; and the knowledge that you are 'looking the part' will give you poise and confidence.

EXERCISES

1. Explain the following words and expressions:

   (*a*) foyer
   (*b*) a business card
   (*c*) an appointments book
   (*d*) a reception register
   (*e*) looking the part
   (*f*) the consignor
   (*g*) delivery note
   (*h*) a window envelope
   (*i*) Goods Received Book
   (*j*) consignment note

2. People are usually concerned about the ways their names are pronounced. A caller at your office will be favourably impressed if you know the right way to pronounce his name—and especially if you can remember it correctly the next time he comes in. Look up the following words in the dictionary and copy next to them an accented and divided phonetic pronunication. Make sure you know what all the marks mean and how the stressed syllables are indicated. Then write out the list of names and write the phonetic pronunciation alongside each name.

Words	*Names*
phthisis	Cadogan
analogous	Belvoir
precedent	Charteris
sanguine	Cholmondeley
hover	Farquhar
desiccate	Slough
orgy	Einstein
pestle	Pepys
trait	Jaeger
lachrymose	Featherstonehaugh

3. Rule a Reception Register page and record the following callers on Thursday, 15 February 1973:

9.40 am   F G Hodd, Capital Carbons Ltd, 4 South Street Hull. To see Chief Buyer. Left 10.05 am.

10.15 am   E S Cole. Job applicant. 62 Station Road, Hull. To see Personnel Officer. Left 11.30 am.

10.20 am   R C Parker. Apex Designs Ltd, Manor Way, Hull. To see Advertising Manager. Left 11.05 am.

11.40 am   E B Schön, Baltic Trading Co, Park Terrace, Hull. To see Sales Manager. Left 12.15 pm.

4. You are asked to take over the receptionist's duties each day from 1.00–2.00 pm whilst she is at lunch. What procedure would you follow if:

(a) A parcel was delivered by the supplier's van driver.

(b) A salesman who had no appointment asked to see the Purchasing Manager.

(c) A caller arrived and said he had an appointment at 1.00 pm with the Company's Transport Manager. You try to ring the Transport Manager's office but can get no reply.

(d) A caller arrived and said he had an appointment with the Personnel Officer. The Personnel Officer says he has no record of an appointment and in any case he will be occupied for the next hour or so.

(e) A visitor arrived and said he had an appointment to see the Publicity Manager at 1.30. The Publicity Manager's secretary says she will come down to escort the visitor to her chief but by 1.40 she has not come and the visitor is looking impatient and cross.

5. You have applied for a post as receptionist/typist and have been called for interview. How would you dress for the interview and how would you try to show the interviewer that you were the right person for the job?

6. Using the words given below write an account to describe the work of a receptionist in a busy office.

telephone	intercom	business card
diary	visitor's book	company literature
messages		(RSA, OP, I)

7. Certain points should be borne in mind when dealing with callers. Mention:

(*a*) three such points in relation to personal calls at the reception desk;

(*b*) two in respect of telephone calls. (RSA, OP, I)

8. (*a*) What do you regard as the main personal qualities and abilities necessary for:

(i) a receptionist;

(ii) a copy typist;

(iii) a filing and records clerk.

(*b*) Explain the advantages of a typing pool. (RSA, OP, II)

Chapter 3

Office Machinery

THERE has never been a greater need for efficiency in business than there is today. All kinds of businesses must employ modern methods in their offices. The raw material of an office is information, and the responsibility of an office is like that of a clearing house, receiving and sending out information, processing and storing facts in various forms. Mechanisation of office work has come about as a result of the need for greater speed and accuracy, and the characteristic picture of modern office efficiency is the successful integrated use of machines and equipment into what are called 'systems'—that is, the machines and equipment are grouped or linked to achieve a higher value of usefulness.

As the number of machines available increases rapidly, we can only indicate which machines a junior office worker might be expected to operate, describing briefly the purpose and method of operation of some of the more commonly found machines. Some are simple and can be operated after a few minutes' instruction, whereas others require many months of specialised study.

We begin by studying typewriters; although not all office workers are typists, nearly all office workers require the services of typists and should, therefore, know something about the varieties of machines available and the kind of work they can produce.

(a) TYPEWRITERS AND TYPEWRITING

First of all there are a few 'vital statistics' common to all typewriters which should be learnt by all typists, and also by those who may at some time have to call upon their services.

These statistics concern line-spacing, that is, the number of vertical line-spaces on a page, and pitch, which means the size of type on a typewriter, i.e. the space occupied by a single letter, figure or character. The figures vary according to the size of the type and the dimensions of the paper, and govern the paper size chosen for any particular piece of work, especially work involving the display of statistical tables.

PAPER SIZES

Until about twenty years ago, typewriting paper was manufactured in sizes which conformed to British Standard specification BS 730 originally issued in 1937. The most common sizes used in typewriting were foolscap, 8 in × 13 in,* and quarto (4to) 8 in × 10 in, which when halved provided an additional two sizes, sexto (6to) 6½ in × 8 in and octavo (8vo) 5 in × 8 in. These sizes, together with two larger sizes (draft, 10 in × 16 in, and brief, 13 in × 16 in, convenient for legal and accountancy work) catered for almost all office requirements in the United Kingdom and other countries of the Commonwealth.

During the 1960's typewriting papers and letterheads cut to conform to the International Paper Sizes,† referred to as IPS, were introduced into the United Kingdom and an increasing number of British firms adopted them.

Recommendations for the IPS series were made by the International Organisation for Standardisation (ISO), the international authority on standardisation responsible for the international development of industrial and commercial standards in almost every field of technology. It is supported by 55 nations, including the United Kingdom and the United States of America. The members of ISO are the national standards organisations; the United Kingdom member is the British Standards Institution.

The IPS system is based on a series of three sizes all of the same proportion, called Series A, B and C. The most widely used is the A series, IPS-A. The B series is intended for larger items such as posters and wall charts. The C series is a series of dimensions used for envelopes. Details of the sizes were published in British Standard specification, BS 3176, in 1959 and the A series were adopted shortly afterwards by several large British firms and professional institutes. The IPS-A series of sizes are based on the A0 sheet which has an area of approximately one square metre (841 mm × 1189 mm, approx.

---

* In quoting paper sizes, the first measurement refers to the width.
† *Paper at Work*, No. 4: 'International Paper Sizes', Spicers Ltd.

33·1 in × 46·8 in). The A1 size equals half of A0 (that is, an A0 sheet folded in half with the two short edges brought together), similarly A2 is half of A1, A3 is half of A2 and so on. The relationship between the sizes is shown by the charts below.

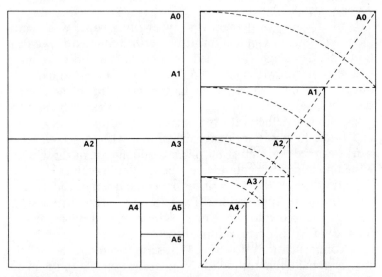

All International Paper Sizes are based on a perfectly proportioned rectangle whose longer side is the diagonal of a square, i.e. in the ratio $1 : \sqrt{2}$ or $1 : 1·414$. Following this formula, one can continue to halve the longer side or double the shorter one and still retain the same proportions. There are three ranges of sizes, prefixed A, B and C. The most widely used for general printing and stationery is the A series. The basic size A0 is approximately one square metre (841 mm × 1189 mm). A1 is exactly half A0 in the same proportions, A2 is half A1, and so on. (The B series is used for posters and larger pieces of print, the C range for envelopes.) The diagram on the left demonstrates the constant ratio between the long and short sides of each successive division. As the basic A0 size is one square metre, the substance is readily expressed in grammes per square metre (gsm or g/m^2). The diagram on the right shows how halving each size produces a division in exact proportion to the original sheet.

When it was suggested that the United Kingdom should adopt the metric system a further British Standard, BS 4000: 1968, was prepared under the authority of the Paper Industry Standards Committee. The compilers of BS 4000 recognised that there would necessarily be a period of transition from British to metric paper sizes but hoped that this would not last beyond the end of 1970. Although an increasing number of

British firms adopted the IPS-A series of sizes during the 1960's, paper and envelope manufacturers are still manufacturing Imperial sizes because of the big demand for them. In 1972 a representative of a leading paper manufacturer said that in his opinion, 'Imperial sizes will be with us for a long time yet, although they will slowly be ousted by the International sizes. Meantime, we and the Stationer must make and stock both to meet all tastes'. And an article in *Management in Action*, June 1972, included the passage:

> 'Having set out to simplify, standardise and reduce the variety of sizes of paper with which we have to cope, we shall, instead, have added even further to the existing range. If you have any doubts about this, then try checking your own stationery store. *We* find that we have all sizes, shapes and descriptions of paper, including British, International and American. Worse still, the problem is creeping into stocks of such things as binders, files, folders, notebooks, forms and envelopes. Presumably we shall eventually find ourselves with a similarly diverse range of filing cabinets and equipment to house all of these different varieties of paper.'

The author had hoped to omit all references to foolscap, quarto, inches and so on in this edition, but in view of the present situation it has been thought useful to list all paper sizes, British, International and American,* in both metric and British units. Two further developments should be noted.

1. Owing to the American influence in the computer industry and because the United States is a non-metric country, computer stationery will remain non-metric. *Computer print-out* has been internationally adopted on a non-metric basis, viz. six lines to the inch down and ten characters to the inch across the page.

2. The A sizes did not suit every office need. There were communications for which A4 was too large and A5 too small; so a new size, similar to the old sexto, has been introduced.

* American quarto, $8 \cdot 75 \times 11$ in (223 mm $\times 282$ mm) is used in the United States, in overseas offices of American companies and in large international organisations like UNESCO.

43

This is known as $\frac{2}{3}$A4, 210 mm × 198 mm, approx. 8·3 in × 7·8 in. Short letters can be attractively displayed on $\frac{2}{3}$A4, which folded singly exactly fits into a DL envelope (see p. 78).

PAPER SIZES*

Designation	Inches	Millimetres
A Series		
A0	33·1 × 46·8	841 × 1189
A1	23·3 × 33·1	594 × 841
A2	16·5 × 23·3	420 × 594
A3	11·7 × 16·5	297 × 420
A4	8·3 × 11·7	210 × 297
$\frac{2}{3}$A4	8·3 × 7·8	210 × 198
A5	5·8 × 8·3	148 × 210
A6	4·1 × 5·8	105 × 148
A7	2·9 × 4·1	74 × 105
A8	2·1 × 2·9	52 × 74
A9	1·5 × 2·1	37 × 52
A10	1·0 × 1·5	26 × 37

Designation	Inches	Millimetres
B Series		
B0	39·3 × 55·7	1000 × 1414
B1	27·8 × 39·3	707 × 1000
B2	19·7 × 27·8	500 × 707
B3	13·9 × 19·7	353 × 500
B4	9·8 × 13·9	250 × 353
B5	6·9 × 9·8	176 × 250
B6	4·9 × 6·9	125 × 176
B7	3·5 × 4·9	88 × 125
B8	2·4 × 3·5	62 × 88
B9	1·7 × 2·4	44 × 62
B10	1·2 × 1·7	31 × 44

	Designation	Inches	Millimetres
British	Foolscap	8 × 13	205 × 330
	Quarto (4to)	8 × 10	205 × 254
	Sexto (6to)	8 × 6·5	205 × 165
	Octavo (8vo)	5 × 8	127 × 205
	Memo	8 × 5	205 × 127
	Draft	10 × 16	254 × 410
	Brief	13 × 16	330 × 410
American	Quarto	8·75 × 11	223 × 282

* When quoting paper sizes, the first measurement mentioned is the width of the paper. A chart, *Office Practice Chart No. 2—Sizes of Notepaper—British and International*, is available from Teaching Aids Ltd.

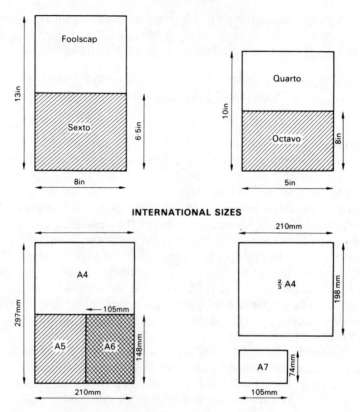

BRITISH SIZES

INTERNATIONAL SIZES

Use A4 for long or medium length letters.
Use ⅔A4 for medium length letters.
Use A5 for short letters.
Use A6 for postcards.
Use A7 for compliment slips, business cards.

LINE-SPACING

This indicates the number of lines of type measured vertically, i.e. down the page. There are six line-spaces to the inch on all British typewriters, most Continental typewriters and all business machines. Some Continental machines were manufactured with a ratio of two line spaces to the centimetre, but now that six line spaces to the inch has been internationally agreed for computer print-out, most typewriter manufacturers will conform to this ratio.

To calculate the number of line-spaces available on any sheet of paper, simply take the length of the sheet in inches and multiply by six; round off to the nearest whole number.

Example: A4 = 11·7″ long   11·7 × 6 = 70·2   Answer: 70
A5 =   8·3″ long   8·3 × 6 = 49·8   Answer: 50

The term 'pitch' is used to indicate the size of type on a typewriter, i.e. the space occupied by a single letter, figure or character. When a typist plans a piece of columnar display such as a large complicated schedule composed mainly of columns of figures, she has to calculate the number of character spaces available across the width of the paper she is using. This is done either by multiplying the width of the paper by the pitch of the machine, or by dividing the width of the paper by the size of one character. It is obvious that the same units must be used for this calculation—you cannot multiply 210 mm (the width of A4) by 10 (the British pica size which gives ten letters to the inch) and expect to get the right answer.

Before the introduction of IPS into the United Kingdom and the decision to change to the metric system of measurements (which it is hoped will have been adopted by all industries by 1975) the two most common British pitch ratios were:

1. British pica   10 letters to an inch
2. British élite   12 letters to an inch

These figures used in conjunction with quarto and foolscap paper—both 8 in wide—enabled typists to calculate simply and quickly:

Pica pitch and 8 in wide paper   10 × 8 = 80
Elite pitch and 8 in wide paper   12 × 8 = 96

During the 1960's as the A series of paper sizes was increasingly widely adopted and as attempts were made in some schools and colleges to metricate British pitch ratios, a complicated situation developed which was further confused by the supply of increasing numbers of typewriters of Continental manufacture. Traditionally, metric type sizes are quoted in millimetres, the commonest being 2 mm, 2·12 mm and 2·54 mm.*

For a typist using a Continental 2 mm pitch machine it is a simple calculation to divide the width of A4 (210 mm) by 2: the answer—105—is the number of spaces available across an A4 sheet used in a Continental élite machine.

As we noted in the section on paper sizes, whilst IPS is being used by more and more businesses in the United Kingdom, British quarto and foolscap are still being manufactured and used in many offices; and ten spaces to the inch has been internationally adopted as the standard pitch for computer print-out. These two facts, added to the implications of Britain's entry into the European Economic Community, have caused some interesting developments:

1. Typewriters of European manufacture will in future be built with either a 2·12 mm or 2·54 mm type size; 2·12 mm pitch resembles élite and 2·54 mm resembles pica. The larger size will enable the machines to be used for computer print-out.

2. An increased range of type sizes (10, 11, 12 and 16 pitch) is available on machines marketed by British companies but 'The use of 6 lines to the inch for vertical spacing and 10 and 12 characters to the inch (see BS 2481), has an almost world-wide acceptance and certainly is predominant for office machines and computer printers, and present international standardisation discussions recognise this established situation'.†

RECOMMENDATIONS

It is hoped that the following recommendations will enable typewriting calculations to be made as quickly as possible using any paper size in any machine:

* 2·6 mm character pitch is a standard introduced in Germany. It is intended to be the nearest to 2·54 mm (10 to 1 in pitch). There are typewriters imported from West Germany with this pitch in use in the UK. However, because of the requirements of OCR, most standard typewriters will be 2·54 mm (10 to 1 in) pitch with portable typewriters at 2·6 mm. The differences are small but could be meaningful over the width of a page.

† *Metrication in Business Equipment*: A **beta** 'Guide to Users' publication. Published by Business Equipment Trade Association.

1. Using British pitch machines, multiply the decimalised inch width of the page by the inch based pitch ratio.

Example   A4 paper in an 11-pitch machine
Paper width 8·3 in
$$8·3 \times 11 = 91·3 \quad \text{Answer: 91 spaces}$$

2. Using Continental pitch machines with IPS paper, divide the width of the paper by the size of the type.

Example   A4 paper in a 2·5 mm pitch machine
Paper width 210 mm
$$210 \div 2·54 = 80·2 \quad \text{Answer: 80 spaces}$$

3. Using Continental pitch machines with British paper, take the metric width of the paper and multiply by one of the following:

Continental pica   3·8 characters per centimetre
Continental élite   4·5 characters per centimetre   *or*
Continental élite   5·0 characters per centimetre

Example   Quarto paper in a Continental pica machine
Paper width 205 mm (20·5 cm)
$$20·5 \times 3·8 = 77·9 \quad \text{Answer: 78 spaces}$$

LETTER AND LINE-SPACES AVAILABLE ON SOME COMMONLY USED PAPER SIZES WHEN USED WITH BRITISH PITCH TYPEWRITERS

The calculations demonstrate the application of the following recommendations:

1. Decimalise all paper depths in inches and multiply by six; round off to the nearest whole number.

2. When working with the 'A' series or American quarto *and British pitch machines*, multiply the decimalised inch dimensions by the standard British ratios; round off to the nearest whole number.*

* The recommendation to use *decimalised inch* dimensions when working with *British pitch machines* is based on the simplicity of the arithmetic and the accuracy of the answers.

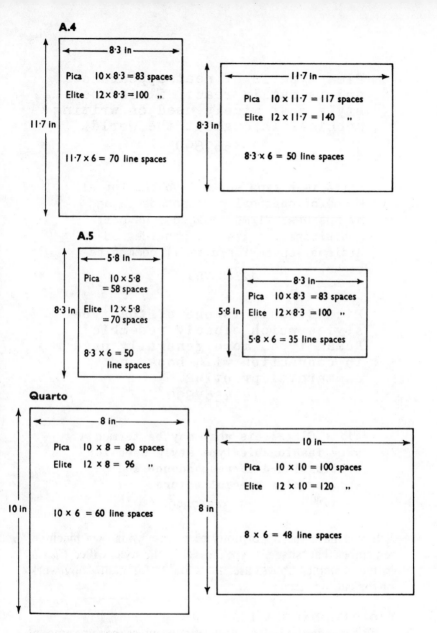

A.4

8·3 in

Pica 10 × 8·3 = 83 spaces
Elite 12 × 8·3 = 100 „

11·7 in

11·7 × 6 = 70 line spaces

11·7 in

Pica 10 × 11·7 = 117 spaces
Elite 12 × 11·7 = 140 „

8·3 in

8·3 × 6 = 50 line spaces

A.5

5·8 in

Pica 10 × 5·8 = 58 spaces
Elite 12 × 5·8 = 70 spaces

8·3 in

8·3 × 6 = 50 line spaces

8·3 in

Pica 10 × 8·3 = 83 spaces
Elite 12 × 8·3 = 100 „

5·8 in

5·8 × 6 = 35 line spaces

Quarto

8 in

Pica 10 × 8 = 80 spaces
Elite 12 × 8 = 96 „

10 in

10 × 6 = 60 line spaces

10 in

Pica 10 × 10 = 100 spaces
Elite 12 × 10 = 120 „

8 in

8 × 6 = 48 line spaces

TYPE FACES

The terms 'type face' or 'fount' are used to indicate the style of type. It would be impossible to give examples of all the different styles, but the examples below give some idea of the various type faces available.

49

Pica type is of neat appearance
and is easily read; it is the
style most widely used on writing
machines throughout the world.
1234567890

Elite is a type style favoured for all
kinds of personal correspondence and
by business firms engaged in export
activities, as its use provides additional space for airmail communications. 1234567890

Pica Classic is one of the type
styles which closely resemble
Roman type, more generally used
in connection with book and
commercial printing.
1234567890

Elite Classic is what may be termed a
very fashionable type style used for
distinguished correspondence and
writing of a special nature.
1234567890

If you have the opportunity to choose your own machine,
remember that 'shaded' type faces (like the styles called *Classic*
in the examples above) are not suitable for multi-copy work
or for cutting stencils.

PROPORTIONAL SPACING

With standard type faces each letter occupies the same amount
of space; for example, the letter 'i' occupies the same amount
of space as the letter 'w' although the actual width of the letters
is quite different. However, machines are available with
proportionally spaced type; on these machines the space
occupied by each letter varies according to the size of the letter.

A specimen of a proportionally spaced typeface is shown in the illustration. All lower case characters, punctuation marks, and the space bar, operate on one unit of space, except for j, i, l, f and t, which have $\frac{1}{2}$ space value, and m and w which have $1\frac{1}{2}$ space value. All the upper case characters are worth $1\frac{1}{2}$ units

This is a sample of proportionally
spaced type as produced by the Avon
typeface of the Underwood "Raphael"
typewriter which is described in the text.
It will be seen that different letters
occupy different units of space producing
a pleasing impression.

Other typefaces have different proportional spacing.

In this example, the proportional spacing has been used in conjunction with a
justified right-hand margin. It will be
seen that the space between the words
has been varied in order to achieve this
effect. Because letters take up different
units of space, the variation of spacing
between the words is not so apparent as
it would be on standard typeface.

Type displayed in this way is often
used to type plates for off-set printing
in order to produce a neat and professional
appearance.

Proportional spacing. The space occupied by each letter varies according to the size. All the lower case characters, punctuation marks, and the space bar, operate on one unit of space, except for j, i, l, f and t, which have $\frac{1}{2}$ space value, and m and w, which have $1\frac{1}{2}$ space value. All the upper case characters are worth $1\frac{1}{2}$ units, and the apostrophe has a space value of one unit.

and the apostrophe has a space value of one unit. Proportional spacing is often used in conjunction with a justified right-hand margin, that is a margin which is as even as the left-hand one. You will find more information about margin justification on pp. 53 and 55.

STANDARD TYPEWRITERS

When we speak of a 'standard' typewriter, we generally have in mind a machine fitted with a 'Universal' four-bank keyboard, a tabular mechanism, choices of line-spacing (1, 1½, 2, 2½, 3),

four ribbon positions (top, centre, bottom and stencil) and a carriage length from 30 to 35 cm or 11 to 13 in. All manufacturers claim special features for their machines, and it would be impossible to enumerate them all here. By 'special features' we mean, for example, the interchangeability of the platen and carriages (see illustration on p.54), a notebook holder incorporated in the front cover (see photograph above), and also the inclusion of a dual ribbon device.

The dual ribbon device on this Hermes Electric Varia is used to switch over from fabric to carbon ribbon for work requiring particular care such as executive correspondence and the preparation of offset masters. This device also allows typing in three colours or use of white corrector ribbon.

MARGIN JUSTIFICATION

You will probably have noticed that the right-hand margin of most typewritten matter is uneven, whereas the right-hand margin of printed material is as even as the left-hand one. When both margins are even the page presents a very pleasing appearance, and many firms like to be able to produce pamphlets and booklets and important letters with justified margins. There are several ways of doing this.

On certain machines in use (manual and electric), there is a mechanism which enables the right hand margin to be automatically justified. When the required length of writing line has been decided, a draft is typed. At the end of each typewriting line a reading is taken from a scale. When the final copy is typed, the justification lever is used in conjunction with the previous readings, and the right hand margin may be automatically justified.

Another way in which justified margins can be produced in some machines is in conjunction with proportionally spaced type. With standard typewriters each letter occupies the same amount of space. Proportionally spaced type varies the space occupied by each letter according to the size. The margins on such machines may be justified by varying the spaces between the words, but the proportionally spaced type causes these spacing variations to be less obvious than they would be in work produced on standard typewriters.

53

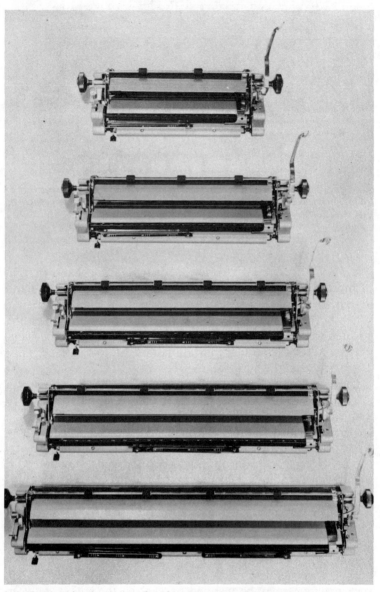

Interchangeable platens reading from the top: 12 inch for standard correspondence; 15 inch for legal and professional work; 18 inch for insurance and shipping work; 22 inch for balance sheets; 26 inch for special forms and returns.

THE JUSTOWRITER produces justified copy automatically, after the first draft, by means of paper tape. During typing the Justowriter punches a code (to represent the text) into paper tape and at the same time records the variation of spacing needed to make all lines of type of equal length. When the tape is 'played-back' the lines are all of equal length.

Although more expensive than normal typewriters, machines which can give straight right-hand margins are invaluable for setting up masters for reproduction by spirit, ink and offset litho methods, and for any kind of displayed work which can be undertaken in an office.

The ambitious typist may have the opportunity of learning to use a composer, which has basically a typewriter keyboard, and is described on pages 65 and 66 as part of the equipment of a reprographic department.

PORTABLE TYPEWRITERS

As their name implies, portable typewriters are light-weight machines which can easily be carried from one place to another.

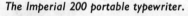

The Imperial 200 portable typewriter.

They take up very little room and are of great use to people who have to travel in connection with their business, e.g. reporters, journalists and representatives. The machine illustrated is only 7·5 cm high and weighs 4 kilogrammes. Some portable machines have no tabular mechanism, and this is a point to query if you are thinking of buying one.

LIGHTWEIGHT TYPEWRITERS

Lightweight machines such as that shown below are used for correspondence in many offices and possess nearly all the features of a standard model. They weigh approximately 10 kilogrammes as opposed to 17·5 kilogrammes for a standard model and are considerably cheaper.

ELECTRIC TYPEWRITERS

Most typewriter manufacturers are now producing electric machines, in which the typebars and carriage return are motivated by electricity. A small electric motor is fitted inside the machine, and a movement of the key of 3 mm is sufficient to set the typebar mechanism in motion. The carriage is returned by depressing a key on the keyboard. Since variable finger pressure on the keys does not affect the momentum with which the typebars hit the paper, electric typewriters produce work of a very uniform appearance. An indicator at the side of the machine increases the typing impression, and, with

(Above) An electric typewriter. Note that there is no carriage return lever.

(Below) The IBM 72 electric typewriter has no typebars. The characters are mounted on a small typing head, like a metal ball, which moves across the platen when the keys are pressed. The typing head can be changed quite simply for another bearing a different type style.

suitable paper and carbon paper, up to twenty legible carbon copies may be obtained at one typing. By extra pressure on the space-bar, hyphen and underscore keys, a repeat action is obtained.

VariTyper segments

The VariTyper is a type composing machine with power assisted keyboard. Type faces are easily interchangeable and are available in a wide variety of printer's type styles and sizes. This machine is also able to rule forms and justify margins automatically.

The VariTyper has no typebars. The characters are moulded on a segment and the segment swings to the printing point for the appropriate letter when a key is struck.

The segment can be changed at any stage during the course of a piece of work; hence several different styles of type can be produced on the same document.

AUTOMATIC TYPEWRITERS

Automatic typewriters are operated by electricity; they type prepared information in a predetermined display style, without a typist striking the keys, returning the carriage or operating any of the standard machine controls.

The first automatic machine, the 'Auto-Typist', was made in America in 1932. The philosophy underlying the invention of the machine was that people react more favourably to typed originals (that is, letters which are clearly 'top copies' written personally to the addressee) than they do to duplicated or printed letters even though an attempt may have been made in a second operation to 'match-in' the name and address of the addressee.

As it is impossible to distinguish between a letter typed by an automatic typewriter and a letter typed by a typist, automatically typed 'originals' were found to be very effective when used for chasing overdue accounts, for direct mail advertising and for 'begging letters'. In addition to their effectiveness, automatically typed letters have three more advantages: 1) they can be produced at speeds ranging from 145–180 words per minute, 2) they need never be checked, and 3) they are very much cheaper to produce than hand-typed letters.

All automatic typewriters have a standard keyboard and, in addition, a number of function or control keys which are used to give the machine instructions such as STOP, START TAPE, EDIT, PARAGRAPH. The function keys may be on the keyboard or front casing of the machine, or they may be built into a separate control unit.

All the machines work on the same general principles:

1. The information to be automatically typed must first be 'recorded' or fed into the typewriter and the machine must be given the necessary display instructions. This is done by

putting a sheet of paper in the machine and typing in the normal way; as this is being done, the whole document is being recorded —some machines record on punched paper tape, others use punched cards or magnetic tape or magnetic cards.

2. The machine is instructed to print-out the recording which is then checked for accuracy, edited and amended as necessary.

3. The 'record'—whether tape or card—is numbered, indexed and stored for future use.

4. When needed, the tape or card is threaded or put into the control attachment of the machine, top copy paper with carbon pack as required is inserted into the machine and the START key is depressed. When used for producing individual letters, the typist types the date (although some machines can be 'programmed' with the date at the start of the day's work) and the name of the addressee; she then instructs the machine to start. The machine can be programmed to stop so that the typist can type in variable information such as numbers or sums of money in the body of the letter, and then continue automatically when instructed.

The keyboard of the Flexowriter 2345 automatic typewriter. This machine is operated by punched paper tape; the standard model has a 16 in carriage and types out error-free work at 145 words per minute.

The 2301 Flexowriter.

uses punched paper tape

or edge-punched cards

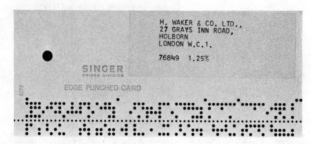

or tabulating cards

The 'Auto-Typist' is controlled by a roll of perforated paper, similar to that used in old-fashioned pianolas. Standard paragraphs are typed automatically when the appropriate control buttons are pressed.

Following the success of the 'Auto-Typist', the next range of machines was marketed under the name of 'Flexowriter' and used edge-punched cards or punched paper tape or tabulating cards. Some of the newest machines use magnetic tape or magnetic card.

The IBM Magnetic Card 'Executive' typewriter consists of a modified Magnetic Card 72 typewriter and a Magnetic Card Unit which contains the read/record mechanism. The first typing of a document is recorded as it is typed on a reusable magnetic card—one track for each line of type and a card for each page. Alterations and amendments are made by locating the line and word on the magnetic card and then typing in the revision. Corrections may be overtyped. The machine types out the final copy at 180 words per minute.

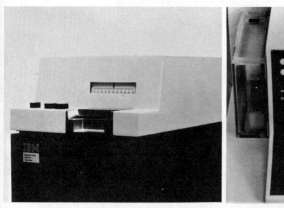

The IBM Magnetic Card Control Unit (left) and the Magnetic Tape Control Unit (right).

The printing mechanism of automatic typewriters is either the IBM golfball or the conventional type-basket with typebars. Typebars are claimed to be strong and reliable, and are used on moving carriage machines so that the positioning of the carriage can be programmed to form part of the machine's functions. On the other hand, a golfball printer is usually quicker than a type-basket machine; it is also quieter because there is no carriage movement. The outstanding advantage of the golf-ball head is that it can be changed very easily to give a variety of type-faces; this factor is of great importance in some display work.

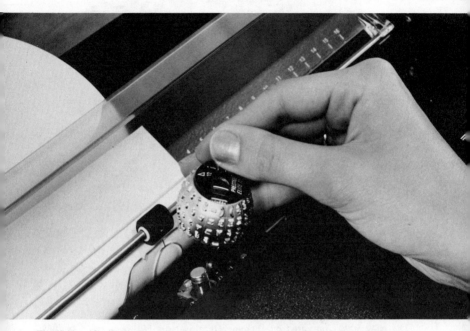

The IBM golfball which can be changed to give a variety of typefaces. Ribbons are supplied in a closed cartridge so that ribbon changing is quick and clean—carbon or fabric ribbon may be used. The machine is fitted with a transparent hood which reduces the noise of typing.

Most manufacturers of automatic typewriters offer a variety of carriage lengths and the machines can be fitted with either carbon or fabric ribbons.

The most recent applications of automatic typewriters are in connection with computer input and print-out, the standardisation of business correspondence, and cold-type composing.

Computer input and print-out. Information is fed into computers in a form which they can 'read'. This information may be in the form of the punched tape, punched cards, or magnetic tape produced by automatic typewriters. Output from computers is in a similar form and can be fed into automatic typewriters and typed out. (For further information, see Chapter 3, (*j*) COMPUTERS.)

The UDS 5000, marketed by Ultronic Data Systems Ltd, comprises an IBM golfball electric typewriter, a tape punch and a tape reader. It can be programmed to produce all sorts of commerical documents and correspondence. The output tape can be used for computer input.

Standardisation of business correspondence. It is claimed that up to 70 per cent of business correspondence is made up of repetitive phrases and similar sentences. When the correspondence requirements of a firm have been assessed by analysing and collating the contents of the filed carbon copies over a given period, it is possible to prepare a series of standard paragraphs, which can be fed into an automatic typewriter. A series of handbooks are produced which contain the printed paragraphs, indexed by number and divided into subjects and sub-sections; for example, under the heading 'Accounts' might be sub-sections for reminders, covering-letters and so on. Instead of dictating full letters, the dictater gives his secretary the numbers of the relevant paragraphs together with any details which have to be inserted manually.   It is claimed that this method reduces the total cost of each letter from £1 to $9\frac{1}{2}$p.*

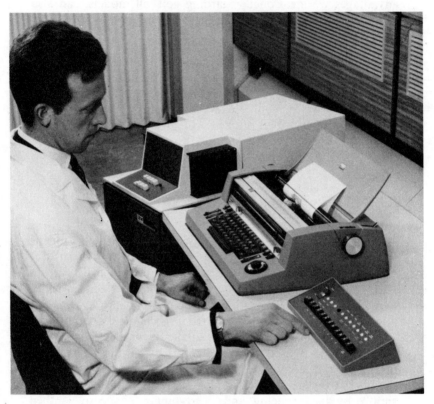

The IBM Selectric Composer.

Cold-type composing.   The expression 'cold-type composing' means the preparation of copy from which offset-litho plates may be produced; it is used to distinguish this method from the conventional 'hot metal' composing for print, and from the processes of photo-composition on to sensitised material.

The function of the IBM Selectric Composer is not as with other automatic typewriters to produce 'original letters' or

* 'In Europe—The automatic typewriter', *Management in Action*, July 1970.

correspondence; its function is to produce displayed copy in a wide variety of printing founts for plate-making in Inplant Printing departments. The following text was produced by the IBM Selectric Composer, which, in addition to the other advantages we mentioned regarding golfball models, can also produce copy with a justified right-hand margin.

All characters in fine printing are proportionally spaced. Composer spacing is based on a 9-unit system with each character taking a prescribed number of units. This proportional-spacing feature, plus the capacity for changing type styles, sizes, and weights, enables you to produce high-quality copy for reproduction.

The IBM Selectric Composer allows a space of 9 units for the widest letter. (Other composers and photo-composers use an 18 unit basis.) In both systems, each letter regardless of its style and shape, must be designed to fit within a certain width in relation to the 9 or 18 unit maximum width. Thus the quality and appearance of print from mechanical composers is very high, and even more precise in alignment and colour when magnetic tape is used to record information and instruct the machine. The copy is produced visually (hard-copy) and on to the tape at the same time, corrections being made at this stage simply by back-spacing and overtyping. The copy is then checked or printed-out. Further or extensive corrections can be made by producing a second tape which is automatically merged with the first during the process of composing. Print out can be on to paper or translucent masters or negatives from which plates are made. The whole process is very quick and error-free, because once the initial keyboarding and correcting phase is passed, the whole process including display is an automatic one. Operators do not have to type the final form of the master material. Nevertheless, familiarity with the typewriter helps operators to learn the new technique more easily.

CARE OF THE TYPEWRITER

1. Keep the type faces clean by daily brushing with a stiff brush. Always clean the type face before and after typing stencils.

2. Use a long-handled soft brush to remove dust from the type basket, the ribbon vibrator and other exposed parts of the machine. Dust the platen.

3. When typing on a single sheet of paper, protect the platen by using a backing sheet.

4. Move the carriage clear of the type basket when erasing so that no eraser dust falls into the machine.

5. Cover the machine at night.

6. To move a typewriter, first lock the carriage by moving both margin stops to the centre and then place your hands under the base of the machine before lifting it.

TYPEWRITER ACCESSORIES

There are many accessories which help the typist to work more quickly and more accurately. Copyholders assist accurate line-by-line reading when complicated schedules are being copied. They range from the most simple devices for keeping a shorthand notebook upright and easier to see, to the more complicated machines which move automatically down the printed page, guiding the typist's eye to that part of the material to be typed. These appliances are sometimes controlled by the foot.

Continuous stationery attachments enable paper or forms to be fed into the machine from the rear and torn off as completed. The next sheet remains at the appropriate position for typing and the carbon paper remains interleaved. Because these sets of stationery are made up beforehand, there can be no chance of error in the number of documents typed, or of the only too usual mistake of putting a carbon sheet 'the wrong way round'. The stationery is printed to the choice of style of the user, and is made in different colours to indicate the purpose of each document typed. Continuous stationery can be numbered consecutively, for reference.

Another group of accessories increase the variety of work the typist can produce on an ordinary typewriter. Two of the

An electrically operated copyholder. A footswitch moves the line-guide so
that the typist need not move her hands away from the keyboard.

The Economatic attachment can be fitted to the standard typewriter for the feeding of continuous stationery.

Sets of continuous stationery like this one by Alacra are made in a variety of sizes with carbon interleaved, or in Duscript carbonless and N.C.R. papers.

The BTA Universal Carbon ribbon Attachment Mk I fitted to a portable typewriter.

most useful are the BTA universal carbon ribbon attachment and the 'Typit' range of symbols.

The BTA carbon ribbon attachment enables almost any typewriter, portable, standard or electric, to produce the crisp black print-like typing normally associated with only the expensive carbon ribbon electric machines or machines fitted with a dual-ribbon device (see p. 53). The BTA unit consists of a carbon ribbon container which has an adjustable ribbon guide arm with four slots and a universal take-up spool. The attachment holds one roll of 960 ft 8 mm carbon ribbon and is fixed to the typewriter by means of a permanent adhesive pad. The carbon ribbon is fed through the appropriate slot on the guide arm and ribbon carrier in the normal way and wound on to the universal take-up spool on the left. When the spool becomes full, it can be lifted off, emptied over the waste-paper bin and the carbon ribbon wound on again ready for further use. The BTA attachment can be fitted to almost any typewriter. The switch-over from carbon ribbon to fibre ribbon for typing less important documents is quick and simple.

The Typit attachment enables the typist to type symbols, letters or characters which are not included on the keyboard of her machine. This avoids the necessity to spoil the professional

√ Radical 75	V Radical 2112	∛ Cube root 2116	√A Sq. root of -1 76	⌒ Arc 108
∠ Angle 65	⊿ Angle 2110	*cos* Cosine 2427	° Degree 113	| Single parallel 83
‖ Double parallel 84	⊥ Equilateral 85	⊥ Perpendicular 788	℄ Centerline 800	∞ Infinity 114
∞ Large infinity 1080	*ln* Natural log. 1066	*f* General function 491	∇ Nabla 86	∂ Nabla (var.) 814
∇ Modified nabla 812	∮ Integration of quaternion 119	W Vector 584	ℋ Hamiltonian 376	J Jacobian 811
∂ Partial 87	′ Prime 77	″ Double prime 78	‴ Triple prime 79	∝ Varies 104
ℵ Transfinite cardinal no. 373	ℬ Steradiancy 592	Ⅎ 530	∨ Or (Logic) 366	∧ And (Logic) 367
∪ Union 369	∩ Intersection 370	⋃ Union (Lge.) 1039	⋂ Intersection (Lge.) 1040	⊂ Is contained 371
⊃ Containing 372	⊆ Contained or equals 617	⊇ Containing or equals 618	¬ Not 374	∈ Membership 375
∋ Reversed membership 393	⇔ Bi-conditional 407	⇒ Implication 408	→ Yields 80	← Is formed from 81
♂ Male 142	♀ Female 143	⌒ Eye 144	ℳ Minim 141	℥ Ounce 167

Some examples of Typit symbols.

A Typit typebar being held in position while the typist strikes any key on the keyboard. The rising typebar forces a special slide into the platen and prints the special symbol on the Typit.

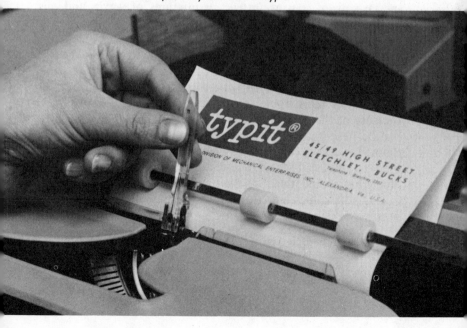

appearance of technical documents by inserting special signs and symbols by hand.

Typits are simply separate typebars. The standard typebar guide on the typewriter is replaced by a special type guide which will hold and line-up the typits. When the modification has been fitted (a simple operation which does not affect the normal operation of the typewriter) the typist selects the appropriate Typit symbol and inserts it into the modified type guide. She then strikes any key and the rising typebar forces a small slide into the platen, thus printing the special symbol. This operation takes only a few seconds. Each Typit is marked on the handle for identification. There are more than 1000 typit symbols available for both 10 and 12 pitch machines, ranging from scientific and mathematical letters and symbols to symbols used in pharmaceutics, astronomy, meteorology and linguistics.

TYPISTS' SUPPLIES

*Carbon paper** is available in many qualities and weights. The choice of weight depends upon the number of copies to be taken at one typing; a lightweight carbon paper used with lightweight ('flimsy') typewriting paper gives up to twelve legible copies.

The newest type of carbon paper is made by applying a special solvent coating instead of mixtures of waxes and oils. The solvent coating can be compared to a very thin layer of sponge saturated with ink; it can be applied to either a film or a paper base. With conventional carbon paper, the carbon coating breaks away at the point of impact, but when a typebar strikes a solvent-coated copying sheet ink is squeezed out and immediately redistributed from the surrounding area when the pressure of the typebar is released.

Film-base solvent carbons are extremely durable and it is claimed that they can be used over a hundred times before being thrown away. The solvent coating prevents smudging and off-setting, while the film base prevents curling, tearing and treeing; the copies are clean to handle and easy to erase. The sharpness of the image depends upon the density and hardness

* The term 'carbon paper' is used colloquially to refer to either conventional carbon-coated paper or solvent-coated film or solvent-coated paper.

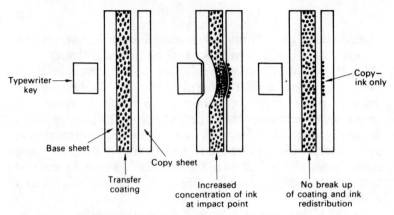

This diagram shows how the ink is redistributed at the point of impact when a typebar has struck a solvent-coated sheet.

of the solvent coating. A hard coating gives a greyer but sharper image which is easier to erase than a really black copy.

The number of clear copies which can be made at a single typing, called manifolding, depends upon several factors:

a) The weight of the carbon paper; more copies can be made using a thin, lightweight copying sheet.

b) The weight and finish (smoothness) of the typewriting paper, both original and copy; the lighter the paper, the more copies can be taken.

c) The hardness of the typewriter platen or cylinder—a hard platen enables more copies to be taken.

d) The hardness and density of the carbon or solvent coating; a hard coating gives a greyer but sharper image which is easier to erase than a really black copy.

e) The typist's touch—a firm, staccato touch is best for multi-copy work.

f) The action of the typewriter keys; most typewriters have an adjustable pressure control gauge and the harder the keys hit the platen, the more copies can be taken at one typing.

g) The style of type face or fount; sharp type styles such as 'standard' pica and élite give better copies than 'shaded' styles.

h) The thickness of the ribbon material—the finer the ribbon, the more copies can be taken. A fine ribbon also gives sharper copies.

73

Ribbons are made from carbon-coated paper or film (carbon ribbons) as well as cotton, silk or nylon (fabric ribbons).

Carbon ribbons are used only once. They produce crisp, black impressions similar to normal printing. Carbon ribbons are also used to create offset-litho plates by direct typing, and they also produce excellent originals for copy by heat, photo or dyeline processes. There are several special carbon ribbon attachments which enable the typist to switch-over quickly and simply from carbon ribbon to fabric ribbon (see pp.53 and 70). Carbon film ribbons are also supplied on twin spools for easy ribbon changing.

As the ribbon acts as a buffer between the typefaces and the paper, the sharpness of the typed characters depends upon the weave and thickness of the fabric; the finer the fabric and weave, the sharper the imprint.

Silk ribbons are very strong and absorbent. They produce a fine impression and last longer than cotton ribbons.

Nylon ribbons are considered to produce work of excellent appearance. As the nylon fabric is very fine, it is possible to wind more on the spool, so instead of the usual 10 metres, nylon ribbons can be made up to 20 metres long, so the typist does not have to change the ribbon so frequently.

When ordering typewriter ribbons, it is important to state: the make and model of the typewriter to ensure that the correct spool is supplied; whether a carbon-paper, carbon-film, cotton, silk or nylon ribbon is required; the degree of inking—this varies from light to medium and medium-heavy; whether a bi-chrome (two colour) or single colour ribbon is needed, and the length (if silk or nylon).

Erasers. Typewriting erasers are made in various shapes and styles to help the typist to erase neatly and quickly. Some typists prefer the circular erasers, others prefer the pencil-stick types.

Erasing shields are made of thin plastic or metal, with differently shaped 'cut-outs'. The shield is placed over the incorrect letter or letters so that the typist can use the eraser without spoiling any of the surrounding words.

Correction papers. These enable typing mistakes to be corrected without using an eraser. One side of the correction

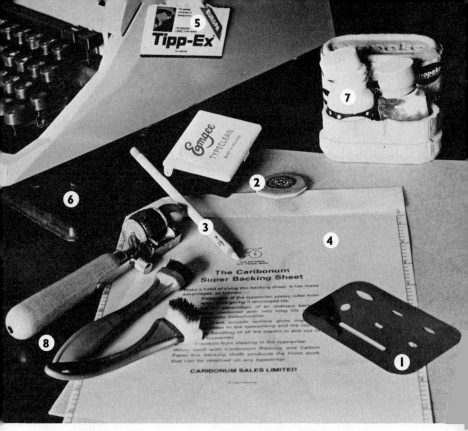

A selection of typist's aids.　1. Erasing shield.　2. Circular eraser.
3. Pencil-stick eraser.　4. Backing sheet.　5. Correcting paper.　6. Typewriter mat.　7. Correction fluid.　8. Brushes and type cleaners.

paper is coated with a white substance.　The strip of correction
paper is placed between the ribbon and the original over the
'wrong' letter, with the coated side against the paper.　The
'wrong' letter is then typed again; this covers the mistake with
the white substance, thus blanking it out.　The correct letter is
then typed.　Different correction papers are normally used for
correcting top copies and carbons.　This method of error correction is completely satisfactory only when the original (top
copy) paper has the same degree and shade of whiteness as the
coating on the correction paper.

Backing sheets are used to place behind the paper in the
machine.　They protect the platen from wear and improve the

quality of the copy by preventing the platen from absorbing some of the force of the impact of the typebar. They also help the typist assemble and feed in the 'carbon pack' as they have a turnover flap at the top which acts as a stay. Backing sheets marked with scales showing lines of typewriting and inches along the left-hand and right-hand edges help the typist to gauge when the work is approaching the bottom of the page. The use of a backing sheet marked off with line or inch calibrations is the best way to make sure that the upper and lower margins are uniform on successive sheets of typing.

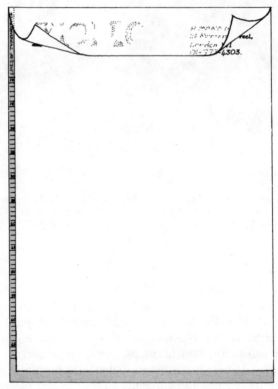

A backing sheet, calibrated in lines of typewriting along the left-hand edge and in inches along the right-hand edge.

Platen restorer. Sometimes the platen of a typewriter becomes pitted. This gives an uneven surface and produces poor carbon copies. A platen restorer in an aerosol container

76

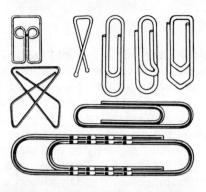

   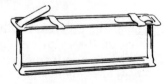

A selection of paper clips, letter clips and paper fasteners.

is now available. The typist inserts into the machine a sheet of paper wide enough to cover the full width of the platen, but sufficiently short to expose the front surface of the platen. Then, using the sponge from the top of the restorer, the typist rubs across the platen, turning it until the whole surface has been treated. Badly pitted platens may need several applications, but if the restorer is used regularly on new machines the platens should keep in good condition. The platen restorer can also be used on other machines, such as teleprinters and accounting machines.

OFFICE SUNDRIES

Under this heading are grouped a large number of small items used in offices, such as paper and letter clips and stapling machines.

Paper clips and letter clips are usually made of metal and are used for holding together small quantities of paper.

Stapling machines. There are many different kinds of machines used to staple sheets together. Some are very small (pocket or miniature staplers), others are more suited for thicker work ('heavy duty' and 'long-arm' staplers). Nearly all staplers work on the same principle and give two alternative fastenings:

1. *Permanent fastening*: In this position the prongs of the staples are pinched inwards.
2. *Temporary fastening*: In this position the prongs are pressed outwards to produce a 'pin' which can be easily removed.

Temporary and permanent fastening.

The main difference between the various makes is in the loading of the strips of staples. There are three main types: rear loading, top loading and front loading.

There is a small gadget called a 'staple remover' which takes staples out of papers without tearing them.

78

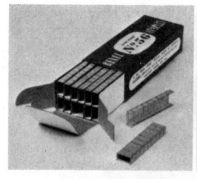

Staples.

Rear Loading Stapler.

Top Loading Stapler.

Front Loading Stapler.

1. REAR LOADING: Access to the loading platform is from the back of the machine, and usually involves first removing the push bar and mechanism.
2. TOP LOADING: Loading of this type of machine is effected on the open-book principle, the top of the body hinging back to allow access.
3. FRONT LOADING: As the term implies, the loading platform is released by a touch of a button, and then projects forward, allowing one or more strips of staples to be placed in position. The platform is then pushed back, and locks automatically in position.

N.B—Methods (1) and (2) are considered preferable, as there are no loose parts involved which can become lost or damaged.

Here is an illustration of a group of office sundries. Can you name them, and say when and how you would use them?

Envelopes are manufactured in a variety of styles, shapes and sizes.   There is also a wide choice of quality (weight), cutting and sealing.

Styles and sizes.   Envelopes are divided into two main styles:

1. *Banker* envelopes have the opening on the longer side.
2. *Pocket* envelopes have the opening on the shorter side.

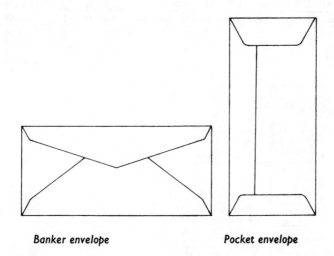

Banker envelope   Pocket envelope

Envelope measurements are quoted to indicate the length and breadth in relation to the opening.   The first measurement is that which is at right angles to the opening, or in other words, the last measurement indicates the side which opens.   Thus a 9 in × 4 in envelope would be a pocket envelope having the opening on the shorter, the 4 in, side.

There is a British Standard specification covering envelope terms and sizes* which suggests that with increasing emphasis on the standardisation of national specifications to conform with international recommendations, traditional British sizes will eventually be superseded by the sizes recommended by the International Organisation for Standardisation.   As we noted when discussing paper sizes (see p. 41), ISO size B is recommended for envelopes.

* British Standard 4264:1967, Specification for Envelopes for Commercial Official and Professional Use (Terms and Sizes).

As you can see from the following illustration an A4 sheet—
slides flat into a C4 envelope without folding
fits into a C5 envelope folded once
fits into a C6 envelope folded twice.

Envelope size symbol	Size in	Size mm	Envelope size symbol	Size in	Size mm
C3	$12\frac{3}{4} \times 18$	324 × 458	B6	$4\frac{7}{8} \times 7$	125 × 176
B4	$9\frac{7}{8} \times 13\frac{7}{8}$	250 × 353	C6	$4\frac{1}{2} \times 6\frac{3}{8}$	114 × 162
C4	$9 \times 12\frac{5}{8}$	229 × 324	C5/6 (DL)	$4\frac{1}{4} \times 8\frac{5}{8}$	110 × 220
B5	$7 \times 9\frac{7}{8}$	176 × 250	C7/6	$3\frac{1}{4} \times 6\frac{3}{8}$	81 × 162
C5	$6\frac{3}{8} \times 9$	162 × 229	C7	$3\frac{1}{4} \times 4\frac{1}{2}$	81 × 114
B6/C4	$4\frac{7}{8} \times 12\frac{5}{8}$	125 × 324			

One of the most popular envelope sizes is the C5/6 (DL)—
usually designated DL—which will take an A4 sheet folded
twice, and a $\frac{2}{3}$A4 sheet or an A5 sheet folded once.

Shapes, cuttings and gummings. Envelopes may be bought in various shapes and cuts and fastenings. Here are some examples:

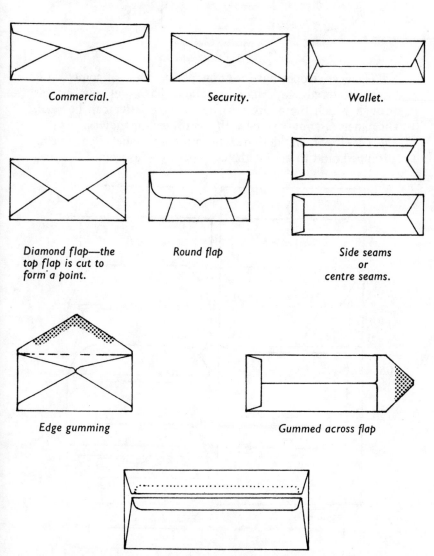

Commercial.

Security.

Wallet.

Diamond flap—the top flap is cut to form a point.

Round flap

Side seams
or
centre seams.

Edge gumming

Gummed across flap

Latex sealed. The two latex-treated surfaces on the flap and body of the envelope seal immediately they are pressed together. This method has been applied to both banker and pocket envelopes and is hygienic, quick and secure.

Window, aperture and anti-trap envelopes.

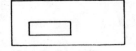

A window envelope.

Window envelopes have window panels made of some transparent material. *Aperture* envelopes have cut out panels through which the address written on the letter can be read. The panels are not covered with any protecting material. *Anti-trap* envelopes are designed to prevent smaller items being entrapped, and to permit the contents to be examined.

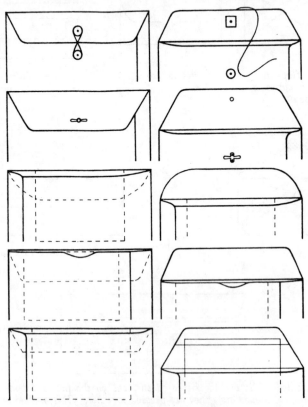

Examples of anti-trap envelopes.

Quality. As airmail postage rates are based on weight, air-mail envelopes are made of very thin strong paper. Sometimes the paper has a faint pattern printed on the inside to ensure that the envelope is completely opaque. Most airmail envelopes have a red and blue border on both sides and are printed with the words BY AIR MAIL set in a solid blue rectangle in the top left-hand corner.

Business firms usually have envelopes of the same quality paper as their noteheads; they are frequently printed with the name of the firm either in the top left-hand corner or on the reverse side.

Manilla (buff-coloured) envelopes are cheaper than envelopes made from high-quality bond and cartridge papers. Manilla envelopes are frequently used for bills and general commercial correspondence.

Post Office Preferred (POP) range. In March 1966 the Post Office announced a Post Office Preferred (POP) range of envelope sizes and asked the public to post their mail, whenever possible, in envelopes conforming to the Preferred range. At some future date inland mail weighing up to 4 oz posted in envelopes outside the POP range of sizes will be liable to an additional charge. POP regulations will not apply to Overseas Post.

To fall within the range envelopes should be:

a) at least $3\frac{1}{2}$ in × $5\frac{1}{2}$ in (90 mm × 140 mm) and not larger than $4\frac{3}{4}$ in × $9\frac{1}{4}$ in (120 mm × 235 mm);

b) oblong in shape, with the longer side at least 1·414 times the shorter side;

c) made from paper weighing at least 63 grammes per square metre.

85

The two most popular ISO size envelopes DL and C6 are within the POP range. Packets and boxes of envelopes which fit in with the POP range are usually marked with a special Post Office Preferred symbol.

All *aperture* envelopes, irrespective of their size and shape, will be classed as outside the POP range.

More information on POP envelopes and cards will be found on p. 132).

POST OFFICE

PREFERRED

So that people may readily recognise Post Office Preferred envelopes, this special symbol is used on packets and boxes of envelopes within the Preferred range.

(b) DUPLICATING EQUIPMENT

The purpose of these machines is to produce many copies of a document from one 'master'. Each method has its own advantages, and you should be able to suggest the most suitable and economic method for any particular job. Most duplicator manufacturers produce both electrically and manually operated models; the electrically operated models are more expensive, but this extra expense may be justified if many thousands of copies are frequently required.

INK DUPLICATORS

The first step in ink duplicating is to prepare a stencil (see illustration) of the document to be duplicated. An ink stencil is prepared in one of three ways:

      a) by typing,
      b) using a thermal heat copier,
      c) using an electronic stencil-cutting machine.

86

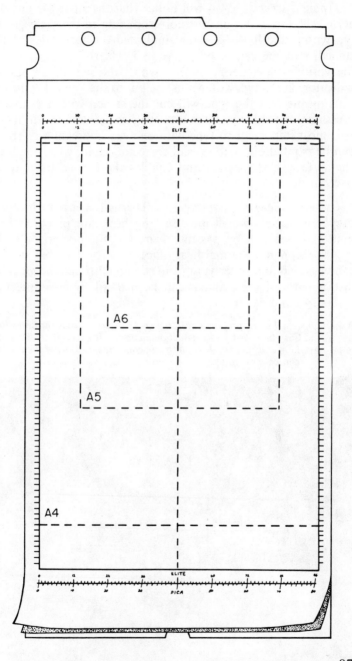

Typing a stencil. You will notice that the stencil is marked across the top with numbers corresponding to the scale on the typewriter; the line spaces are indicated on both sides of the stencil, and the centre of the page is clearly marked, as are the various paper sizes. Before typing the stencil, the ribbon indicator on the typewriter must be put to the 'stencil' position (this means that the type will cut the stencil with a clear impression), and the type faces must be cleaned with a stiff brush. It is most important to type with an even impression. Errors can be painted out with special correcting fluid, which replaces the surface of the stencil and enables the correct letter to be overtyped.

Using a thermal heat copier. Thermal stencils, specially prepared stencils which are 'cut' by heat, are prepared in a matter of seconds by passing them and the document to be copied through a thermal heat office copier. Thermal stencils can be added to by overtyping and running through the machine again; parts of the original can be masked by covering with ordinary bond paper.

A thermal stencil being prepared in less than 15 seconds, ready for immediate transfer to Gestetner Model 460 stencil duplicator. The stencil can be added to by overtyping and running through the machine again: parts of the original can be masked by covering with ordinary bond paper.

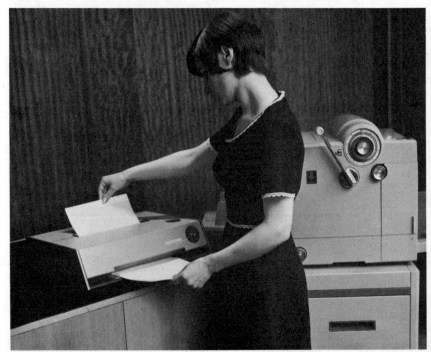

Using an electronic stencil-cutting machine. With the electronic stencil cutter it is possible to produce a stencil from almost any form of document and even photographs. The electronic stencil cutter consists of a rotating cylinder on which the original to be copied and a specially coated stencil are placed side by side. As the cylinder rotates, the original document is scanned by a photo-electric cell synchronised with a cutting stylus (an electrode) scanning the stencil. When the photo-electric cell senses a dark area, a series of pin-point holes is burnt in the stencil thus forming the same pattern as the original.

The Rex-Rotary 2202 electronic stencil cutter.

When it has been prepared the stencil is fixed over the cylinder of the duplicator, and a stack of clean paper is placed in the feed-tray.

Stencil duplicating paper should be used as it is manufactured to specifications that give maximum acceptance to the absorption of stencil duplicating ink, which dries only by this means. Good modern stencil duplicating papers, however, can be written on with water-based fountain pen and writing inks without feathering, although with some inferior stencil duplicating papers you may have to play safe by using a ball-point pen.

When the paper in the feed-tray has been raised to the appropriate position and the machine switch turned to the 'On' or 'Print' position, a rotation of the handle will cause printed copies to be delivered into the receiving tray.

When one or two copies have been 'run off' they should be carefully inspected to see if the material is being printed too high or too low on the paper. On most machines there is an

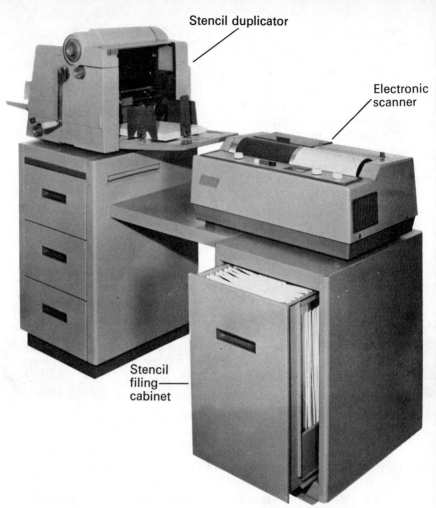

Stencil duplicator

Electronic scanner

Stencil filing cabinet

The Gestetner Combi-Unit includes a stencil duplicator, a Thermal Copier or Electronic Scanner, a cabinet for keeping master stencils and storage drawers for ink, paper and other accessories.

adjustment which enables the printed material to be raised or lowered an inch or two from the normal position.

The papers fences on the feed tray can be moved to left or right to allow you to place the right and left hand margins as you want them.

When you are satisfied that all is well, set the counting mechanism to the number of copies required, and start turning the handle (on a manual machine), or turn the switch to 'On' on an electric machine. When the required number of copies has been printed, the machine will stop feeding paper.

Additional points

1. Up to 7000 good copies can be printed from one stencil.

2. Up to 150 copies per minute can be produced on an electric machine.

3. It is possible to print in more than one colour, but the inking unit and the stencil carrier must be removed and a fresh carrier and unit inserted.

4. Lines may be drawn and names may be signed on stencils by means of a special stylus pen shown below, using a suitably surfaced plastic writer's sheet under the stencil.

5. Stencils may be stored and used again when required. Most duplicator cabinets have a storage tray to hold used stencils placed in absorbent filing folders; but other methods are available, for example Flexiform, where the stencils hang on two parallel rods.

SPIRIT DUPLICATORS

The first step in the spirit duplication process is to prepare a special 'master'. The 'master' sheet is a thick piece of paper, one side of which is shiny. Spirit masters are prepared either by typing or by using an infra-red office copier; they can also be handwritten or drawn.

Typing a spirit master. The master sheet is inserted in the typewriter with a specially produced carbon paper facing the back, or shiny, side, so that the typing appears on the front, or dull, side, and the image appears as 'mirror' writing on the under-side of the master. It is not necessary to switch off the ribbon, but the type should be kept clean. Errors are corrected by erasing the copy (which will appear as 'mirror' writing) from the back of the 'master', inserting a clean slip of carbon behind the word to be corrected, and overtyping the right letters.

Spirit duplicators are so called because the copy is transferred to the paper by means of a special spirit, instead of ink as with

Some spirit duplicators allow selected parts only of the master to be reproduced. This very sophisticated model is the Block & Anderson Selectomatic AP/AF— a single or multiple line selection machine with automatic programming.

stencil duplicators. When the 'master' is placed round the cylinder, and the paper put in the feed-tray, the method of operation is similar to that on the stencil duplicator. Electric and hand-operated models are available.

Spirit masters can be prepared very quickly with infra-red heat office copiers by passing the original and the special master-pack through the copier.

Additional points

1. Up to 300 good copies can be produced from one 'master'.

2. By using different coloured carbons, 'masters' can be prepared in several colours.

3. This method is ideal for the reproduction of drawings, charts and sketches, providing the 'master' sheet and carbon are placed over a very hard surface and a hard pencil or ball-point pen is used.

4. Copies are not 'run off' on absorbent paper, so this method is especially suitable for the production of forms which have to be completed in ink.

5. 'Master' copies are dry and do not require special storage facilities.

6. The printed result tends to fade if exposed to the light for any length of time.

(c) OFFICE COPIERS

Office copiers are machines which produce facsimile, that is exact, copies of original documents. Formerly referred to as photocopiers, office copiers are now classified as a sub-division of Reprography, the name given to the subject which includes the study of all machines which copy or reproduce documents.

The methods of reproduction which we have already discussed—taking carbon copies, and stencil and spirit duplication —all require the document to be copied to be re-written or re-typed, or the use of a machine to cut a stencil or prepare a spirit master. The great advantage of office copiers is that there is no need to re-write or re-type the original; provided it is in a fit state to be reproduced, copies can be made using one of the office copying processes, which are still usually called 'photocopying' or 'photostatting'.

In addition to their obvious use for making one or two copies of a document very quickly, some office copiers can also be used to produce stencils, spirit masters and offset-litho plates. The latest machines, called 'copier/duplicators', can produce up to 3000 or more copies an hour; some will also collate the copied sheets.

There are many firms manufacturing office copying equipment and most firms produce several models. Each process and each model is not suitable for all purposes. It is outside the scope of our studies to describe all the different machines and their applications, so we shall describe them according to the processes used and indicate the type of work for which each is most suitable.

There are four main processes: electrostatic, heat copying, diffusion transfer and dyeline (Diazo); there are also machines which are described as reflex and direct-positive.

Electrostatic copiers. During the past fifteen years there has been a rapid development in electrostatic copiers and their simplicity and convenience has caused them to become more widely used than almost any other process. There are two electrostatic processes (1) Xerography and (2) the Electrofax process. The main difference from the user's point of view is that Xerography copies on to plain paper, but specially coated paper has to be bought for use with the Electrofax process.

93

HOW XEROGRAPHY WORKS

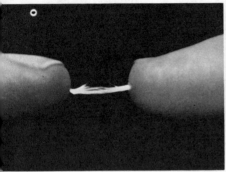

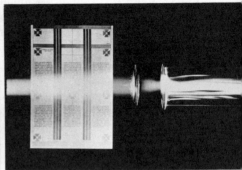

Remember the spark that snapped at your finger-tip after scuffing your slippers across a thick carpet? Or the way you could pick up bits of paper with a comb that had been run quickly through your hair?
Both of these familiar experiences are examples of static electricity, a natural phenomenon. This same electrostatic force is fundamental to the process of xerography.

2. *The process starts with the three units displayed here. An image of the document to be copied is projected onto a light-sensitive surface. An electrostatic charge, placed earlier on the drum surface, disappears from the exposed areas, which were white on the original document. The charge is retained on the drum in the area which corresponds to the black or printed parts of the original document.*

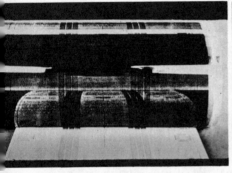

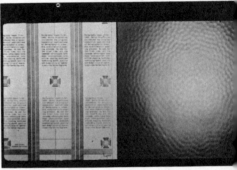

Special developer powder, poured over the drum, clings to the charged portion of the drum (just as the bits of paper adhered to the comb). A visible image of the original document is thus created on the drum. Ordinary bond paper is brought into contact with the drum and an electrical charge beneath the paper attracts the powder from drum.

4. *The powder image is then softened and fused into the paper, usually by heat creating an exact copy of the original document. The whole process takes only a few seconds from start to finish. The prints, on ordinary bond paper, are clean dry and permanent.*

94

XEROGRAPHY. The Xerographic process was invented in America in 1938. The first popular model, the Xerox 914, was introduced into England in 1960 by Rank Xerox, the organisation which markets Xerox copiers in all parts of the world' except the Americas and Japan.

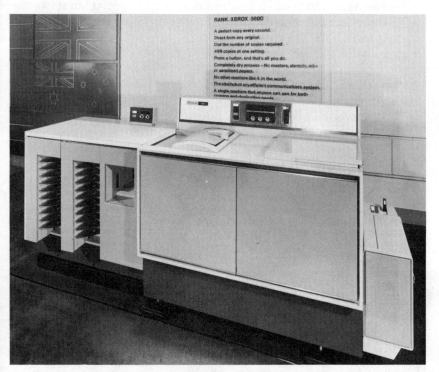

The Rank Xerox 3600 Copier, Duplicator with automatic sorter. It operates at the rate of 60 copies per minute.

Developments during the following years increased the speed at which multiple copies could be made; in 1968 the Xerox 3600, a copier-duplicator, was introduced which produces copies at a speed of one per second. The original document is placed on the platen, the required number of copies is dialled and the 'PRINT' button pressed. Any number of copies up to 499 can be dialled. Accessories for collating and feeding can be fitted to the Xerox 3600. The Automatic Document Feeder selects originals one at a time from a stack of up to 150 and places them on the platen. To produce, for example, twenty copies of a

95

fifty page report, the operator puts the report on the Automatic Document Feeder, dials '20' and presses a button. As the collated copies are delivered the operator removes them from the sorter and staples them together. The whole operation takes less than twenty minutes.

The Xerox 7000 will do the same work as the 3600 but it can also produce copies reduced to 85 per cent, 75 per cent, 70·7 per cent and 61·5 per cent of the size of the original, as well as same size copies. It will accept originals up to 14 in by 18 in but the maximum copy size is 8½ in by 13 in.

The latest Xerox machine, the 4000, has two paper feed trays which enable the machine to copy on to both sides of the paper.

Xerox machines cannot be bought outright; they are hired from the manufacturers. In addition to a fixed monthly rental, the user pays a small charge for each copy made. The number

The Rank Xerox 7000 reduction duplicator. Documents up to 14 in by 18 in can be reproduced on ordinary bond paper at the rate of one a second, at ratios of 100 per cent, 85 per cent, 75 per cent, 70·7 per cent and 61·5 per cent of the original, up to a maximum size copy of 8½ in by 13 in.

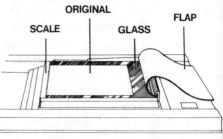

Raise flap. Lay original face down on glass with one edge against scale.

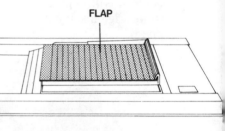

Lower flap.

Set counter. Depress copy switch 'C' (green) and collect your copies from collecting tray. If amber light 'P' lights up, paper tray must be reloaded. If white light 'T' lights up, tissue must be replaced.

The Gestetner FB12 copier (left) produces dry copies at a rate of 12 copies per minute on plain paper, or offset paper plates. The right-hand diagram shows how to operate the machine.

of copies is registered on a meter in the machine. If 100 copies are made per day, each copy costs approximately 2p.

Xerography is a dry copying process; it will copy anything written, typed, printed or drawn, from originals in any colour. The finished result is always black and white. Both the

Xerographic and Electrofax processes will make paper and metal offset plates for offset-litho machines.

As we have seen, the Xerographic process uses a coated drum and copies on to bond paper. Within the past few years one or two other copiers, such as the Gestetner FB12 have appeared which also copy on to bond.

The ELECTROFAX electrostatic process uses paper coated with zinc oxide. The paper may be supplied in a roll and fitted into the copier which automatically cuts off the correct length for the document being copied. The Electrofax process was developed by the Radio Corporation of America who have licensed over 200 copier manufacturers to use their process in one form or another. Electrofax copiers, like Xerographic copiers, will copy anything written, typed, printed, or drawn, from originals in any colour. They will also make metal offset plates.

The A B Dick 625 Copier. Up to 20 copies can be dialled. The toner (black powder) is supplied in an enclosed cartridge and the copy paper fits into a cassette for easy handling. Copies are produced at the rate of ten per minute.

The office copier market today is dominated by electrostatic machines. Offices which do not have sufficient copying to justify the installation of an electrostatic machine tend to use the *heat process* (sometimes called *Thermography*) which, as we discussed in section (*b*) will also produce spirit masters and prepare thermal stencils. The infra-red reflex process, the dual spectrum process and adherography are all heat processes. No liquids or chemicals are used but specially coated paper must be purchased. The copies are dry. Inks or pencils without a

98

graphite content cannot be copied on all machines.   Each copy costs between 2p and 3p.

The *transfer process*, diffusion transfer or gelatine transfer, is wet and comprises two stages—(1) exposure to a light source and (2) processing.   The diffusion transfer process is largely used for making plates for small offset-litho machines.   Good single copies may also be made but the process is comparatively slow and expensive.   The original is first exposed, with a piece of sensitised paper, to the light source; the light-sensitive paper and another sheet of special paper are then passed through a chemical solution, which transfers the copy from the light-sensitive paper to the other sheet of paper.   The two sheets emerge from the machine slightly damp, and in close contact. When they are peeled apart, the copy appears on the sheet of special paper.   Single A4 copies cost about $2\frac{1}{2}$p each.

The *reflex process* produces copies from opaque or transparent originals and also comprises two stages.   It differs from the transfer process in that the first operation of the reflex process produces a negative copy (white print on black) from which a positive print can be made during the second operation. The paper negatives can be stored and used to make as many positive copies as required.   The positive copies are damp after processing and must be allowed to dry.   Reflex is also capable of copying half-tones.   This is the only process which will satisfactorily reproduce photographs.   A4 copies cost about 2p each.

The *dyeline process* uses special diazo paper.   The process also involves two stages.   When the original and the sheet of yellow diazo paper are exposed to light, the chemical coating is bleached away from those areas not covered by the lines of the original image.   During the second stage the diazo paper is passed through chemical liquid or vapour which develops the remaining yellow coating on the printing area, darkening the image, so that a positive copy emerges.   The original must either be translucent (this means that light must be able to pass through the paper) or a translucent master must be produced in the first operation, from which copies can be taken.   A4 copies cost between $1\frac{1}{2}$p and 2p each.   You will note that some firms print on their notepaper 'suitable for making dyeline copies'. Diazo, in spite of the low cost of materials and the introduction of heat developing materials, has not become very popular

99

outside drawing offices. This is probably because only one-sided translucent originals can be copied.

The *direct-positive process* is similar to the reflex process but produces a positive copy without first having to make a negative. A much stronger light source is necessary. Direct-positives, like reflex materials, have to be developed and fixed. A4 copies cost about 2p each.

Examples of photocopying equipment—(left) the Bandaflex Mk II thermal copier; (right) the Ilford Azoflex dyeline copier.

When an office copier is required, these are the questions which must be asked:

1. Should the machine be rented or bought?
2. What will be the average price per copy?* This will depend upon the price or hire charge of the machine, the cost of supplies, i.e. specially coated paper, chemicals or toner (ink), and the average number of copies made per day.
3. Will it make only a single copy?
4. If it will make more than one copy, how many?
5. How quickly are the copies made?
6. Will the machine copy only translucent originals?
7. Will it copy double-sided documents?
8. How long does the machine need to be switched on before using?
9. What accessories, such as automatic feeders and collaters, are available?

* The single copy prices mentioned in the preceding pages vary considerably with the volume of work undertaken and the terms on which the machine is rented or bought.

(*d*) OFFSET-LITHOGRAPHY AND OFFSET-LITHO MACHINES

Offset-lithography, or offset-litho as it is more commonly called, is a further method of reproducing many copies from one master.

The word 'lithography' means 'stone writing', and the process was discovered in 1796 by a Bavarian printer. He found that when he wrote on a stone with a greasy pencil, water would only adhere to the surface of the stone not covered by the writing. When ink was rolled over the stone, only the greasy crayon marks held the ink, the water repelling the ink from the rest of the surface. Since then lithography has passed through many stages of development, and today light metal or paper plates are used for the master copy instead of stone. The process still relies on the fact that when the 'image' (the writing, typing or drawing) is made in a greasy medium and the remainder of the surface is covered with a film of water, the printing ink from the

The Gestilith 200 Offset Duplicator.

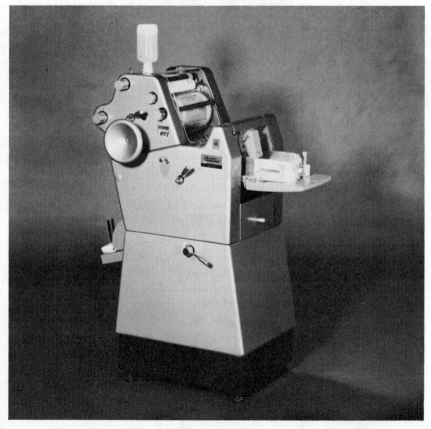

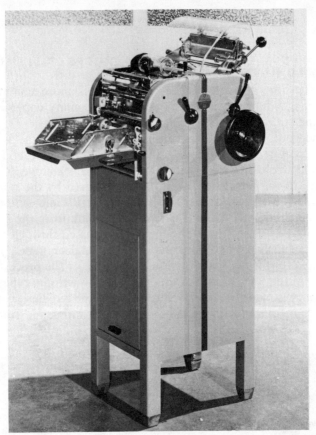

Multilith 85R—the smallest Multilith office duplicator and printer.

inking roller will only adhere to the image. Plates may be prepared in a number of ways:

(1) by writing, drawing or typing through a litho ribbon or litho carbon paper; or 'cold-type' composing:

(2) by photographic or electrostatic processes, including heat type office copying machines utilising paper plates;

(3) by electronic scanners, and special paper plates.

Costs vary but are not high and the time taken to make a plate may be as little as one minute.

When the prepared plate has been fixed to the cylinder of the machine it is first of all wetted with a solution generally known as the fountain solution. Then the inking rollers are brought into contact with it thus inking the image, but not the wetted background. The inked image is then brought into contact

102

with a second roller on the machine, around which is wrapped a soft rubber sheet, known as a 'blanket'. In this way the image from the inked plate is 'set off', i.e. it appears in reverse, on the blanket roller. When the blanket roller is brought into contact with the rolling-off paper, the reversed image is transferred in a readable form. This process is known as 'offset', hence the term offset-lithography.

Today, offset-lithography can take the form of a large multi-coloured printing machine or a small office duplicator, but the original principle of using oil and water still remains. The small office machine is capable of reproducing, in miniature, high-class work equally as good as the large offset machine, but it also has the added advantage of being capable of reproducing inexpensively most of the requirements of the modern office.

The Rex-Rotary 1515 Offset platemaker uses the diffusion transfer method to produce offset plates within minutes.

It is very important to use an even touch and to clean the typeface regularly when typing offset-litho plates, and no grease or dirt from the hands should be transferred to the image area. The plate must only be handled at the ends.

Another point requiring special attention is the correction of errors. Once matter has been typed on a plate, it is unwise to roll back the platen as grease can be picked up and transferred to other areas from the under-platen rollers. Corrections must be made without damaging or removing the surface of the plate. With a paper plate, corrections should be made with a special eraser, obtainable from the suppliers of most types of paper plates. The plate must not be rubbed hard or deeply into its surface. A 'ghost' image will remain, on which the new typing can be superimposed, each letter being typed more than once if necessary. An image on a metal plate can be erased with a glass brush or pumice block.

103

The number of copies obtainable by offset-litho depends upon the type of plate used. From 20 000 to 50 000 copies may be produced from a metal plate, and up to 5000 copies from a paper plate. There are also cheaper short-run plates giving 100 copies.

Advantages of offset-litho duplication are as follows:

(1) The plate can be kept and re-used at a later date.
(2) Copies can be taken on good quality paper (not absorbent paper as in stencil duplication).
(3) Plates using a variety of type-faces can be prepared by several methods.

(e) MAIL-HANDLING EQUIPMENT

FRANKING MACHINES. The bulk of the outgoing mail tends to be sent to the mail room or postal section during the last half-hour or so of the working day, and during this time most of the day's output has to be stamped and despatched. This work is facilitated by franking machines which print on the envelope or label any denomination of postage from $\frac{1}{2}$p to $99\frac{1}{2}$p (small machines) and from $\frac{1}{2}$p to £4·99$\frac{1}{2}$ (large machines).

Roneo-Neopost's new fast all electric decimal franking machine with a detachable meter. The machine can be bought outright or rented. Known as the '505', this machine franks and seals all sizes and classes of mail at the rate of 5/6000 per hour.

Franking machines may be hired or purchased from the supplying companies licensed by the Post Office. Payment in respect of postage must be made in advance at a specified post office, and the meter on the machine will be set according to the amount prepaid. Most machines are clearly marked with a scale which records the balance in hand. Franking machines can also print an advertising slogan on the envelope. Hand and electric models are available. The electric models also print gummed, franked labels ready to affix to bulky packets or parcels. Franking machines eliminate the task of keeping a postage book, and there are no loose stamps in the office which could be lost or stolen. The machines may be locked when not in use.

Franked envelopes should be posted only at a main post office or sub-post office. If you are late with the mail and the post office is shut, franked envelopes should be put in a large envelope (provided by the supplier of the franking machine); the large envelope containing the franked mail may then be posted in a pillar box.

The Bandafix stamp-affixing machine is used in many small offices where the volume of mail does not justify the purchase of a franking machine. The Bandafix, shown right, guillotines, affixes and counts stamps in rolls of 480, which are purchased from the Post Office.

LETTER-OPENING MACHINES. Machines which open envelopes are of great assistance in postal departments receiving a large number (say over 100) of letters each morning. The machines, which may be hand or electrically operated, cut a narrow strip from the top of the envelope. Some machines operate on the guillotine principle. The edge of the envelope is placed between the blades, the lever is depressed and approximately 1·5 mm is cut off the top of the envelope.

Other machines operate automatically. The feed mechanism draws the envelopes through the cutting blades, and the opened envelopes are stacked in a receiving tray. This type of machine can handle up to 600 envelopes a minute.

The Pitney-Bowes LA Letter Opener—an electrically operated model which opens all types of correspondence.

ENVELOPE-SEALING MACHINES, INSERTING AND FOLDING MACHINES. Machines such as the Bandafold are available which will fold papers and insert magazines in wrappers, documents and magazines into envelopes and seal the flaps. In general, folding machines will give two or three parallel folds and one or more cross folds, but on both manual and electric machines as many as twelve different kinds of folds can be achieved. Machines can also perforate and cut. Envelope-filling machines will enclose documents of many different sizes by being adjusted, and they will also stack the envelopes. In some cases the envelope is 'created' around the document to go through the post. As many as 3000 or 4000 envelopes can be dealt with hourly by these various methods.

The Bandafold 350 Document Folding Machine.

(f) ADDRESSING EQUIPMENT

Addressing machines print addresses on envelopes, cards and invoices from previously prepared plates. They are also used for listing. Two methods use stencil or spirit masters, which can be prepared on the typewriter. An attachment, which fits any standard typewriter, is available for preparing the address stencils. The stencils are stored in drawers, and provide an index: they are made in various colours for identification, and only the ones required to be printed can be selected quickly. A drawing of an address stencil is shown below. A third method, the Addressograph, uses embossed metal plates which have to be made on an embossing machine. It is quite easy to blank out parts of an embossed plate and re-emboss it with new information.

The plates are stacked in the machine and the envelopes or cards to be printed are placed in the feed tray. When the 'print' lever is depressed, the address from the first stencil is printed on the first envelope, each is passed on to its own receiving tray, and the second plate and second envelope move into position. A 'skip' lever enables some plates to pass through without printing, if this is required. Both stencils and plates can be 'punched' to allow an attachment similar to a punched card sorting machine to select automatically only those stencils or plates requiring printing.

In some cases the frame of the stencil may be used for recording additional information, and, as has been said, the plates or stencils can form a card index, which can be notched, punched or flagged for reference.

(g) CALCULATING MACHINES

There are five basic forms of calculating machines:

(1) Adding or add-listing machines.
(2) Key driven adding-calculators.
(3) Rotary calculators.
(4) Electronic calculators.
(5) Programmed desk computers.

The choice for use obviously depends upon the nature of the task to be performed.

The Point 11KNS—amounts to be added are set up on the keyboard in the sequence in which they are normally read and written. To add and print a complete amount, the operator has merely to use slightly firmer pressure when setting up the last figure. This eliminates the use of a motor bar, saving time, reducing hand-movements and simplifying the operation.

ADDING OR ADD-LISTING MACHINES. These machines will total groups of figures. When the appropriate keys have been pressed, the amount is transferred into the machine by pressing the operating lever. The amount put into the machine is shown clearly on the register. When a second amount is put into the machine, total of the first and second amount appears automatically on the register. As soon as the machine is cleared the total is 'lost'. You will note that there is no record of the amounts or figures which have been totalled.

Add-listing machines do the same work as an adding machine, but the figures are printed line by line as the keys are pressed, and the total is printed on the tally-roll when the *total key* is pressed. The tally-roll can be used for checking the figures that have been put into the machine. Various types of keyboard are available in adding and add-listing machines. They may have the full keyboard which has digits from 0–9 in each column, or they may have a simplified keyboard, which requires that the operator shall strike two keys for the digits which do not appear. Keyboards vary in capacity, that is, the amount which can be recorded, up to £1 million or more.

KEY DRIVEN ADDING CALCULATORS. Key driven adding calculators can add, subtract, multiply and divide, and carry out such book-keeping functions as calculating the cost of so many articles at a certain price, e.g. 465 articles at £1·84½ each. A percentage can also be calculated and deducted. Further examples of the use of these machines are the calculation of wages (so many hours at so much per hour), and currency conversion. Key-driven adding calculators operate by adding the number depressed immediately into the accumulator, and these machines are particularly fast in the hands of specially trained operators, who use both hands.

ROTARY CALCULATORS. There are two types: the main feature of the one most commonly used is the crank handle which works in two directions—for subtraction and division or for addition and multiplication. They are small, and very useful for such people as engineers or draughtsmen, who wish to keep an easy means of calculation on their desks.

ELECTRONIC CALCULATORS. The fourth type of calculator— the electronic calculator—has no moving parts. It is silent and

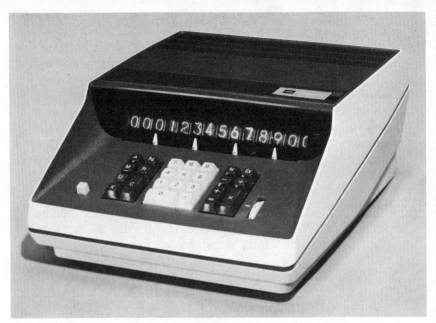

The ADM Toscal 1412 is a fast, silent desk-top 'brain' for use by all personnel, from managing directors to office clerks.

fast, and has an illuminated display register. Multiplication and division are far more easily and quickly carried out. The lightning speed of electronic circuits makes these machines by far the fastest and most simple of calculators, and some models have high speed printing (5 lines a second) to check what is being calculated.

PROGRAMMED DESK COMPUTERS. The fifth type of calculator has been described in advertisements as a 'desk-top computer'. It is basically an electronic calculator, but it is programmed by the preparation of a magnetic card of instructions (devised by the user and prepared by the manufacturer) which will instruct it to carry out a whole pre-arranged programme of calculations. The cards can be stored and used again and again, and it is not difficult to imagine the large number of routine calculations which could be undertaken in such a manner.

(h) ACCOUNTING MACHINES. Large accounting machines with special 'registers' can carry out the sales and purchase accounting of a firm, and at the same time produce printed invoices and statements, delivery notes and other documents. The word 'register' on these machines has a special meaning.

110

The NCR Point SD 31 accounting machine.

The registers can be compared with small adding machines within the one accounting machine; in other words each register is a small adding box. A register is also a memory unit, as it will 'hold' the amount put into it until it is needed when it can be brought into play by pressing the appropriate key.

For example, when a typist is typing an invoice, she will not want to use the customer's previous balance until the new purchases have been listed and totalled. When she has totalled the new purchases and set these against the amounts paid in, she will bring into play the register which has been 'holding' the previous balance, and the machine will calculate and print the new balance.

(*i*) PUNCHED-CARD ACCOUNTING

How a card can record information. The card shown in the illustration on p. 108 has 80 columns ranged horizontally and ten columns ranged vertically; by using the margin above the row of noughts, two more rows can be accommodated, bringing the total number of vertical rows to twelve.

The cards can be printed to suit the business of a firm and the columns allotted according to the type of information to be recorded. For example, if a card was being used by an

111

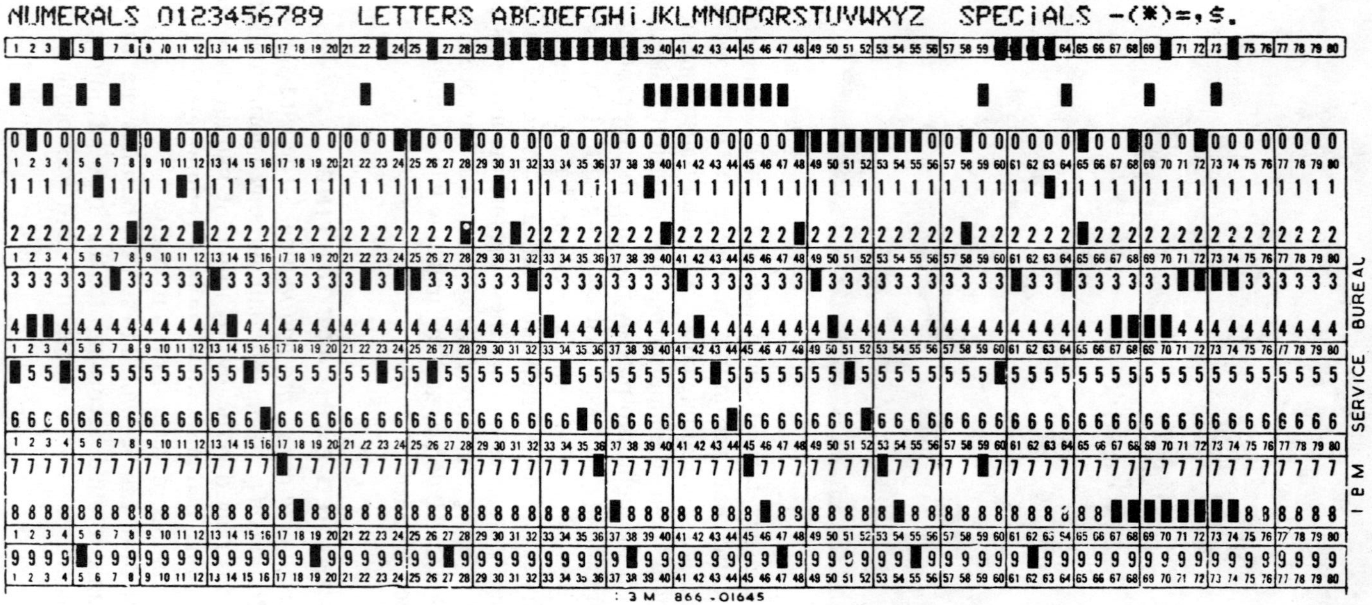

NUMERALS 0123456789 LETTERS ABCDEFGHIJKLMNOPQRSTUVWXYZ SPECIALS -(*)=,$.

I B M SERVICE BUREAU

3 M 866 - 01645

112

An operator working an ICL 072 automatic key punch.

The IBM 084 sorter which can sort punched cards at the rate of 2000 a minute.

insurance company, the first column might record the policy number. In the second column the type of policy could be recorded by the use of a code number. The third column might record the amount of the policy, the next column the agent's number, and so on.

The work of punching the holes is carried out by girls who are known as *punched-card operators*. It is vital that the holes have been punched accurately, so the next operation is to check the punching. This is done by a machine called a *verifier*.

The sets of punched-cards can be put into a machine called a *Sorter*, which can 'read' the information on them and sort them into piles as required.

How the Sorter can 'read'. Within the machine the cards are passed over metal feelers (known as 'brushes') or light beams which can detect where a hole has been punched. These contacts begin a series of electrical operations which makes the machine sort the cards into piles, according to the way it has been instructed to sort them.

How the Sorter is given its instructions. The control panel of the Sorter makes the machine select some cards and reject others. The wiring of the control panels is a very specialised job. The panels are detachable, and separate panels are put into the machine according to the type of sorting required. The cards similar to that shown in the illustration could be sorted under the headings: all the policies sold by agent no.

An operator watches the tabulated results being printed on a tabulator.

919132; or all the policies sold by branch no. 218; and in many other ways.

How the cards are used for accounting. Information regarding accounts can be punched into the cards, e.g. the customer's ledger number, the customer's balance last month, the new purchases, etc.

Just as the registers in the accounting machine operate when the keys are pressed, the registers in a punched-card accounting machine are brought into play when the presence of the holes is detected by the 'brushes' or light beams.

A *Tabulator* is a combined printing and sorting machine which will print the customer's invoice and record a list of all the invoices; it will also punch a new card recording the new figures. The printing is carried out usually a line at a time. As the sensing mechanism reads the holes in the cards, it causes hammers to hit the selected typebars. The machine can go on adding or calculating while the printing is going on.

(*j*) COMPUTERS

Computers have been used by scientists for many years to carry out complicated mathematical problems. They are known as 'analogue' computers.

Computers which will carry out commercial calculations have also been invented and are used by many large firms. These are known as 'digital' computers; as they are mainly used to carry out clerical processes dealing with a huge amount of data (i.e. facts) they are frequently referred to as 'Electronic Data Processing' machines (EDP for short) or 'Automatic Data Processing' machines (ADP for short).

Computers are similar to punched-card accounting machines in two respects: firstly, information is fed into them in the form of punched holes which they can 'read'; and, secondly, they can add, subtract, multiply and divide. But there are several differences:

(1) The computer works electronically—if you looked inside the various units you would see transistors and wires, whereas punched-card accounting machines are operated by electrical and mechanical devices such as switches and levers.

115

(2) The computer receives its instructions in the form of punched cards, punched tape, Magnetic Ink Character recognition (as seen on all cheques), optically readable characters or marks, direct keyboard entry, light pen. Information to be processed is fed in by the same means. This is called the 'programme'.

(3) As well as adding, subtracting, etc., the computer can also make judgments and decisions, and vary its calculations according to the data it is processing. For example, a computer calculating salaries and wages can calculate how much tax should be deducted for the month or week by comparing the 'tax due' amount with the 'tax paid' amount; if the tax paid is greater than the tax due, it will work out the amount of the re-fund and add this to the salary for the month.

(4) Recorded information is most usually stored on magnetic tape, with magnetic discs used in cases where random access (widely scattered references) is required rather than serial access (starting at the beginning of the tape until the required part is reached).

(5) Output from the computer is by means similar to input, including the use of light-screens like T.V. screens. The most common is the high-speed line printer, printing a line at a time.

Computers are used in business for two distinct types of work. The first of these is to carry out very quickly, accurately and automatically, a great deal of detailed, often very dull routine work, freeing staff for other constructive work. Much of this type of work can also be done on the punched-card systems we have already mentioned. The second use of computers is to provide for the management of a business accurate forecasts of the position of their businesses in the future; how much stock will be required at certain times, what additional staff and materials will be required for particular tasks; how many machines will lie vacant or be occupied at particular times. It provides the data, or information, for planning and controlling business.

The use of a computer is only one way of getting the office work done, and the expression 'electronic brains' is not a good description because the machines cannot think. Those firms

The ICL magnetic tape data recorder, used to prepare input data rapidly and accurately.

ICL 1901A computer installation.

In this picture you see details of an engineering drawing being encoded on the drawing measuring machine. The resultant punched tape produced by the system will be processed by computer to produce detailed production drawings from the original design layout.

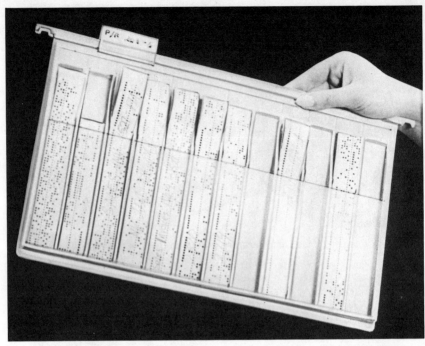

Twinlock runners for suspension filing cabinets, each fitted with 12 clear plastic pockets, designed to hold lengths of punched tape.

using computers to help to carry out their office work have to use the brains of men to devise the programmes that the machines will use. The office jobs are analysed, and a programme written which the machine accepts and acts upon.

A computer can be thought of as a man sitting at his desk planning his work, and carrying some of it out. He has his files for reference, his 'In' tray and his 'Out' tray, and his mind or calculating machine. He may also have some last-minute reminders as rough notes scribbled on his blotting pad.

The computer has files or 'storage' units: it has an 'input' and an 'output', and an arithmetic or calculating system. The information is fed in; the machine works upon it in the manner directed by the programme; and the results are printed out, either by tabulators or by electric typewriters, teleprinters or high-speed printing devices. The results may also be stored on punched-cards, or on magnetic tape, or in the machine itself, and the files of the future may well look like the illustrations above and on p. 119.

Office work has always consisted of receiving, sorting, storing and passing on information, after calculations and other work

118

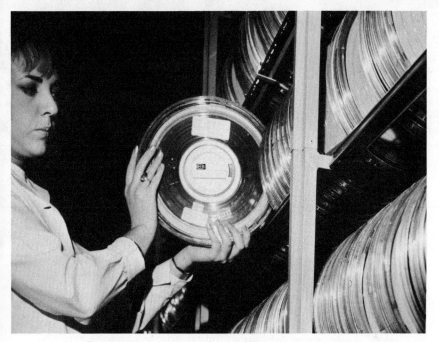

Storage cabinet holding reels of magnetic tape records.

have been done on it; electronic computers really do only this, but they do it very quickly and, unlike men, can begin another set of calculations while the first is being stored and put into printed form.

(*k*) DICTATING MACHINES

Instead of dictating their letters to a shorthand-typist, some employers prefer to dictate into a machine which records their dictation on to a tape, disc, plastic belt or sheet. In the illustration you can see typists typing from recorded dictation. They are known as audio-typists. You will notice that they are wearing headphones (sometimes called stethophones) through which they can hear what they have to type. Each audio-typist has a control attached to the dictating machine. The control has two types of action. Pressure on one part will start the machine while pressure on the other part will cause the machine to back-space, so that the typist can hear the previous sentence again if she has not understood it correctly. Most audio-typists prefer to use a foot control, but hand controls which fit under the front of the typewriter frame are also available.

119

A comprehensive centralised dictation system.

Recording media. The material on which the dictation is recorded is known as the medium (plural—media). The various makes of machines use different media. Some use plastic belts, some use discs (similar to gramophone records), some use specially prepared sheets which look like a heavy type of carbon paper and others use tape or wire.

Some media are magnetic. These can be used again and again, as new dictation automatically erases the previous dictation. The dictater can make corrections by talking over the original dictation.

Non-magnetic media can only be used once and corrections cannot be superimposed. The typist must therefore listen to

Recording media—a belt, disc and magnetic tape.

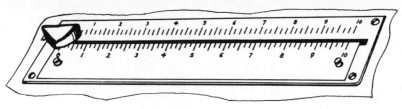

An index strip in position.

the corrections before she starts to type the letter. Her attention is drawn to the corrections by a mark on the *index slip*. The index slip will also indicate the length of the letter and the number of carbon copies required.

Some machines both record and play back what is dictated. These are known as dual-purpose machines. A few manufacturers produce two machines—one for recording dictation and another for the typist; the typist's machine is known as a transcribing machine.

Remote dictation systems. In a firm using a remote dictation system the executives may dictate either into hand microphones or into special telephones in their offices, and the dictation is recorded on to one of the machines in the audio-typing room. As each record or tape is finished, the supervisor puts a new one on to the dictating machine, and distributes the full records to the typists for transcription.

A Philips 84 Automatic Dictation machine which uses tape as its medium.

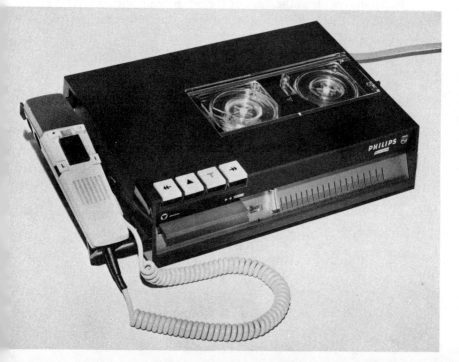

Advantages of dictating machines.

1. While the dictation is being given, the typist can be doing other work.

2. Dictation can be given at any time convenient to the employer, for example, after normal office hours. If he has a portable machine, he can use it at home.

3. Some media can be sent through the post. Reports can be posted to the typist and will be typed ready for the employer when he returns to the office.

4. In a large office, work can be distributed evenly amongst the typists.

(*l*) STENOTYPING

Not to be confused with dictating machines are stenotyping machines. Stenotyping is a system of note-taking, like a system of shorthand. It is an alternative for handwritten shorthand, and the operator uses a machine instead of a notebook and pen. The notes, though printed, still have to be transcribed just as shorthand notes have to be transcribed.

Stenotyping is often known as 'machine-shorthand', but in fact no shorthand symbols are used. Instead, ordinary letters of the alphabet are printed in type on a band or roll of paper which moves on as the keys of the machine are struck. Unlike a typewriter, the keys of a stenotyping machine can be struck

The Palantype stenotyping machine.

with both hands simultaneously, just as a chord is played on a piano. Stenotyping systems are based on phonetics, and each time the keys are struck, the operator prints a syllable or word.

The machines of England, America and France differ; the keyboards are different, and while the French operator uses a roll of paper, the English and American stenotypists use packs of paper. Some machines are used on tripods or tables: the English machine, the Palantype, illustrated on p. 118, is used on the knees, and the perforated paper pack folds back into the lid of the machine.

You may have seen stenotypists at work in court and conference scenes both on films and television. Because of their phonetic basis, systems of stenotyping lend themselves readily to high speed or verbatim work, to technical matter and foreign languages. But stenotypists do not only work in conferences or in the courts; many, perhaps those who do not reach such high speeds, or wish to work the erratic hours of the verbatim writer, work in offices and carry out the same type of work as any shorthand-writer or secretary.

Recently experiments have been made to use stenotyping as an imput to computers.

(m) COLLATING MACHINES

When a report running into many pages has been duplicated the sets have to be sorted and stapled together. The collection of the sets is known as collating.

This common office task used to take up a lot of time and space. The stacks of each page were spread out on a table and each set was collected by hand. It was found that the placing of the piles in a certain order made the job easier.

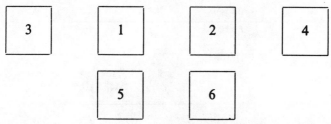

The invention of collating frames and machines has speeded and simplified this task. Collating machines work on several different principles. The simplest principle is that of a number

123

The Multicollect marketed by Block and Anderson Ltd, is a fully automatic collating machine which can simultaneously collate individual sheets, folded sheets, card or carbon paper of varying sizes and weights. Production speed is between 1500 and 5000 sets per hour depending upon paper weight.

Manual collating machine.

of trays (corresponding with the piles of paper) into which the piles of each numbered sheet are placed. A foot or hand lever lifts the top sheet of each pile and allows the operator to use both hands freely for gathering up the papers in their right order. Many modern machines will run for several hours automatically, delivering five or six sheets of paper in their correct order at a speed of several sets per minute. Collating machines are used in connection with joggers, which shake the papers into alignment.

EXERCISES

1. What kind of typewriter (manual, portable, etc., type face, pitch) would you recommend:
   (a) for occasional use at home,
   (b) for use in a general office,
   (c) for use in an office where large balance sheets are typed,
   (d) for use in an office where it was frequently necessary to type forms, programmes and brochures?

2. In what types of office would you expect to find:
   (a) a Flexowriter automatic typewriter,
   (b) a 'cold-type' composer?

3. What are the advantages of continuous stationery and form-feed equipment?

4. What size paper would you use for typing:
   (a) a menu, (b) a programme for a school concert?

5. Make a list of the different makes of typewriters in your typewriting room and note the special features of each make.

6. Calculate the number of line-spaces and letter spaces available on A.3, A.4, and A.5 paper (a) using the shorter side horizontally, and (b) using the longer side horizontally, when using (1) a 3·8 letter per centimetre Continental pica machine, and (2) a 2 mm Continental élite machine.

7. Explain the following terms:
   (a) franking,
   (b) a verifier,
   (c) recording media,

(*d*) collating,
(*e*) an audio-typist,
(*f*) a dual-purpose dictating machine,
(*g*) an index strip,
(*h*) a transcribing machine,
(*i*) a remote dictation system,
(*j*) a computer programme.

8. The Post Room in your firm is not mechanised. Write a report for submission to the Company Secretary, suggesting what equipment should be purchased. The volume of mail has increased to about 300 letters a day.

9. Write short notes on the following:
(*a*) addressing machines,
(*b*) dictating machines,
(*c*) add-listing machines,
(*d*) punched-card accounting,

10. Give examples of the uses of *three* of the following:
typewriter with an 18-inch carriage;
automatic typewriter;
dictating machine;
typewriter with a continuous stationery attachment;
intercom. (RSA, OP, I)

11. (*a*) Describe three different processes of photocopying.
(*b*) Summarise the circumstances in which each would be used. (RSA, OP, II)

12. Your firm's mailroom is over-worked and under-mechanised. Suggest three machines which might help the situation and write about their uses. (RSA, OP, I)

13. (*a*) When would you use the following office machines?
(i) Photo-copier.
(ii) Ink Duplicator.
(iii) One type of continuous Stationery Machine.
(iv) Add-Listing Machine.
(*b*) Describe in detail the functions of ONE of these machines.
(RSA, OP, I)

14. Write notes on the preparation of a stencil for ink duplicating, and the use of the duplicator for subsequent

production of 200 copies. State the method and advantage of storing the stencil. (RSA, OP, I)

15. State the functions and advantages of the use of *either:*
    (*a*) an adding-listing machine
    or
    (*b*) an addressing machine. (RSA, OP, I)

16. (*a*) List the machines used in an automatic punched-card installation and explain the function of each.
    (*b*) Why are many automatic punched-card installations being replaced by electronic computers? (RSA, OP, II)

17. (*a*) To remain efficient, an office typewriter needs to be well cared for. Suggest three ways in which a typist can, in her daily use of the machine, take care of her typewriter.
    (*b*) What are the advantages of an electric typewriter? (RSA, OP, I)

18. Name and explain the uses of three keyboard machines (other than typewriters) which you might find in an accounts department of a medium-sized organisation which did not have the use of a computer or automatic punched card equipment. (RSA, OP, II)

19. Write about some of the uses in the office of EITHER calculating machines OR dictating machines. (RSA, OP, I)

20. (*a*) Give an example of the use made in an office of each of the following international stationery sizes: A4 A5.
    (*b*) Name two other examples of international stationery sizes and give their uses. (RSA, OP, I)

21. (*a*) List the important points which should be borne in mind when incoming office mail is being opened and sorted, in order to ensure that all items receive proper attention.
    (*b*) Name two items of mechanised equipment which you would expect to find in the mailing department of a large organisation and explain the uses of these items. (RSA, OP, II)

22. Explain the importance of each of the following items in the handling of mail in a large office:
    (*a*) franking machine;
    (*b*) addressing machine;

(c) letter opening machine;

(d) postal scales. (RSA, OP, I)

23. What type of office copying machine could you choose to make:

(a) one copy of this page;

(b) ten copies of this page;

(c) seven thousand copies of this page?

Give reasons for your answers. (RSA, OP, I)

24. (a) Below is an illustration (not life-size) of a large sheet of paper folded to show the International Paper Size A6 in section (a). Write in on the dotted line the IPS. for the other four sections.

(b) What information would you expect to obtain from a firm's headed notepaper? (RSA, OP, I)

Chapter 4

The Post Office

IN this chapter we shall study the services of the Post Office under two headings: (*a*) Postal Services, (*b*) Miscellaneous Services, e.g. licences, pensions. Since 29 September 1975, weights and measures for Post Office letters and parcels have been metricated. All weights are now in grammes and kilogrammes instead of ounces and pounds, and size limits are in millimetres and metres instead of inches and feet.

The Telephone and Telegraph Services are also administered by the Post Office, but these will be studied in Chapter 5, Communications. Post Office facilities for making payments are studied in Chapter 7.

(a) POSTAL SERVICES

In many offices the despatch of mail is the responsibility of the typist, and it is essential that she should have a thorough knowledge of the postal regulations. The *Post Office Guide* contains complete information covering all the services rendered by the Post Office and is a reference book which should be available in all offices. Further information is given in the publications *Postal Addresses, London Post Offices and Streets, Post Offices in the United Kingdom* which are available from H.M. Stationery Office or from the London Chief Office at King Edward Street, LONDON EC1A 1AA, or through any Crown Office.

To ensure that your correspondence is correctly addressed, pay attention to the following points:

(1) Show the name of the POST TOWN and the POSTCODE in block capitals, so that they can be read quickly and accurately.
(2) Leave about 4 cm above the address so that it will not be obliterated by the postmark.

129

THE JOURNEY OF A LETTER

COLLECTION

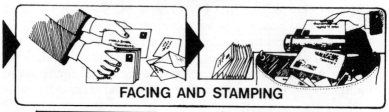

FACING AND STAMPING

PRIMARY SORTING

SECONDARY SORTING

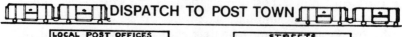

DISPATCH TO POST TOWN

SORTING TO LOCAL POST OFFICES

SORTING TO STREET

DELIVERY

(3) Put the postage stamp in the top right-hand corner of the envelope.

(4) Do not use words like 'Local', 'By' or 'Near' in the address.

(5) Write county names in full, unless there is a recognised abbreviation, e.g. 'HERTS.' for Hertfordshire.

How to write the address

The address should contain:

(1) The name of the addressee.

(2) The name of the house or block of offices, if any.

(3) The number of the house and name of the road.

(4) The name of the village, if any.

(5) The name of the post town, in BLOCK CAPITALS.

(6) The name of the county where shown.

(7) The Postcode in BLOCK CAPITALS.

```
Miss K White              Messrs William Brown & Co
100 South Street            600 Grand Street
PURLEY                           LONDON
Surrey                           W1N 9UZ
CR2 4TJ
```

POSTCODES should always appear as the last item of information in any address. If it is necessary to restrict the number of lines used, the post town and the county name may be written on the same line, but the Postcode should appear on a line by itself. Occasionally it may not be possible to place the Postcode on a line by itself and it may have to share a line with other information. If so leave a space of at least two characters, preferably six, between the Postcode and whatever precedes it. Never underline the Postcode or join the characters of a Postcode in any way. Do not use full stops or any other punctuation marks between or at the end of the Postcode.

```
Mr J Fisher
55 Cod Street
FRASERBURGH
Aberdeenshire     AB4 8YZ
```

131

These are liable to change, and you should learn the rates in force at the present time. The INLAND LETTER SERVICE offers two speeds, or classes, of service (First and Second Class) for any correspondence sent to addresses in the United Kingdom and Irish Republic. The postage rate depends on the speed of service required. There is no weight limit in the first class service, but in the second class service there is a weight limit of 750g. The maximum size for *1st Class Letters and Packets* as well as for *2nd Class Letters and Packets, Registered Letters, Recorded Delivery Letters, Railex, Railway* and *Airway Letters* is 610mm length, 460mm in width and 460mm in depth.

POST OFFICE PREFERRED (POP) ENVELOPES AND CARDS. The Post Office asks all its customers to post their mail, whenever possible, in envelopes within a preferred range of sizes which have been recommended for use by postal administrations all over the world, so that much more of the mail can be handled by the latest electronic sorting machines. This should help to speed up the work, keep costs down and reduce demands on manpower.

At a later date only the Post Office Preferred range of envelopes (POP Envelopes) will qualify for the lowest rate of postage for inland letters. Mail weighing up to 60g posted in envelopes outside the Preferred Range will be liable to an additional charge. A firm date from which the higher postage will be charged will be announced later. Mail weighing more than 60g will be unaffected by the choice of envelope.

To fall within POP range, envelopes should be at least 90 mm × 140 mm and not larger than 120 mm × 235 mm. They should be oblong in shape (the longer side at least 1·414 times the shorter side), and made of paper weighing at least 63 grammes per square metre.

Postcards will be treated as letters and as if they had been posted in an envelope of the same dimensions as the card itself. Postcards outside POP sizes and those sent folded with the edges not sealed together will require the higher postage. Postcards must be not less than 250 micrometres thick.

Irrespective of their size and shape, all aperture envelopes (that is envelopes where cut-out address panels are not covered

132

with a transparent material) will be classed as outside the POP range.

Window enevelopes (where cut-out address panels are covered with transparent material) will be treated as falling within the POP range provided they conform in size, shape and weight of paper.

All unenveloped matter weighing up to 60g except cards, will be classed as outside the POP range and will be liable to the higher postal charges. Fold-and-tuck forms and items enclosed in wrappers are in this category. Folders and letter-cards with all the open edges sealed down will, however, be treated as falling within the POP range provided they conform in size, shape and weight of paper.

PREPAYMENT OF POSTAGE CHARGES. Many companies and firms take advantage of the facility by which postage on any postal packets may be prepaid, especially when a large number of packets must be despatched on one day. The conditions under which such packets may be posted are given in the Post Office Guide, and the arrangement is one which is mutually advantageous to both the Post Office and the senders. If the facility does not normally exist at certain Post Offices in the provinces, application for it can be made to the local postmaster, stating the exact date of posting and the approximate number of articles to be posted.

POSTE RESTANTE. Postal packets and letters may be addressed to any post office (except a town sub-office) to await collection by the addressee. The words 'Poste Restante' or 'To Be Called

```
        Miss J Hawkins
        POSTE RESTANTE
        The Post Office
        RICHMOND
        Surrey
        TW9 1JA
```

For' must be written clearly in the address, and the addressee will be asked to prove his identity when he collects the letters. This service is of great use to travellers, but it must not be used in the same town for more than three months.

BUSINESS REPLY SERVICE. Under this service business firms may enclose in their communications an unstamped reply card, letter card or envelope and thus obtain a reply from a client without putting him to the expense of paying postage. It is not available in the overseas post.

FIRST CLASS DESIGN

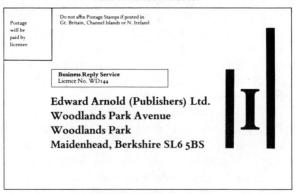

SECOND CLASS DESIGN

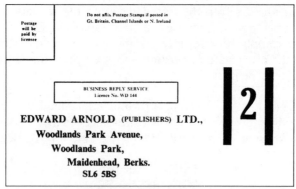

Reply-paid cards

Before using this service a licence must be obtained from the local Head Postmaster, and the licensee will be required to pay in advance a sum of money sufficient to cover the amount of the charges likely to accrue. A fee of $\frac{1}{2}$p in addition to the normal postage will be charged on each card or envelope returned by post to the licensee. The design of the card or envelope must conform to certain standards, and the proofs of the design must be approved by the local Head Postmaster before the cards are printed.

FREEPOST. The Freepost service is a new reply method designed to encourage public response to advertising and sales promotion campaigns.

Although the Freepost service is similar to the Business Reply service in that it enables prospective customers to reply to advertisements without using postage stamps, it has the advantage that the licensee (the firm promoting the advertising

campaign) has not first had to go to the expense of having Business Reply cards printed and mailed to prospective customers.

A firm wishing to use a Freepost address must first obtain a licence from the Head Postmaster of the district in which it is situated. The licensee pays an annual fee of £5 for a Freepost address; he also has to pay in advance a sum of money sufficient to cover the amount of postal charges likely to accrue during the period of approximately one month, and to make further payments to renew his credit from time to time. The licensee is charged the standard second-class mail postage (at present $2\frac{1}{2}$p) plus $\frac{1}{2}$p on each Freepost item delivered to him. Freepost packets are treated as second-class mail.

The Freepost address is included in all the firm's press and television advertisements and prospective customers can send for further information by enclosing their replies in envelopes or using postcards on which they have written the advertiser's Freepost address. No postage stamp is needed—the cost of postage is paid by the holder of the Freepost licence.

LATE POSTED PACKETS. Mail trains provided with travelling Post Offices will accept letters prepaid at current first class postage rates with an extra postage of 1p. Registered letters and recorded delivery packets are accepted up to five minutes before the departure times on payment, in addition to the registration or recorded delivery fee and first class postage, of extra postage of 10p, which must be affixed in stamps before a letter is presented. In London the posting times on the trains are exhibited on the special posting boxes provided at those main line terminal stations from which the Travelling Post Offices depart. Letters and packets can also be accepted at stations where the travelling Post Offices stop. The local Head Post Office will give details of posting times.

EXPRESS SERVICES

The following express services are available:

(1) By Post Office messenger all the way.
(2) Delivery at the addressees' request, by Post Office messenger from the delivery office after transmission by post.
(3) Railex—conveyance of a letter or packet to a railway station by Post Office messenger for despatch by the first available train, and for its delivery by messenger from the station of destination.

Express letters and packets sent under (1) must have the word 'EXPRESS' clearly written above the address in the left-hand corner of the cover; these items must not be posted in a posting box. The charge for the service is 50p a mile or part of a mile from the Post Office to the place of delivery. Items sent by this service may be registered or sent by Recorded Delivery (see p. 138). Railex letters and packets cannot be registered.

Persons or firms who wish to have their mail delivered by service (2) before the ordinary time of delivery may make an application on a form obtainable at most post offices. The fee

136

for this service is 50p a mile for one packet and a further charge of 2½p for every 10 or up to 10 additional packets beyond the first. The express fee on at least one packet must be prepaid in stamps affixed to the application form.

CASH ON DELIVERY (C.O.D.). Under this service the 'Trade Charge' (that is, the amount specified by the sender) can be collected from the addressee when a parcel or first class letter is delivered, and remitted to the sender by means of a special order. The following conditions must be fulfilled:

(1) The amount to be collected must not exceed £50, or contain a fraction of 1p.
(2) The name and address of both sender and addressee, and the amount of the trade charge, must be clearly shown on the cover in ink. A special adhesive address label may be obtained from the post office.
(3) The sender must complete the trade charge form and prepay the C.O.D. fee of 40p.
(4) The sender will obtain a certificate of posting from the post office for a registered letter packet or a compensation fee parcel, and for an unregistered parcel if required.
(5) The C.O.D. service must not be used to send unsolicited goods.

The C.O.D. parcel service operates to some overseas countries. For details see *Post Office Guide*.

REGISTRATION. All inland letters (except airway letters, Railex or railway letters or parcels) and parcels and packages

REGISTERED

Bennett & Campbell (Kent) Ltd
74 St Vincent Street
GLASGOW
G2 5TS

may be sent by First Class letter post provided they conform to certain size regulations (see pp. 132 and 142), and all letters containing coins, treasury notes, jewellery or certain watches, must be registered. The minimum registration fee of 45p provides compensation for loss or damage up to £200. Higher

137

compensation may be obtained by paying higher fees shown in a schedule in the *Post Office Guide*.

All letters and parcels intended for registration must be handed to an officer at the post office, and a certificate of posting, giving an acknowledgment that the fee for registration has been paid, must be obtained. A receipt is obtained for a registered letter or parcel when it is delivered. The word 'REGISTERED' must be clearly marked on the packet and two blue lines drawn across it, as shown. The string on registered parcels must be secured with sealing wax or by means of a lead, steel, or strong metal seal crushed with a press. Overseas parcels cannot be registered but may be insured.

CERTIFICATES OF POSTING. These may be obtained from post offices when the letters or parcels are posted. Certificates of Posting for overseas parcels are issued free of charge. A Certificate of Posting for a letter or packet or an ordinary inland parcel costs 1p.

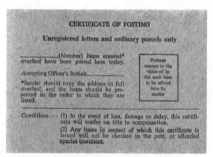

RECORDED DELIVERY SERVICE. Any inland postal packet, except a parcel, Railex packet and C.O.D. packet, railway or air letter, can be sent by this service which provides proof of posting and of delivery.

Letters and packets for recorded delivery must be taken to the post office. A fee of 8p per packet, additional to the postage, is payable. The name of the addressee must be written on the recorded delivery receipt, and the gummed label at the end of receipt must be detached and affixed to the left-hand top corner of the envelope. The officer at the post office will date-stamp and initial the receipt, which should be kept by the poster. Recorded delivery packets must not be posted in a letter-box.

The receiver of a recorded delivery packet must sign a receipt. If the sender completes an advice of delivery form and

138

THE SIX FASTEST POST OFFICE METHODS OF DELIVERY FOR INLAND LETTERS AND PACKETS[1]

	Service	Input	Arrival	Cost	Notes[2]
FAST	1st class	Any postbox (see note)	Next day (in nearly all cases)	8½p up to 60g	Valuables or money should not be sent. Metered items must be posted in accordance with special regulations
FASTER	Special Delivery	Hand in at Post Office	Possibly same day	Postage plus 60p	The letter will travel by ordinary mail but may be sent out by special messenger
FASTER	Railway Letter	Hand in at Railway Station	Possibly same day if collected by addressee	1st class postage plus railway fee (24p to 40p)	Weight limit is 450g (60g to Republic of Ireland). Valuables or money may not be sent
FASTER	Airway Letter	Hand in at British Airways (European Division) **Air Terminal**	Possibly same day if collected by addressee	Postage plus airway fee (55p)	Weight limit is 450g. Available only on certain inland services
FASTEST	Railex	Hand in at certain Post Offices	Same day if posted in time	£4 flat rate	Weight limit is 450g (60g in Northern Ireland). Valuables or money may not be sent
FASTEST	PO Messenger all the way	Hand in at certain Post Offices	As soon as journey is completed	50p a mile	Registered or Recorded Delivery is available and a reply service can be arranged

[1] Packets are bulky envelopes and larger items which are paid for at letter rate. They are subject to the same weight and size regulations as 1st and 2nd class letters. Above a certain weight parcel post may be cheaper, but there are no express or registered parcel post services. A CF (Compensation Fee) service replaced the registered service for inland parcels on **4 September 1972**.
[2] **Refer to the Post Office Guide** for more detailed information.

pays an additional 10p fee, he will be notified when the packet has been delivered.

Recorded delivery packets must not contain bank notes, coins or jewellery.

Enquiries regarding the non-delivery of packets sent by this service must be made on a form which is obtained from the post office. A fee of 20p is charged unless the advice of delivery fee has been paid. The original receipt must be produced if an enquiry is made. Compensation up to a maximum of £2 may be paid in cases of loss or damage.

CALLERS SERVICES

The Post Office provides the following four Callers Services through which mail may be received earlier or at a more convenient time than normal delivery by the postman. Each service involves the addressee (or his authorised representative) calling at the post office which serves the address to which the mail would normally be delivered. All mail must bear the full address including the Box number if a Private Box is used, for example:

> T Smith & Co Ltd
> PO Box 100
> 9 High Street
> HULL
> HU9 1HF

1. The *Private Box Service* (town districts) allocates a Box number for use in the address. Mail is usually handed to the addressee when he calls at the post office but at some offices the mail is placed in a locked box to which the addressee holds a

140

key. The standard fees for using this service during the daytime are:

> Letters—£20 per year
> Parcels—£20 per year
> Letters and Parcels—£40 per year

2. *Private Bags.* The post office will sort mail into a lockable private bag ready for collection. The addressee must provide the bag. Although arrangements can be made for the Private Bag to be delivered to the addressee (provided it does not weigh more than 1·1 kg when empty) it must normally be taken to the post office. The annual charges for town districts are:

For letters—£20	For letters and parcels—£40
For parcels—£20	Delivery of Bag by postman—£20 for each regular daily delivery

3. *Callers Service.* In a rural district the addressee may call regularly at the post office for correspondence without the need to provide a Private Bag. The annual fee for this service is £20 covering both letters and parcels, but if the addressee needs to call after 6.0 a.m. and before the first delivery by postmen begins and when the public office is normally closed, an additional annual fee of £20 is payable.

4. *Registered and Recorded Delivery—Delivery to Callers.* The addressee may call regularly for Registered and Recorded Delivery packets during office opening hours on payment of a fee of £5. This fee is not charged to Private Box or Bag renters.

SELECTAPOST

A company's or an organisation's mail can be subdivided before delivery into separate departments. An indication of the division must of course be shown in the address so that mail may be sorted and delivered direct to different departments. The charges for this service are set separately for each customer and the minimum period for which the service is charged is a year. Applications for the Selectapost service should be made to the local Head Postmaster.

DELIVERY AT ANOTHER ADDRESS

This service enables mail addressed to a person at his office to be delivered to his private address or vice versa; or mail can be diverted from one branch of a business to another. The annual fee is £52 for each address from which mail is to be diverted.

COLLECTIONS FROM PRIVATE POSTING BOXES

Arrangements may be made for letter mail to be collected from Private Posting Boxes. The customer must provide, fix and maintain the box. The Post Office provides the lock and retains the keys. Boxes must conform to a design laid down by the Post Office and charges vary according to the situation of the box within the building and the frequency of collections.

THE POST OFFICE PARCELS SERVICE (INLAND)

Compensation Fee (CF) Parcels. The registered parcel service was withdrawn on 4 September 1972 and replaced by a Compensation Fee service. Under the new arrangements compensation for loss or damage can be claimed if a compensation fee has been paid at the time of posting. Compensation fees payable in addition to postage are:

    7p   limit of compensation £10
    12p limit of compensation £50
    20p limit of compensation £100 maximum

A 'Certificate of Posting' form must be completed for each Compensation Fee parcel. Give the parcel and the Certificate of Posting to the counter clerk at the post office. When you have affixed stamps to the value of the fee you wish to pay, the clerk will initial and date stamp the top portion of the Certificate of Posting and hand it to you to keep.

Other parcels. If you are posting a parcel and do not wish to pay a compensation fee you may still obtain a Certificate of Posting. There is a fee of 1p per parcel.

Parcels and packages may still be sent as First Class registered letters provided they conform to the size regulations for First Class letters (see page 132). The registration fees are:

    45p limit of compensation £200
    50p limit of compensation £400
    55p limit of compensation £600 maximum

COMPENSATION FEE (C.F.) PARCELS
CERTIFICATE OF POSTING

Enter below in ink the name and full address as written on the parcel and tick the appropriate box at the bottom of the form

Name...

Address...

....

....

PLEASE SEE NOTES OVERLEAF
KEEP THIS RECEIPT – It must be produced if you need to make a claim.

STAMP(S)		Date Stamp
		Inland COD form No.
	Fee	Accepting Officer's Initials

COMPENSATION

Up to	£10	£50	£100	Date Stamp
Fee	5p	10p	20p	
Tick fee ► required				

PP 89B

How to post Compensation Fee parcels. Fill in the name and address of addressee and tick the appropriate box showing the fee you wish to pay.

Local Parcels are those which have in their address the same post town as that of the office of posting. The rates for Local Parcels are cheaper than those for other parcels, for example:

Not over	Ordinary Parcels	Local Parcels
1kg	48p	39p
2kg	62p	53p
5kg	98p	89p
10kg	142p	132p

Datapost is an overnight door-to-door collection and delivery service which is suitable for computer material, wages records and medical supplies. Datapost charges are arranged by negotiation as each contract is specially geared to the customer's requirements.

143

The Postage Forward Parcel Service is useful for companies who run a 'free approval' service. The Postage Forward service enables customers to return goods at no cost to themselves. The cost to the company is £15 for a yearly licence and 5p per parcel over the usual rate.

Special Collections. Firms who regularly despatch at least 20 parcels each day can make arrangements for them to be collected by Post Office van.

Under the *Railex* service packages (up to a maximum weight of 450g) are collected and despatched on the first available train. At the arrival station, the parcel is taken straight to the addressee by Post Office messenger.

Parcels may also be sent by the C & D, TCF or Red Star services provided by British Rail. These services are described on pp. 12–15.

OVERSEAS POSTAL SERVICES AND RATES

Full postal rates and regulations are given in the *Post Office Guide* and in various leaflets available at post offices.

There are different postage rates for the categories of mail in the overseas postal service. The main categories are letters, postcards and printed papers, but there are others. There are airmail and surface mail services to all countries for all categories. However, under the *All-up Service*, letters and postcards to Europe paid at the surface mail rate go by air at no extra cost when this speeds delivery. The letter rate of postage should be paid on other categories of mail sent to Europe if air transmission is required.

A special *Air Mail Leaflet*, obtainable from any post office, gives full details of all air services.

Air Letters, which can be bought at any post office for 10½p and 11p, may be sent to any address in the world outside Europe. They must not contain enclosures.

Blue air mail labels must be affixed to all letters and packets for transmission by air to destinations outside Europe. Air rates are assessed according to the weight of the letter or package, therefore special light-weight paper and envelopes should be used.

PRINTED PAPERS sent in the overseas post must conform to the regulations published in the *Post Office Guide*. In particular, it should be remembered that they must not be sealed against inspection. The same applies to some other categories of overseas post (small packets, phonopost packets and samples).

REPLY COUPONS. If you wish a friend or client abroad to reply to your letter, without his having to pay postage, you cannot, of course, send a stamped, addressed envelope bearing a British stamp. You can, however, buy an International

Reply Coupon (price 13p) from a post office, and enclose this with your communication. These coupons may be exchanged abroad for stamps representing the minimum postage payable for a letter from that country to this country.

EXPRESS DELIVERY (OVERSEAS)

In many countries postal packets can be delivered to the addressee by express messenger as soon as possible after they are received in the office of delivery. A special fee of 60p must be paid in addition to the normal postage. The envelope or cover, and the despatch note in the case of parcels, must bear the word EXPRESS in capital letters in red ink or red pencil, above the address.

145

COD PARCELS (OVERSEAS)

Many countries will arrange for the price of the goods (the 'Trade Charge') to be collected before delivery and sent to the sender. The maximum trade charge collected by any country is £50. The COD fee is £1 per parcel and must be prepaid in addition to the postage.

AIR PARCELS

Air parcels may be sent to almost all parts of the world. The maximum weight is 10kg. A Customs Declaration is needed and in some cases a Despatch Note also.

OVERSEAS PARCELS

The senders of parcels to some countries may arrange to pay all customs and other charges normally collected from the addressee. The service is known internationally by the title 'Franc de Droits' (Free of Charges) or by the initials FDD. There is no additional fee for this service but the sender is asked to pay a deposit on account of the charges. The parcel must be marked 'To be delivered free of charges' or 'Franc de Droits' and applications for this service should be made to Postal Finance Department, Cashier's Section, Postal Headquarters, St. Martin's-le-Grand, London EC1A 1HQ.

(b) MISCELLANEOUS SERVICES

National Insurance stamps may be bought at any post office. The following pensions and allowances are paid at post offices:

Widows' pensions,
Retirement pensions,
War pensions,
Sickness benefit,
Supplementary pensions or allowance,
Maternity allowances,
Family allowances.

SAVINGS AND INVESTMENTS. As well as transmitting money, Department for National Savings business may be transacted at Post Office counters.

The National Savings Bank is an ideal place to deposit your savings. You may open a Savings Bank Ordinary account with 25p at any of the 21000 savings bank post offices in the

United Kingdom. You will be given a bank book in which your deposits are recorded. Interest at the rate of 4 per cent per annum is paid on deposits.

When you wish to withdraw some money from your account, you may obtain any sum up to £30 by filling in a withdrawal form and giving it (together with your bank book) to the officer at any savings bank post office.

If you wish to withdraw more than £30, you should complete a Notice of Withdrawal form, obtainable at the post office, and send it in the envelope provided to the Savings Bank Headquarters, who will return the form to you within a few days. You may then take the withdrawal form and your bank book to the post office which you have named on the form, and the money will be paid to you.

Investment Accounts are designed for bigger, longer-term saving. The current rate of interest is 9 per cent per annum. You may open an Investment Account with £1 but 1 month's notice is required for withdrawals.

You can also buy National Savings Stamps, National Savings Certificates, British Savings Bonds, Premium Savings Bonds and make monthly payments into the SAYE scheme at the Post Office.

National Savings Stamps cost 10p each and are an ideal way of saving small amounts towards an investment in National Savings.

National Savings Certificates cost £1 per unit and each unit increases in value to £1·25 at the end of four years.

British Savings Bonds are sold in units of £5. An interest rate of 9½ per cent per annum is paid twice yearly on the current issue, and the Bonds are repayable at the rate of £103 for each £100 held at the end of five years.

Premium Savings Bonds may be bought in units of £1, subject to a minimum purchase of £2, but no person may own more than 2000. These Bonds earn no interest for individual holders, but the owner of a Bond has the chance of winning a tax-free prize in monthly and weekly prize draws. No Bond is included in the draw until it has been held for three clear months. The serial numbers of prize-winning Bonds are selected by an electronic machine and the winners are notified by post. The serial numbers of the winning Bonds (but not the names of the owners) are published in the newspapers.

147

The National Savings Bank operates a scheme called Save As You Earn or SAYE. The saver signs an agreement to save a fixed amount from £4 to £20 each month for five years. If at the end of five years the saver wishes to withdraw his money from the National Savings Bank each of the 60 contributions will be adjusted in line with any change in the Retail Price

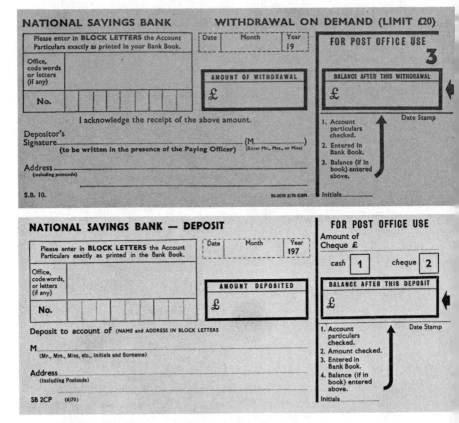

Index which has occurred between the time of making the contribution and completion of the agreement. Alternatively, the saver can leave his money in the Savings Bank for a further two years without making any more payments. If he chooses to do this his contributions will be adjusted in line with the RPI on the 7th anniversary of the start date of the contract. A tax-free bonus equal to two monthly contributions is also paid.

The saver is allowed to withdraw his money before the end of the five years. If the money is withdrawn during the first year, no interest is paid. If it is withdrawn after the first year but before the end of the fifth year, the saver receives 6 per cent interest on the amount he saved.

Anyone 16 or over can save with SAYE in one of three ways:

1. *Through the Post Office.* The saver can make cash payments each month at the post office or he can have the amount transferred to the National Savings Bank from his National Giro account every month.

2. *Through a bank.* A saver with a bank account can use a standing order to pay the monthly amount (see p. 241).

3. *Through his employer.* If the saver's employer participates in a SAYE scheme, the monthly amounts are deducted from the saver's wages or salary and paid directly to the National Savings Bank.

The SAYE contract forms are available from post offices, banks and participating employers.

Note: If you wish to apply for repayment of British Savings Bonds or to make a withdrawal from an Investment account you must give one month's notice. It is therefore sensible to use these forms of investment for money which you can afford to put aside as long-term savings.

The Post Office issues broadcast receiving licences, motor licences and dog licences.

Note that although forms of application for Driving Licences are obtainable from post offices, the completed form must be sent to the Taxation Department of your local county council. A form of application for a Driving Test is also obtainable from a post office. This form, when completed, must be sent to the Clerk of the Traffic Area where the test is to be taken. The names and addresses of the traffic areas are listed on the back of the application form.

EXERCISES

1. In what circumstances might you wish to use the Poste Restante service?

2. What procedure is necessary before a firm can print Business Reply Cards?

3. You have to despatch 350 circulars and have insufficient stamps in the office. What would you do?

4. Consult the *Post Office Guide* for the following information:
   (*a*) articles which may not be sent by post,
   (*b*) packets which the Post Office classifies as 'Embarrassing',
   (*c*) regulations regarding window, and aperture envelopes,
   (*d*) 'trap' packets,
   (*e*) redirection of postal packets by the Post Office,
   (*f*) the minimum registration fee.

5. What are the postage rates in force at the present time for:
   (*a*) inland postcards,
   (*b*) a letter to France,
   (*c*) a postcard to Italy,
   (*d*) airmail letters to Australia,
   (*e*) surface parcel post to Ceylon,
   (*f*) airmail parcel post to Finland?

6. What are postcodes?

7. Explain the 'two-tier postal system' and its importance to the office.   (RSA, OP, I)

8. (*a*) Describe the Post Office services which can be used to ensure that written communications are received (i) speedily, (ii) safely.
   (*b*) Explain the Business Reply Service offered by the Post Office.
   (*c*) How would you arrange to prepay a reply to a letter sent overseas?   (RSA, OP, II)

9. Give an example of an address with a postal code. In what ways are we asked to assist the Post Office in improving the handling and delivery of mail?   (RSA, OP, I)

10. (*a*) Complete the relevant part of the Recorded Delivery form below for a packet which you are sending to:
    John Green & Co. Ltd., 13 Cheshire Street, Millston, M16 8CC
    (*b*) When would you use the Recorded Delivery Service?
    (*c*) When would you use Registered Post?   (RSA, OP, I)

11. The Post Office guide gives definite instructions on how
    mail should be addressed.   Make specimens, to show your
    familiarity with these instructions, of
    (*a*) A Poste Restante letter.
    (*b*) An Air Mail letter.
    (*c*) A tie-on label.   (RSA, OP, I)

Chapter 5

Communications

COMMUNICATIONS are an essential part of our lives. Nearly every day we send or receive information and messages. If we have something to say to somebody and cannot see him and speak to him directly, we have to choose an alternative means of communication; we can write a letter, make a telephone call or send a telegram. The method we choose will depend upon the circumstances.

Very much the same thing happens in the business world. In Chapter I we learnt that part of the clerical function of an office was to receive and pass on information. This information may also be transmitted by letter, telephone or telegram; but business firms frequently use other methods (like the teleprinter) which are not available to private individuals.

In this chapter we shall study these methods of communication. You must know how to use them correctly and how to choose the most suitable method in any given situation.

(a) LETTERS

We all have to write letters. The letters we write to our friends and relations are called *personal letters*. Sometimes we need to write *business letters*; letters arranging holiday accommodation or letters to your local council, your insurance company, gas or electricity company would come under this heading.

Nearly all the letters written in offices are business letters. If, however, an executive is writing on his firm's behalf to an executive in another firm who happens to be a friend of his as well as a business associate, he may write a *semi-personal letter*, that is, a business letter using less formal language. Whereas a normal business letter starts 'Dear Sir', a semi-personal letter will start 'Dear Jim' or 'Dear Mr. Williams'.

A fourth type of letter is known as an *official letter*; this means a letter written by a government department.

The ability to write a good letter is highly valued in the business world. A letter which is clearly and concisely written, correctly spelt and pleasantly displayed, will convey to the recipient a better impression of the writer and his firm than an untidy, rambling letter containing grammatical errors and spelling mistakes.

It is the responsibility of the dictater to see that the information contained in the letter is correct and that the wording is polite and clear. The typist's responsibility is to type the letter accurately and to display it so that it presents a pleasing appearance.

One of the distinctions between a shorthand-typist and an experienced secretary is that the secretary is able to compose a letter from brief outline instructions. As soon as an employer realises that a typist can compose letters without his having to dictate every word, he will begin to consider promoting her to a more responsible position.

The requirements of a good letter can be summarised as follows:

(1) The information, grammar and spelling should be correct.

(2) The wording should be polite and simple to understand.

(3) The letter should be displayed pleasantly and in accordance with accepted procedure.

When you start work you will be shown how your employer likes his letters displayed. This is called the *Rule of the House*, and you must follow it.

Letter display styles have changed rapidly in recent years. Until about ten years ago, the style known as semi-indented was the most common. During the late 1960's increasing numbers of organisations adopted the fully-blocked style, frequently with open punctuation, that is no punctuation marks after any of the lines above and below the body of the letter. In the fully-blocked style, which has been accepted American practice for many years, *every* line begins flush with the left-hand margin.

However, after a short trial of the fully-blocked style some firms decided to move the date back to the right-hand side for the sake of clarity and to facilitate filing and reference work.

A style now seems to be evolving (which might be termed

'simplified British' but is referred to as 'blocked' by some writers) which combines the efficiency and modern appearance of left-axis designs and open punctuation, with the need for the date to be in a conspicuous position on the right-hand side of the page when handling carbon copies or looking through files. Examples of this layout can be seen on pages 153, 161 and 208.

In the layout referred to as NOMA (because it is recommended by the National Office Management Association of America) there is no salutation or complimentary close; the punctuation style is 'open' and every line starts flush with the left-hand margin. This style is frequently recommended by O and M specialists but so far it has not been widely adopted in Great Britain.

BUSINESS LETTERS
1. Printed heading
Business firms have a heading printed on their letter paper. The printed heading will state: (*a*) the name of the company, (*b*) the address, and (*c*) the telephone number.

It may also state:
> (*d*) the telegraphic address (a shortened name to be used on telegrams),
> (*e*) the names of the directors, and nationality, if not British.
> (*f*) the telex number (if any),
> (*g*) a description of the firm's business,
> (*h*) the words 'Our ref.' and 'Your ref.' Alongside 'Your ref.' may be typed the reference of the person to whom you are writing, if this is known. Alongside 'Our ref.' may be written the departmental reference or name of the person writing the letter. A common type of reference is the initials of the dictater followed by the initials of the typist, e.g. AKT/BMS would indicate that AKT had dictated the letter and BMS had typed it. Sometimes the reference includes the name of the department and a reference number, e.g. Claims/9307/PGP/EVK.
>
> If the printed heading provides no space for the reference this may be typed at the left-hand side of the page underneath the heading; sometimes references are typed at the bottom left-hand corner of the page.

Until 1 January 1973 the information to be shown on letter headings was governed by Section 201 of the Companies Act 1948 and the Registration of Business Names Act 1916.

To comply with the European Communities Act 1972 and Value Added Tax legislation, additional information must now be given on business stationery, i.e. letter headings, order forms, trade catalogues and circulars, tax invoices and credit notes.* Section 9 (7) of the European Communities Act 1972 which came into force on 1 January 1973 requires letter headings to show:

(*a*) Registration number, i.e. the number appearing on the company's certificate of incorporation,

(*b*) Place of registration,

(*c*) Address of company's registered office,

(*d*) The words LIMITED LIABILITY in the case of a limited company exempt from the obligation to use the word 'limited' as part of its name,

(*e*) Reference to paid-up capital when reference is made to the amount of share capital.

* *Business Stationery Must Meet E.E.C. And V.A.T. Requirements*, published by the British Federation of Master Printers.

Directors: A B Brown, C D Cobb, J D Green, R U Shaw (USA)

CLASSIC WHOLESALERS LTD

Registered number 000 000 England
Registered office 24 Market Street Anytown Anyshire   *Telephone* 00–123 4567

SCIENTIFIC PROMOTION ASSOCIATION

LIMITED LIABILITY

Registered number 000000 Scotland
Telephone 00–321 7654

10 High Street
Oldtown
Oldshire
(Registered office)

Fully-indented (*rarely seen nowadays*).

Semi-indented or indented (*now considered rather old-fashioned*).

Semi-blocked (*for some organisations the adoption of this style was a sort of half-way stage towards the adoption of the fully-blocked*).

Fully-blocked or blocked (*this style has been accepted American practice for many years and was adopted by an increasing number of organisations in the late 1960's*).

```
Our ref:  FGB/RMD                              10 January 1976


Miss Margaret Mansfield
The Wool Centre
High Street
BANFIELD
Essex
ES6 4BA


Dear Miss Mansfield

Thank you for your order dated 3 January, no. 221, for 'Alpine'
and 'Modale' wool and instruction leaflets.  This order will be
despatched to you by passenger train within the next few days.

We should like to bring to your attention our new range of
knitting accessories, full particulars of which are shown on
the enclosed leaflet.  Many of these are very suitable for small
gifts and you may like to include them as a special feature in
your Easter window display.

Our representative hopes to call on you during the last week of
this month.  He will be pleased to show you samples of our
knitting accessories; he will also give you advance information
of the leaflets we are producing of new spring and summer styles.

Yours sincerely



F G Beckwith
Sales Promotion


Enc:  1
```

After a short trial of the fully-blocked style, many firms decided to move the date back to the right-hand side for the sake of clarity and to facilitate filing and reference work.   The style illustrated above and on pp. 165, 212, and 213 (which could be termed simplified British *but is referred to as* blocked *by some writers) now seems to be evolving and may become the standard layout of the future; it combines the efficiency and modern appearance of left-axis designs and open punctuation with the need for the date to be in a conspicuous position on the right-hand side of the page.*

157

kores

manufacturing company limited

Kores Carbon Papers and Typewriter Rib
Plastofoil Carbon
Plastograph Waxless Carbon F
Drytype and Nylotype Ste
Kores Duplicator Inks and Sur
Korofax Self-Copy F
Contractors to H M Governe

Harlow 20411 (10 lines) ● STD Code 0.

Telegrams Korescarbo Ha
Cablegrams Korescarbo Ha
Telex No. 8

Registered Office:
West Road Temple Fields Harlow Essex CM20 2AL
Registered No: England 252960

An example of a clear letter heading.

2. The date

This is written on the right-hand side of the page opposite the reference or slightly lower. The following form, which starts with the smallest unit of time and progresses to the largest (day, month, year) is most usual:

29 December 1976

The following form is also acceptable:

December 29 1976

3. The inside address

The name and address of the person to whom the letter is being written (the addressee) is known as the inside address.

An individual may be addressed in one of the following ways:

E J Harris Esq
Mr E J Harris
Mrs P W Midwood
Miss J C Frost

'Esq' is the abbreviation of 'Esquire' and is considered more courteous in writing than 'Mr'. The full form is never used. If you do not know the initials of the person to whom you are writing (and cannot look them up), it is necessary to use 'Mr' in the address.

There are special forms of address for titled people (lists of which are given in most typists' reference books and in *Titles and Forms of Address*, published by A & C Black) and an accepted order for titles and professional qualifications. A conferred or hereditary title (such as *Sir* or *Lord*) must immediately precede the name of the person and follow any other title, for

158

example, Colonel Sir Charles Reddaway. Initials after a name are arranged in the following sequence:

1 Orders of chivalry, civil honours and decorations conferred by the Queen, eg VC, KCMG. (The VC and GC precede all other honours.)
2 Military decorations, eg DSO, DFC.
3 Academic and professional; letters standing for degrees, such as MSc, precede letters standing for membership of a professional association, such as AMIMechE. Lower university degrees precede higher ones.

Examples:

```
Field-Marshal Viscount Montgomery, K.G., G.C.B., D.S.O.,
                         or
Field-Marshal Viscount Montgomery KG GCB DSO


Sir Solly Zuckerman, C.B., M.A., M.D., D.Sc., F.R.S.,
                         or
Sir Solly Zuckerman CB MA MD DSc FRS
```

Messrs. When people form a partnership, the courtesy title 'Messrs' is used. This is an abbreviation of the French word 'Messieurs' and is used in this country as the plural of 'Mr'. Thus Mr Dawson and Mr Phillips, trading together, would be addressed in writing as Messrs Dawson and Phillips.

The majority of business letters are addressed to limited companies[1] and no courtesy prefix is necessary:

```
            Johnson and Teape Ltd
            The Metal File Co Ltd
            Sir James Baker & Co Ltd
```

Whenever possible it is better to address a letter to an official of the company. If, however, this is expressly forbidden in the

[1] A limited liability company is a form of business organisation, in which a number of people called shareholders have invested their money, and appointed directors to run the business for them. When the company is registered it is given a 'life' or independent existence of its own, and in law it is the company and not the shareholders who are responsible for its activities. As it is an artificial person it is necessary for the company to act through one of its officers, usually the company secretary in official matters, and this is why letters to the company may be addressed to him.

159

SUGGESTED LAYOUT FOR GENERAL BUSINESS LETTERS

1(h)
xxxxxxxxxxxxxxxxxxxx

2
xxxxxxxxxxxxxxxxxx

3
xxxxxxxxxxxxxxxxxxxxxxxxxxxxxx
xxxxxxxxxxxxxxxxxxxxxxxxxxxx
xxxxxxxxxxxxxxxxxxxx
xxxxxxxxxxxxx

4
xxxxxxxxxxxxxx

6
xxxxxxxxxxxxxxxxxxxxxxxxxxxxxxxxxxxxxxx

7
xxxxxxxxxxxxxxxxxxxxxxxxxxxxxxxxxxxxxxxxxxxxxxxxxxxxxxxxxxxxxxxxx
xxxxxxxxxxxxxxxxxxxxxxxxxxxxxxxxxxxxxxxxxxxxxxxxxxxxxxxxxxxxxxxxx
xxxxxxxxxxxxxxxxxxxxxxxxxxxxxxxxxxxxxxxxxxxxxxxxxxxxxxxxxxxxxxxxx
xxxxxxxxxxxxxxxxxxxxxxxxxxxxxxxx

xxxxxxxxxxxxxxxxxxxxxxxxxxxxxxxxxxxxxxxxxxxxxxxxxxxxxxxxxxxxxxxxx
xxxxxxxxxxxxxxxxxxxxxxxxxxxxxxxxxxxxxxxxxxxxxxxxxxxxxxxxxxxxxxxxx
xxxxxxxxxxxxxxxxxxxxxxxxxxxxxxxxxxxxxxxxxxxxxxxxx

xxxxxxxxxxxxxxxxxxxxxxxxxxxxxxxxxxxxxxxxxxxxxxxxxxxxxxxxxxxxxxxxx
xxxxxxxxxxxxxxxxxxxxxxxxxxxxxxxxxxx

5
xxxxxxxxxxxxxxxxxxxxxx

8
xxxxxxxxxxxxxxxxxxxxxxxxxx
xxxxxxxxxxxxxxxxxxxxxxxx

9
xxxxxxxxxxx

Suggested layout for general business letters. 1(h)—Reference 2—Date 3—Inside address 4—Salutation 5—Complimentary close 6—Subject heading 7—Body of letter 8—Signature and designation of writer 9—Enclosures.

printed heading by some such instruction as 'All communications must be addressed to the company and not to individuals', the letter may be addressed to the Secretary, or be marked for the attention of the official who will deal with it, if his name is known.

<u>For the attention of Mr J Gorman Sales Manager</u>

The Amalgamated Plastic Co Ltd
Torpedo Works
Long Lane
YORK
YO1 6EB

Many American companies have the abbreviation 'Inc' included in the title. This stands for 'incorporated'. French firms use 'et Cie', and German firms 'GmbH' in place of 'Ltd'.

The word 'Mesdames' is used for the plural of 'Mrs'. Two sisters may be addressed thus: The Misses J and C Brown.

The inside address is written two line spaces below the date on the left-hand side of the page. Nowadays the block method (each line starting at the left-hand margin) is preferred. The indented form (the second and succeeding lines starting 5 spaces to the right of the previous line) is permissible but nowadays considered old-fashioned.

4. The salutation

The salutation is the greeting which commences the letter and precedes the message. The most usual salutation in business letters is 'Dear Sir', or 'Dear Sirs', or 'Dear Madam'.

	Salutation	Complimentary close
GENERAL BUSINESS	Dear Sir Dear Sirs *Dear Madam	Yours faithfully Yours truly (*note small* f *and small* t)
OFFICIAL	Sir Gentlemen *Madam	Yours faithfully
SEMI-PERSONAL	Dear Mr Harris †Dear Harris Dear Ted	Yours sincerely With kind regards Yours sincerely
PERSONAL	Dear Ted My dear Ted	Yours very sincerely Very sincerely yours ‡Yours affectionately

* Used for single or married women.

† The omission of the courtesy title 'Mr.' and the use of the surname alone between men is an indication of closer acquaintance. Thus '**Dear Harris**' is more friendly than 'Dear Mr. Harris'.

‡ More affectionate terms than those given can, of course, be used in personal letters.

5. The complimentary close

This is the closing remark of the letter. The most common form in business letters is 'Yours faithfully', but others are sometimes used. The choice of the complimentary close is governed by the salutation, which in turn is governed by the relationship between the two correspondents. The plan on page 161 will give some guide as to the forms of salutation and complimentary close having similar degrees of familiarity.

```
Yours faithfully
THE ANDERSON RECORD CO LTD

    F. A. White

General Manager
```

```
Yours faithfully
pp DUBLIN ENTERPRISES LTD

    PM. Murphy

P M Murphy
Sales Manager
```

```
Yours faithfully
per pro TAVISTOCK ENGINEERING CO LTD

    G Reynolds

G Reynolds
Chief Accountant
```

```
Yours faithfully
EVES EXPORT CO LTD

    G. M. Drake

G M Drake (Mrs)
Director
```

If she is given permission by her employer, a secretary may sign letters thus:

```
Yours faithfully

(Mary G Barker)
Private Secretary to
Mr D F Tomlinson
```

6. Subject heading

A subject heading is frequently included in a business or official letter. As its name implies it states the subject of the letter and is of assistance when the letter is opened in the postal room and when the letter is being filed. The subject heading should be typed two line spaces below the salutation and flush with the margin in a left-hand axis display style.

7. Body of the letter

The body of the letter conveys the information or message to the addressee. It should be arranged in paragraphs. Each paragraph should start flush with the left-hand margin.

Some business letters are very brief and only occupy one paragraph. When you start writing letters you may find the 'Three-Paragraph' rule helpful: the first paragraph is an acknowledgement or introduction; the second paragraph conveys information and is factual; and the third paragraph suggests future action.

The examples given on pages 157 and 213 show this form of arrangement.

8. Signature

Directly under the complimentary close it is usual to write the name or position held by the person who is writing the letter. Sometimes the name of the company is also included; if so, it should be typed under the complimentary close and four or five spaces should be left before the designation or name of the signatory is typed.

9. Enclosures

When catalogues, price-lists or other leaflets and documents are enclosed with a letter, the word 'Enc.' or 'Encs.' is typed at the foot of the page at the left-hand side. Some offices prefer to use a red sticky label, sometimes shaped like an asterisk with the word 'Enclosure' printed on it, for this purpose. Boxes of these labels may be bought from shops selling office sundries.

Both these methods have two purposes: one, to remind the typist to enclose the documents in the envelope; and two, to draw the attention of the person who opens the packet to the fact that something has been enclosed.

Continuation sheets

Unless printed continuation sheets are provided, the second page of a letter should be typed on a plain sheet. The name of the addressee, the page number and the date should be typed at the top of the continuation sheet.

```
J.M. Jones, Esq.          - 2 -        11 September, 1976


have reached a stage where we feel able to assure you of
production dates in the future.
```

Style suitable for semi-block or semi-indented letters.

```
Page 2

11 September 1976

J M Jones Esq


have reached a stage where we feel able to assure you of
production dates in the future.
```

Style suitable for letters typed in full-block or fully-blocked styles.

```
                              Page 2
                              11 September 1976
                              J M Jones Esq



have reached a stage where we feel able to assure you of
production dates in the future.
```

Style suitable for letters typed in the style sometimes referred to as Simplified British, that is fully-blocked except for the date which is typed on the right-hand side of the page.

BUSINESS LETTER

PRINTED HEADING

Our ref JRS/CMW   2 August 1972

The Conference Secretary
British Association for Business Education
Union House
13 Bristol Street
LONDON
WIN 9UZ

Dear Sir

Thank you for your letter of 29 July 1972. We note that
you propose to hold a one-day conference on the subject
of machine dictation on Saturday 14 March 1973, and wish
to exhibit some equipment.

We shall be pleased to show examples of our Regal Recorder
dictating equipment and can arrange to have a demonstrator
present.

We look forward to receiving full details of the venue and
programme in due course.

Yours faithfully
for REGAL DICTATING MACHINES LIMITED

J R Sanderson
Sales Manager

OFFICIAL LETTER

 HER MAJESTY'S STATIONERY OFFICE
Establishments and Organisation Division
Sovereign House, St Georges Street, Norwich, NOR 76A
Telephone Norwich 22211 ext.   60

J Doe Esq
CSD
Sanctuary Buildings
Westminster
LONDON
SW1

Our reference
E 73/2
Your reference
MS(OM) 33/02
Date
June 1969

Dear Doe

PAPER PRICE ADVISORY SERVICE

I thought it might be helpful, in view of the forthcoming
O & M investigation, if I set out very briefly the basic
purpose of this Service. Its main functions are

    a. to collect and process details of the paper
        prices currently, ie day by day, being asked
        and paid in each region, and

    b. to pass this comprehensive information as
        quickly as possible to all regional trade
        associations.

I enclose 4 copies of a draft paper giving fuller details
which has been specially compiled for you and the other
members of the review team by the Secretary to the Service.

Yours sincerely

A N Other
Assistant Director

ENCS 4

An official letter.   Note the blocked inside address, the open style of punctuation, the subject heading in block capitals, and the way the enclosures are indicated.   The printed letter-head is completed by typing the telephone extension number, the references and the date in the spaces provided.

Until a few years ago official letters were displayed quite differently from business letters; for example, the inside address was typed at the foot of the page in an indented form, the salutation and complimentary close were 'Official', enclosures were indicated by a row of full-stops in the left-hand margin of the letter, and the last word on a page (known as a catchword) was set underneath the last line of typing and repeated again at the top of the next page.

A suggested new format was recommended by the Civil Service Department O and M Division in 1969* and this has been adopted by most government departments. With two exceptions:

(1) All numerals over *one* and all fractions to be typed in figures, except where a numeral is the first word of a numbered paragraph or sub-paragraph in which case it should be spelt out to avoid confusion

(2) Pages are numbered at the foot of each page when there is more than one sheet; the second page is typed on the back of the first

the recommended display is identical to that suggested on page 157. The list of simplifications includes 'blocking' the inside address, omitting all punctuation above and below the body of the letter, no indentation of paragraphs, no catch-words, enclosures to be indicated by typing 'ENCS' at the bottom left-hand corner of the page and the subject heading to be typed in block capitals, not underscored.

As you can see from the illustration on page 166, an official letter is now displayed in almost the same style as a business letter.

SEMI-PERSONAL LETTERS

1. In many offices it is the practice to type the inside address (blocked) at the foot of the page on the left-hand side in semi-personal letters.

2. The salutation is Dear Mr Jones, or Dear Bill.

* 'Typing Topics—Towards a Simpler Letter Layout', G H E Fowler, *O & M Bulletin*, August 1969.

3. The complimentary close is
> Yours sincerely

or

> With kind regards
> Very sincerely yours

4. Some employers like to write the salutation and complimentary close by hand on semi-personal letters; this is known as 'topping and tailing' and sufficient space must be left for it when the letter is typed.

PERSONAL LETTERS

Personal letters are frequently hand-written. As they are not business records, it is unnecessary to take carbon copies. The inside address is usually omitted.

(*b*) INTERNAL MEMORANDA

Officials working for the same firm or organisation use memoranda forms to communicate with each other in writing. They are generally known as 'memos'. No salutation or complimentary close is used. It is customary for memoranda to be initialled, not signed in full.

Memorandum are sometimes typed on pre-printed forms, but when these are not provided, the information can be displayed as shown in the following example:

INTERNAL MEMORANDUM

FROM: J M Ramsay, Claims Department, Head Office   DATE: 5 May 1976

TO: Claims Department, Birmingham   REF: CPC/JMR

MR J FOSTER - CAR ACCIDENT

The estimate for repairs to Mr Foster's car has been approved. Please inform him accordingly.

INTEROFFICE MEMORANDUM

FROM: J M Ramsay, Claims Department, Head Office

TO: Claims Department, Birmingham

DATE: 5 May 1976

SUBJECT: MR J FOSTER - CAR ACCIDENT

The estimate for repairs to Mr Foster's car has been approved. Please inform him accordingly.

CPC/JMR

The memorandum on the left is typed in a centred style; the one on the right is blocked.

168

The parts of a memorandum are:

1 THE HEADING—INTERNAL MEMORANDUM or INTEROFFICE MEMORANDUM
2 FROM
3 TO
4 DATE
5 REFERENCE
6 SUBJECT HEADING
7 MESSAGE

No salutation or complimentary close is used. Memoranda may be initialled, not signed in full, but some managers prefer a full signature thinking that this gives the message a more personal touch.

INTERNAL DISTRIBUTION. Sometimes letters, memoranda and literature such as trade journals contain information which is relevant to more than one person. There are various ways of dealing with these situations.

Distribution stamp or circulation slip. A rubber stamp or a slip such as the one shown in the illustration is stamped on or stapled to the document or journal which has to be circulated.

A trade journal with a circulation slip stapled to it.

When each person listed has perused the document, he signs his initials in the space provided and passes the document or pamphlet on to the next person listed. The document is eventually returned to the person named in 'PLEASE RETURN TO' for action and/or filing.

An incoming letter stamped with a distribution stamp.

Action slip. Sometimes internal communications are routed by means of action slips. These small slips, frequently brightly coloured for prominence, are used to initiate action within an organisation; they may also be used to accompany a document upon which action is requested.

ACTION SLIP	
TO Chief Transport Officer	**FROM** Cashier
SUBJECT Travel Claim	**DATE** 17·2·73

Please authorise payment of attached & return.

Thankyou.

RMW.

An action slip.

Routing slip. A routing slip is used to accompany documents from one official to another within an organisation. The 'messages' will be compiled and printed to suit the requirements of the business.

ROUTING SLIP			
TO			
FOR APPROVAL		NOTE AND RETURN	
FOR INFORMATION		NOTE AND RETAIN	
FOR SIGNATURE		FOR TYPING	
FOR COMMENT		FOR RUNNING OFF	
FOR REVISION			
DATE		FROM	

A routing slip.

Carbon copies. When carbon copies are being sent to other persons within the firm, their names are usually listed in the bottom left-hand corner of the letter. Each recipient's name is underlined or ticked on one of the carbon copies; sometimes an additional caption is typed across the top of the page.

Sometimes the writer of the letter does not want the addressee to know that copies of the letter have been sent to other people. In these cases, the carbon copy notation is not typed on the original. When the typist has finished typing the letter, she draws out the top copy and types the list of names on the top carbon copy (and thus through all the carbon copies). These copies are known as 'blind copies' and any additions, which may be messages as well as names, may be prefixed with the letters *NOO* (not on original).

Multiple memoranda. If the contents of a memorandum are of interest to more than one official, a separate copy may be sent to each individual concerned or one copy may be routed to each

171

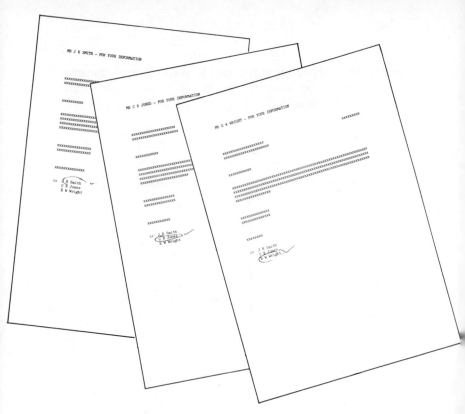

Carbon copies, annotated and ready for distribution.

person. In the latter case it is usual to use a circulation slip or distribution stamp. When a separate copy is sent to each official, the names of all the recipients are listed in the 'TO' section of the memorandum.

There are several ways in which the names of the recipients may be listed: (*a*) alphabetically, (*b*) by location, (*c*) according to rank, (*d*) according to job priority, and (*e*) for information only. The alphabetical method is simple, makes no allowance for rank and no one need feel slighted. Routing by location saves time, but pays no attention to job priority. The advantage of routing according to job priority is that the person who must act on the memorandum's contents sees it first. Sometimes memoranda are routed to certain officials who are not directly affected by their contents; this may be classified as 'informational routing'. It is usual to type the initials *FYI* (for your information) or *FIO* (for information only) next to the name.

172

Possibly the best method of routing is by job priority combined with informational routing, as this allows the person who has to act to see the memorandum first and also helps executives to keep in close touch with company operations. In most offices, the office manager will decide which method is to be used; he will, of course, choose the method best suited to the requirements of the organisation.

(c) TELEGRAMS AND CABLES

If you wished to communicate very quickly with someone who was not available by telephone, you would send a telegram. Telegrams may be sent to all parts of the country through the Post Office—they are called *Inland Telegrams*.

The charge for a telegram is calculated on the number of words used. It is, therefore, important to use as few words as possible. For this reason most business firms have a special abbreviated address for use on telegrams. This is known as a *telegraphic address*. Telegraphic addresses must be registered with the Post Office. The charge is £3 a year. The telegraphic address is usually included in the printed heading on a firm's letter paper (see page 93). Here are some examples of telegraphic addresses:

Ransom and Jones Ltd   Ranjon London
432 Holborn
LONDON
WC1R 4SR

British Steel Co Ltd   Britsteel Birmingham
Chancery Buildings
Old Street
BIRMINGHAM
B5 4LJ

SENDING A TELEGRAM

By hand. The telegrams should be typed or written in block capitals on the special form provided by the Post Office and handed in over the counter of the nearest post office. If it is

If you wish to pay for a reply insert RP here	ADDRESS	BLOCK LETTERS THROUGHOUT PLEASE
		WHISKY SCOTLAND

PLEASE DELIVER SIX CASES WHISKY S.S. EMPIRE
PRINCESS LYING GEORGE FIFTH DOCK GLASGOW

STANMILL LONDON

The particulars on the back of this form should be completed.

LETTER CONFIRMING TELEGRAM

Our ref: Stores/6739/WPD   3 September 1976

John Harper & Co Ltd
KILMARNOCK
K16 3SP

Dear Sirs

S S 'EMPIRE PRINCESS'

We confirm having sent you today the following
telegram: 'PLEASE DELIVER SIX CASES WHISKY S S
EMPIRE PRINCESS LYING GEORGE FIFTH DOCK GLASGOW'

Our official order No. S2310 is enclosed.

We shall be glad to receive your invoice when
the six cases of whisky have been delivered.

Yours faithfully
for STANTON & MILLS LTD

Head of Stores Department

Enc

typed, three or four spaces should be left between each word, and a carbon copy should be made. Remember to write the name and address of the sender in the space provided on the back of the telegram form, and write the full name and address of the addressee on the carbon copy. To keep costs at a minimum a telegram is usually confirmed by a detailed letter, written and posted immediately after the telegram is sent.

By telephone. Telegrams may be sent by telephone, from a private telephone or from a public call box. The dialling instructions will tell you the number to dial. The telegram should be dictated slowly to the post office operator. Remember to keep a copy of the telegram and note on it the time and date it was telephoned.

Greetings telegrams may be used for sending messages of congratulation or good wishes. They are delivered on decorative forms in colourful envelopes and cost more than ordinary telegrams.

Overnight telegrams may be sent between 8 a.m. and 10.30 p.m. for delivery normally by first post the following morning, except on days (Sundays and public holidays) when there is no postal delivery. Overnight telegrams are much cheaper than ordinary telegrams. The word 'Overnight' must be written before the address.

Priority telegrams cost 10p extra and are given priority over other telegrams in transmission and delivery.

Multiple address telegrams. Identical telegrams may be sent to two or more addresses in the same delivery area at a reduced charge.

Reply-paid telegrams. A sender may prepay the reply to his telegram when he sends it. A reply form, showing the amount prepaid, is delivered with the telegram to the addressee.

INTERNATIONAL TELEGRAMS

Telegrams may be sent to most parts of the world, to ships in port, to aircraft at airports and to trains at railway stations abroad. They are sent either by wireless or cable. When the route is not specified by the sender, the Post Office selects the route. International telegrams may be written on an International Telegram Form and handed in at a post office or Post Office international telegraph office or dictated by telephone or sent by Telex.

The Letter Telegram service enables international telegrams to be sent at half the rate for ordinary telegrams, with a minimum charge for 22 words including the indication ELT or LT. European Letter Telegrams (ELT) may be sent to countries in Europe and North Africa. Letter Telegrams (LT) may be sent to most places outside Europe. ELT and LT telegrams take longer than ordinary telegrams but are normally delivered the day following the day of handing in.

Facilities for sending international greetings telegrams, urgent telegrams, and multiple address telegrams are also available.

Details of charges for international telegrams are given in the *Post Office Guide*.

PHOTOTELEGRAPH SERVICES

Pictures, photographs, drawings, typed or written documents and plans may be telegraphed in facsimile from London to many places in the world. (A facsimile is an exact copy.)

The charges are calculated on the size of the item to be transmitted, which must be printed on one side only of the paper.

Phototelegrams are accepted at the more important post offices throughout the country and at International telegraph offices. They are forwarded by post to London for onward telegraphic transmission. Alternatively the sender may post his phototelegram direct to London with the necessary remittance. They are delivered from the office of receipt by post.

RADIOTELEGRAMS

Radiotelegrams may be sent to ships at sea. They may be written on an International Telegram form and handed in at a post office, dictated from a telephone or sent by Telex.

Radiotelegrams may also be sent from ships for delivery to addresses ashore.

(*d*) TELEPRINTERS

A teleprinter resembles a typewriter in appearance and can easily be operated by a typist after a little practice. When the typist types a message on the teleprinter, an identical message is typed on a distant teleprinter with which her machine is connected. Teleprinters enable two separate premises of one business firm to exchange information and messages instantaneously. It is not necessary for the typist to sit at the teleprinter machine all day, as messages received are printed automatically. As soon as a message is received, however, it should be taken from the machine and sent to the appropriate department. If the operator at the transmitting office wishes to attract the attention of the operator at the receiving office, she can press the figures key and a key marked 'BELL' which will ring a bell on the receiving machine.

(e) THE TELEX SERVICE

The Telex service is an extension of the teleprinter system. Formerly a teleprinter could only send a message to another machine with which it was permanently connected.

The Telex service provides a public teleprinter system and subscribers connected to the system can communicate direct with any other Telex subscriber in the United Kingdom and in many overseas countries.

The service operates day and night; providing the machine is switched on it will receive messages even though it is unattended. Each subscriber has a Telex number (which is shown on his headed letter paper) and is provided with a Telex Directory, which gives the numbers of all other United Kingdom Telex subscribers.

As you can see from the illustrations overleaf, a dial similar to a telephone dial is attached to the machine. The operator dials the number, and as she types the message it is automatically typed immediately on the receiving machine.

If you study the keyboard shown in the illustrations, you will see that it is very similar to a typewriter keyboard.

Using punched tape to send messages. A machine which translates information into a series of holes punched in tape can be attached to a Telex teleprinter. The typist can prepare intricate messages or tabulations on punched tape by typing the matter before a call is made. The machine will then transmit the information to the selected subscriber.

The rental for the teleprinter and the line to the Telex exchange is charged quarterly. Inland and dialled International calls are charged in units. The charges in force can be found in the *P.O. Guide.*

Telegrams by Telex. Telex subscribers can send inland or International telegrams directly to the Post Office, including

(Above) *The Telex operator dials the distant subscriber with the dial connected to her machine and types her message.*

(Below) *The operator feeds punched tape into the automatic transmitter on a Telex installation.*

Post Office International telegraph offices, for transmission. Incoming telegrams can be received on the teleprinter from the telegraph office.

(f) THE TELEPHONE

A telephone call is often the cheapest and quickest method of communication.

In recent years several firms have analysed the cost of typing and despatching letters. Apart from postage, the costs of the typist's time, the dictater's time, the typewriter and the stationery were taken into consideration. It was found that each letter typed cost between 35p and 40p. Because of this, much information that was previously sent by letter is now sent by telephone. A telephone call does not, however, provide a written permanent record of a business transaction. Moreover, it is unsuitable for transmitting any information which is detailed, such as statistical tables.

THE SWITCHBOARD. Nearly all firms have more than one telephone. Usually the telephones are connected to a switchboard, which is looked after by a switchboard operator. The first voice heard by an outside caller is that of the switchboard operator, who will announce the name of the firm. The caller will then ask for a certain person or number and by inserting one of the plugs on the switchboard into the appropriate hole or by throwing a switch the operator will connect the caller with the office of the person for whom he has asked.

The telephones in the various offices are called *extensions*. Each extension has its own number. It is recommended to type the extension number underneath the telephone number on the printed letter heading; and when you are calling a person it is better to ask for the extension by number, if you know it, as this enables the operator to connect the call quickly.

Switchboards may be cord-connected or cordless; they may be automatic or manual; and they can vary in capacity from one main line with three extensions to hundreds of main lines with thousands of extensions.

The advantage of cord-connected switchboards is that they can accommodate more extensions and their capacity can be increased by the addition of further boards according to the requirements of the business.

PABXs (Private Automatic Branch Exchanges, often referred

Private Automatic Branch Exchange I (PABX I). This switchboard will accommodate up to 10 exchange lines and 49 automatic extensions. Extensions dial 9 to get an exchange line to make outside calls.

to as 'automatic switchboards') enable internal calls to be dialled direct from one extension to another. External calls are also made direct from any extension by first dialling a special digit (such as '9') to obtain 'an outside line' (that is, access to the national telephone network, indicated by hearing the dialling tone) and then dialling the number required. The operator or operators on the company switchboard can be contacted when needed by dialling a special code or set of digits or numbers.

PMBXs (Private Manual Branch Exchanges) are usually referred to as 'manual exchanges'. Like PABXs they too may be either corded or cordless; but all calls from PMBX extensions have to be made through the switchboard operator. For example, if Mr Jones on extension 39 wants to speak to Mr Smith on extension 51, he must lift his receiver and when the operator answers he will say, 'Would you please connect me with Mr Smith on extension 51', or perhaps simply, 'Connect me to extension 51, please, operator'. External or outside

Private Manual Branch Exchange 4 (PMBX 4). This switchboard will accommodate 10 exchange lines and 40 extensions. The capacity can be increased up to 200 extensions. Extensions provided with dial telephones can dial outside calls direct when the extension is connected to an exchange line.

calls are obtained through a PMBX switchboard either by asking the operator to get the number or by asking the operator for an outside line; in the latter case, as soon as the extension holder hears the dialling tone, he can dial the number he wants.

ANSWERING THE TELEPHONE. If the name of the firm has already been announced by the switchboard operator, the caller will not want to hear it again when the extension telephone is answered. If you are working in a department of a large firm, it is better to announce the name of the department when you answer the telephone. Speak clearly and slowly and never say, 'Hallo.' Say, 'Sales Department. Good morning.' This tells the caller to whom he is speaking and gives an impression of alertness and courtesy.

Some executives like their secretaries to answer the telephone on their behalf. In such cases the secretary will announce the name of the office, thus, 'Mr. Johnson's office. Good morning.'

Small firms sometimes have a switchboard in the general office, and it is frequently part of the typist's duties to answer all incoming calls. In such a case you would announce the name of the firm.

A third arrangement is for the manager's telephone to be on the same line as the telephone in the general office. All outside calls will be answered in the general office. A conversation similar to the following will take place.

TYPIST OR SECRETARY IN GENERAL OFFICE:	Barker and Hunt, Ltd. Good morning.
CALLER:	May I speak to Mr. Barker, please?
TYPIST:	Who's calling, please?
CALLER:	Evans, British Plastics.
TYPIST:	Would you hold the line, please, Mr. Evans. I'll see if Mr. Barker is in his office.

(The typist will then call Mr. Barker by using a special switch on her telephone, which prevents the caller from hearing her conversation with Mr. Barker, but does not cut off the outside call.)

MR. BARKER:	Barker.
TYPIST:	I have Mr. Evans of British Plastics on the phone for you, Mr. Barker.
MR. BARKER;	Put him through, please, Miss Clark.

(Miss Clark, the typist, moves the switch so that she can speak to Mr. Evans.)

MISS CLARK:	I'm putting you through now, Mr. Evans.
MR. EVANS:	Thank you.

(When Miss Clark hears Mr. Barker and Mr. Evans greet each other she will replace her receiver.)

Suppose Mr. Barker had not been in his office, or had been

engaged and did not want to speak to Mr. Evans. Miss Clark might have handled the call like this.

MISS CLARK: I'm sorry Mr. Barker is not available at the moment, Mr. Evans. Can I help you or would you like Mr. Barker to ring you himself when he is free?

MR. EVANS: Would you ask him to ring me as soon as possible please. My number is 01–222 2870 Extension 47.

MISS CLARK: 01–222 2870 Extension 47. Certainly Mr. Evans, I'll give Mr. Barker your message.

MR. EVANS: Thank you. Good-bye.

MISS CLARK: Good-bye. (Replaces receiver.)

Conversations similar to these take place every day in business offices. What action should be taken next? The typist should write down the message and give it to her employer. Always make a note of the time of the call, the name of the caller and his telephone number, and the message. If you write with your right-hand, place the telephone on the left side of the desk. Hold the receiver in your left hand; this leaves your right hand free to write. Always have paper and pencil available.

Telephone Message

Date: *3 November*

Time: *11·15 am*

Telephone call for:
Mr. Barker

Message:

Please ring Mr. Evans, British Plastics, 01 222 2870 Extension 47, as soon as possible.

Message taken by: *S. Clark.*

183

Here are some hints on answering the telephone:

NEVER SAY:	SAY:
'Hallo'	The name of the firm, department or office. When you answer a telephone installed in a private house, announce the number or your identity.
'Who?'	'Who is speaking, please?'
'Who are you?'	'What is your name, please?'
'Mr. Who?'	'Would you please repeat your name?'
'Who do you want?'	'Who do you wish to speak to?'
'He's out.'	'I'm sorry Mr. .... is not available. Can I
'He's not here.'	help you?'
'Hold on.'	'Would you hold the line, please?'
'O.K.'	'Yes, certainly.'
'I'll tell him.'	'I'll give Mr. .... your message.'

INTERNAL TELEPHONES. We have already referred to internal telephones. With some internal automatic systems outside calls are made with a dialled code, usually a single number. Otherwise these telephones are used for making calls between offices within the firm. An Internal Telephone Directory is printed which gives the names and numbers of departments and officials. When you answer the internal telephone, you should not announce the name of the company. State the name of the department or the extension number.

MAKING A TELEPHONE CALL. Before you can dial a telephone number you must wait for the dialling tone. If you are using a telephone with a direct outside line, you will hear the dialling tone when you lift the receiver. If you are using an extension telephone, say to the operator, 'Would you give me a line, please?' She will then plug your extension into an outside line, and when you hear the dialling tone you can dial the number you are calling.

In some firms the switchboard operators dial all the numbers. If you work in such a firm, you should say to the operator, 'Would you please get me ...', and then state the number. There are accepted rules for giving telephone numbers, which assist the operator. These are:

    (1) Pause between each pair of figures, e.g. for 5773, say five seven (pause) seven three.

(2) The word 'double' can be used if a pair of identical figures occurs either at the beginning or end of a number, e.g. for 5573, say double five (pause) seven three; for 5733, say five seven (pause) double three.

(3) When a number ends with three noughts, say 'thousand', e.g. 7000 would be seven thousand.

When you have dialled the number, you will hear either the ringing tone, or the engaged tone, or the unobtainable tone. If you hear the engaged tone (which indicates that the number you are calling is engaged), replace your receiver and wait a little while before dialling the number again. If you hear the unobtainable tone (a continuous high note), check the code and number and dial again. If you hear the unobtainable tone again, report the matter to the public exchange telephone operator.

If you hear the ringing tone, it means that the number you have dialled is being rung. When the telephone is answered, ask for the extension number or person to whom you wish to speak. When connected, introduce yourself and the subject of your call. Speak slowly and clearly; the mouthpiece of the receiver should be an inch or so from your lips.

It is a convention that the person originating the call should bring the conversation to an end. A good plan is to summarise the points covered in the conversation and then say, 'Good-bye.'

Another convention is that the person originating the call will re-establish the connection if a conversation is cut off.

If difficult words have to be spelt out confusion can be avoided by using names for letters, such as:

A	for Andrew	N	for Nellie
B	for Benjamin	O	for Oliver
C	for Charlie	P	for Peter
D	for David	Q	for Queen
E	for Edward	R	for Robert
F	for Frederick	S	for Sugar
G	for George	T	for Tommy
H	for Harry	U	for Uncle
I	for Isaac	V	for Victor
J	for Jack	W	for William
K	for King	X	for X-ray
L	for Lucy	Y	for Yellow
M	for Mary	Z	for Zebra

A *local call* is a call to another telephone number within the local call area. Exchanges within local call areas are shown in the telephone directories and dialling instructions issued to subscribers; they are also displayed in call boxes.

Calls to other exchanges are known as *trunk calls*. The charge for a trunk call is based on the duration of the call and the distance. Trunk calls may be dialled in areas where STD (*Subscriber Trunk Dialling*) facilities are available. In other areas trunk calls are obtained through the operator at the local telephone exchange.

Subscriber Trunk Dialling is now available from over ninety-three per cent of the telephones in the country. STD calls are charged in units; the time you get depends on the chargeable distance of the call and the time at which it is made.

STD COIN BOXES

Incoming calls. If you answer the telephone and hear a rapid series of pips it means that somebody is calling you from a coin box in an area which has Subscriber Trunk Dialling. With this coin box, from which all calls are timed, the caller first dials the number and pays when the connection has been made. The pips are the pay-tone signal, which tells the caller that you have picked up the receiver and it is time for him to put in the coins. When he has done so, you will be able to speak to each other.

When the time paid for is used up, you will hear the pay-tone again. Your caller can then either say, 'Good-bye', or put in more coins.

Making calls. When you wish to make a call from an STD coin box, have your money 2p or 10p ready. Lift the receiver, and when you hear the dialling tone, dial the number carefully, and then wait for a tone. If you hear the engaged tone (slow pips), replace the receiver and try the number again later. If you hear a steady note, the number unobtainable tone, check the number and re-dial. If you hear the ringing tone (burr-burr), wait until the called number answers. The ringing tone will then automatically change to the pay-tone (rapid pips). As soon as you hear the rapid pips, press a coin into the appropriate slot and you will be able to speak to the person you are calling. If you wish to extend the call, you may insert more money during the call or when you next hear the rapid pips. The length of time you are allowed depends upon the time of day and the distance of the call.

A public telephone kiosk with an STD coin-box.

Details of telephone services and facilities available in a particular district are usually given in the preface to the appropriate telephone directory, which also lists subscribers in alphabetical order. Sometimes you will not find entries where you might expect to find them: for example, schools and libraries may be listed under the name of the controlling local or county authority, and hotels are sometimes listed under the name of the

187

manager. Advice on finding numbers is given in the new type of telephone directories.

The Post Office publishes the following types of telephone directories:

(a) Main alphabetical directories printed on white paper;

(b) Classified business (Yellow Page) directories printed on yellow paper;

(c) The Greater London Business Directory printed on white paper;

(d) Local and Community alphabetical directories serving some of the smaller communities, printed on white paper;

(e) Commercial classification directories listing businesses in classified order which are of predominant interest to the business community. These are printed on blue paper;

(f) Where it is convenient, the main alphabetical directory ((a) above) is bound with a classified business directory ((b) above) and the book is then known as a combined directory.

Each subscriber is supplied with a copy of the alphabetical directory, the classified business (Yellow Page) directory and, where issued, a local or Community directory. Business directories and commercial classified directories for his area are issued to each business subscriber.

Additional copies and copies of any directories for other districts may be bought.

It will be seen that there is now more than one type of directory replacing what used to be called 'the buff book'. This was a classified directory which listed all business subscribers under their respective trades or professions, for example, Builders, Builders' Merchants, Building Societies. In the new directories (b) the classified pages are printed on yellow pages with a pink index, but they may be bound up with the alphabetical directory, and called a combined directory. In addition, there are classified directories (e) printed on blue paper, with a pink index, of special interest to business houses.

Every subscriber who has trunk dialling facilities is given a dialling instruction booklet, listing all the exchanges which can be dialled and giving codes and charges.

Transferred Charge Calls. The charge for a telephone call may be put on the account of the subscriber called provided the person answering the telephone agrees to accept it. If you want the charge for a call transferred, you should start by telling the operator when you book the call; she might want to know your name if the called person requires it before deciding whether to pay for the call.

Telephone Credit Cards. A telephone credit card will be supplied to any subscriber on application to the local Telephone Manager. The holder of the card is able to make calls whenever he is away from home or office without paying immediately. He must tell the operator his card number and the cost of the call will be put on his regular telephone account. A quarterly charge is made for a telephone credit card.

Personal Calls. A personal call enables the caller to specify the person to whom he wishes to speak either by name, department or reference number. The call is not charged for until the person you want is available, but a fee is payable whether or not the call is ultimately successful.

Morning and Alarm Calls. Arrangements may be made for the exchange telephone operator to ring a specified telephone number at a certain time. This service is frequently used by people who wish to be wakened very early in the morning.

Freefone. A subscriber may rent a special Freefone number which enables him to bear the cost of incoming calls via the operator from an area specified by him without the need for the operator to offer each call individually.

To make a call to a Freefone number simply tell the operator the Freefone number you require.

Advice of duration and charge (ADC). The cost and duration of a particular call made through the telephone exchange operato will be notified on its completion for an additional fee of $2\frac{1}{2}$p provided the operator is asked to advise the cost and duration when the call is booked.

Additional telephone services. The following information is available by telephone by dialling the appropriate code: the time, the principal events of the day in London (by dialling the appropriate code this information can also be heard in French, Italian, Spanish or German); the scores of Test Matches when these are being played in England; weather conditions on the roads within a radius of about 80 kilometres of certain cities; local weather forecasts.

TELEPHONE ANSWERING MACHINES

There are several machines available which answer the telephone and record a message for the subscriber when he is not there to answer the telephone himself or when it is not necessary for telephone calls to be personally acknowledged.

Most telephone answering machines are obtainable solely on rental because the equipment is connected to the Post Office telephone lines.

Basically, a telephone answering machine is a tape-recorder fitted with two sets of tapes and connected to the telephone. One tape is a continuous loop on which the subscriber has recorded his message or instructions to incoming callers; he can change the message or the wording of the instructions whenever he wishes to do so. The second tape is a standard blank tape; it is triggered into the RECORD position by the answering tape, and starts to record as soon as the message on the answering tape has been completed.

When a caller dials the subscriber's number, he will hear the ringing tone. After a few seonds the ringing tone will stop and the answering machine will 'answer' the caller by acknowledging the call with a pre-recorded announcement, such as: 'This is an automatic telephone answering machine. If you wish to leave a message for Mr Smith'—*or whatever the name of the subscriber is*—'you may do so as soon as you hear the bleep signal at the end of this recorded acknowledgment'.

The caller may then speak into the telephone and his message will be recorded on the answering machine attached to the receiving telephone. When the subscriber returns to his office a light on the machine will tell him that a call has come in. He will then play back the tape and listen to all the messages which have been recorded during his absence.

Telephone answering machines enable shop or store managers to offer a 24-hour service to customers; and for the business man with a small staff or none at all, they provide a method of accepting telephone messages at any time when he himself is not available.

Telephone answering machines have the great advantage that incoming calls can be routed directly to them, thus freeing the

190

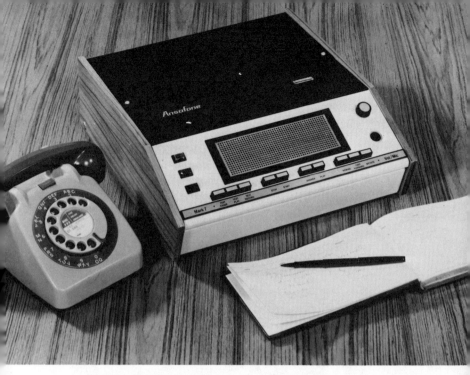

The Ansafone Mark 7 telephone answering machine.

switchboard of the organisation for outgoing calls or incoming calls relevant to a different aspect of the business from that being handled by the answering machines. For example, 125 Ansafone machines installed at Television House were able to deal with 4000 calls made in response to summer holiday advertisements televised on Christmas Day and Boxing Day 1970. The messages were subsequently transcribed, and envelopes prepared and mailed so that callers could receive their brochures within 24 hours of phoning.

This type of service is also useful for factories and head offices that are receiving continuous calls from dealers, agents and branches for spare parts or requests for new deliveries.

Some companies install telephone answering machines in the Telex or teleprinter room so that whilst the Telex or teleprinter operator is transmitting one message another may be received over the internal telephone and recorded ready for handling when the operator is free.

Some firms accept calls from their salesmen or representatives

ORDER PROCESSING

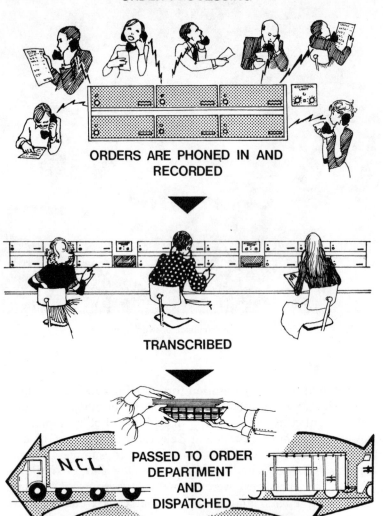

ORDERS ARE PHONED IN AND
RECORDED

TRANSCRIBED

PASSED TO ORDER
DEPARTMENT
AND
DISPATCHED

Agents, salesmen, branches, representatives, depots, regular or account customers can phone in orders at any time convenient to them—for example publicans may find it convenient to phone through their orders at night after closing time. The telephone answering machines record the orders. Next morning the orders are transcribed, and passed to the Order Department and the goods are despatched within a few hours.

192

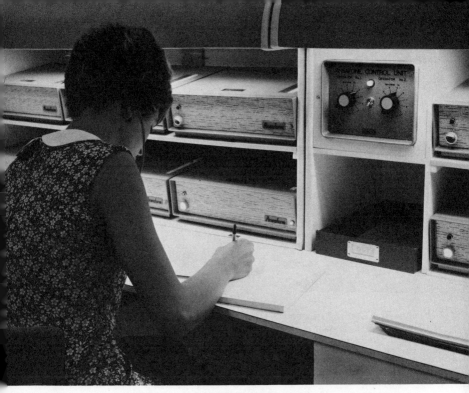

This girl is transcribing messages from the telephone answering machines which are able to receive orders and enquiries at any time of the day or night from any of Vauxhall Motors 350 main dealers.

or regular customers by Transferred Charge Calls or by using the Freefone service. Calls through these services may also be connected to telephone answering machines, in this way orders are dictated at conversation speed and recorded without interruption, so that each call is cleared in less time than is needed for handwritten dictation.

FACSIMILE TRANSCEIVERS

Facsimile transceivers are machines which will transmit and receive facsimile copies of any kind of original document over ordinary telephone lines. An A4 size document can be transmitted in four minutes.

There are several makes of transceiver on the market; each manufacturer uses a different name, for example *Remotecopier* (Plessey Co Ltd), *Telecopier* (Rank Xerox Ltd), *Sendox* (Muirhead Ltd), but the operation of the machines is similar.

193

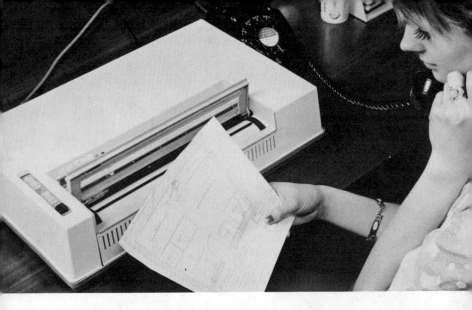

The Rank-Xerox Telecopier III sends facsimile copies by telephone. To send a copy of a document, put the original into the Telecopier, press the SEND button and telephone the recipient. Transmission begins immediately, and in a few minutes a facsimile of the original document emerges from the recipient's Telecopier at the other end of the line. By inserting a multiple-copy pack, the recipient can get up to four copies.

The transceiver is placed on a desk or table top and connected to an adjacent telephone. To transmit, (1) the document is put into the machine, (2) the SEND button is pressed, (3) the recipient is telephoned and told that a copy is being sent to him, (4) the recipient presses the RECEIVE button and switches through to the telephone line, (5) the transceiver signals when the transmission is complete and the two parties can then resume their conversation.*

INTERNATIONAL TELEPHONE SERVICES

International Subscriber Dialling (ISD) enables telephone calls to most European countries, Canada and the United States of America to be dialled direct. International dialling codes are listed in the dialling instruction books issued by the Post Office. The instruction books also list the call charges and contain useful information on the pitch and speed of the ringing and

---

* Transceivers have not yet achieved universal compatibility; in other words, it is not always possible to transmit and receive pictures between machines of different makes.

engaged tones which you will hear when you dial international numbers.

International numbers which cannot be dialled direct are made through the International Exchange, London.

Services similar to the inland telephone services are available with many countries, such as personal calls, transferred charge calls, credit card calls. Person-to-person calls are available to certain countries and the cost of this service is included in the call charge.

Ships' radio telephone services. It is possible to make a telephone call to a person aboard a ship at sea. To obtain a call ask the local exchange operator for the Ships' Telephone Service and when connected to the controlling operator ask for a Ships' Radiotelephone Call. Give the name and position (if known) of the ship, and the name or description of the person required.

(g) TELEXOGRAM SERVICE

Telexograms enable telegrams to be delivered direct from a public telegraph office in one country to the telex machine of a telex subscriber in another country. The service is available between the United Kingdom and certain European countries. Telexograms can be handed over the counter at certain telegraph offices; they can also be sent by telephone by dialling the number for *International Telegrams.* The cost is the same as the European Telegram (ELT) rate with the same minimum charge as for 22 words.

(h) DATEL POST OFFICE DATA TRANSMISSION FACILITIES

The Post Office Telecommunications provide a range of facilities known as Datel Services which deal with data transmission, that is, the electrical transference of information for use by computers.

Basically, a Datel service comprises a *terminal unit* which incorporates a special machine with a typewriter keyboard connected to a *computer centre* by 'a line of suitable quality', that is, a telephone or telegraph line which can transmit electronic pulses or signals at a certain speed.

As you can see in the illustration on p. 196, the operator types (or *keys-in*) the information which is to be transmitted to the computer on a special machine with a typewriter keyboard.

195

Information from cheques is being keyed-in (or typed) on this Burroughs TC 500 Branch Terminal. The operator is transmitting data from a bank headquarters to a computer centre where it will be stored until it is needed.

Before the information (the *input*) can be transferred to the computer centre it must be *encoded*, that is, changed into electronic signals which can be transmitted over the telecommunications network. Similarly, computer output must be *decoded* so that it can be printed out in a readable form at the receiving unit. The machine which performs the technical processes of encoding and decoding is called a *modem*, a word made up from the two words *modulator* and *demodulator*. The modulator encodes the information which is to be fed into the computer, and the demodulator decodes the information into a readable form known as *computer print-out*.

Computers process information by means of a *binary digital process*. (*Binary* means involving a choice between two items, figures or units; *digital* means relating to numbers or digits.) The binary digital process uses an electronic element which has two states—on or off, positive or negative—and the computer

196

Modems mounted in racks in the computer terminal installation of a national bank.

is able to distinguish between these two states. In other words, it can make a decision when presented with a 'yes/no', 'this or that' type of question. Each decision the computer makes is known as a *bit* (from *bi*nary dig*it*), which can be defined as a unit of information. The expression *bits per second* (bit/s) refers to the number of bits that can be transmitted in one second. The fastest Datel service, Datel 48K, can transmit data at the rate of 48 000 bits per second.

The information which is sent to the computer will be of various kinds: letters of the alphabet, decimal digits 0–9, punctuation marks, mathematical symbols, other symbols such as currency signs and special 'function' (or instruction) symbols like 'carriage return' and so on. Each of these symbols or signs may be made up of any number of bits. That is to say, the computer will have to make a certain number of decisions (bits) before it can understand any single item of information such as a letter of the alphabet, a number or a symbol.*

Characters are, therefore, encoded in a series of bits (0 or 1) and in data transmission codes are formed from five, six or seven bits. There are several internationally standardised codes in common use.

Datel services are rented from the Post Office. For example, the Datel 200 service transmits data at 200 bits per second; the modems for this service are rented at £100 per annum and the terminal equipment is obtained from the manufacturers.

Datel services are used by many businesses whose operations demand the constant feeding in and retrieval of information. All the leading banks have now computerised their records; this means that data about each day's transactions is keyed-in to a computer terminal and transmitted to the computer centre where it is stored until needed. For example, the computer terminal stores records of each customer's account making additions (credits) and deductions (debits) according to the data it receives and calculating the new balance after each trans-action. When a customer wants to know his balance the information is produced by the computer terminal and relayed back to the branch terminal within a very short time.

Other firms who find Datel services improve their efficiency are manufacturers or wholesalers who have salesmen or branches or shops all over the country. One large manufacturer of a well-known range of foodstuffs such as tinned cream, soup and instant coffee, has 600 salesmen working around the country in nine sales regions. As the firm manufactures nearly 900 products there are always a lot of orders being processed and the company has to keep track of every transaction. So they have a central computer linked to each of their sales offices. The rapid transmission of information between the offices and the computer enables orders and invoices to be sent out very quickly and the Head Office always knows the up-to-date stock position and the sales records of all its products and salesmen.

As data can be transmitted over ordinary telephone lines the

* You may understand this more easily if you imagine yourself playing a guessing game with a friend. She has thought of a letter of the alphabet and you have to identify the letter. She may only answer 'yes' or 'no' to your questions. You can start, for example, by asking, 'Is the letter in the first 13 letters of the alphabet?'

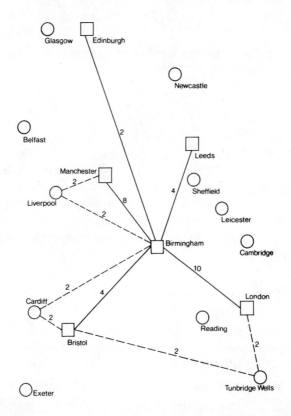

The diagram shows possible future locations of Data Exchanges. The numbers against the transmission links show the probable capacity in Megabit/s (thousand bits per second) of the routes between exchanges.

Datel service is nationwide. Large cities are connected to computer centres throughout the United Kingdom and international services are being co-ordinated by the International Telecommunications Union, a specialised agency of the United Nations Organisation. There are Datel services to the United States of America and 17 European countries, and by using satellite circuits intercontinental services include Australia, Canada and Hong Kong.

Plans are being made for a digital data network which would not require the use of modems in the transmission of data. The diagram above shows the possible location of the specialised exchanges required for this work.

199

EXERCISES

1. Explain the following words and expressions:
   (*a*) the Rule of the House,
   (*b*) headed letter paper,
   (*c*) a courtesy title,
   (*d*) the salutation of a letter,
   (*e*) a catchword.

2. Whilst on holiday at a sea-side resort you bought a length of dress material at a large department store. When you returned home you realised that you would need an extra 0·5 metres of material. Compose a letter to the shop, asking them to post the material to you.

3. Write a letter to a friend congratulating her upon her examination results.

4. Your colleague at the office is in hospital recovering from a minor operation. Your employer asks you to write a letter of sympathy for his signature. Write the letter.

5. A record-player which you purchased recently is not working properly. Write a letter of complaint to the Manager of the shop where you made the purchase.

6. As Manager of the shop, write a reply to (5).

7. Write a letter to the firm responsible for cleaning the windows of your office, complaining about the poor and irregular service and high charges.

8. Your employer has been invited to present the prizes on Speech Day at a local school. Write a suitable acceptance for his signature.

9. Compose a circular letter from a newly-opened hairdresser's shop to prospective clients in the district.

10. Your employer is away on a business trip on the continent of Europe. Among matters dealing with business he writes to you that he will probably be returning one day later than anticipated, but that this is not yet certain. He asks you to tell his wife in case this change affects her plans. You telephone her, but are unable to speak to her. Write a letter to your employer's wife, dealing with the situation.

11. Explain the meaning of the following words and expressions:
    (a) a telegraphic address,
    (b) an overnight telegram,
    (c) a radiotelegram.

12. Refer to the *Post Office Guide* for the following information:
    (a) the current charges for inland telegrams,
    (b) how figures are counted when the charge for a telegram is being calculated,
    (c) the cost of a telegram to Sierra Leone,
    (d) whether a 'De Luxe' (greetings) telegram can be sent to India,
    (e) the charge for a phototelegram to Bonn, Germany,
    (f) the method of address for a radiotelegram.

13. You are employed by Regent Pictures, Ltd, Wardour Street, London, W1A 1AA. Your employer, Mr B K Fox, is taken ill suddenly and cannot travel to Scotland to keep an appointment the following day. He was to have visited Scottish Motion Pictures, Ltd, Dunoon Street, Glasgow (telegraphic address FILMS SCOTLAND). His appointment was with Mr G McIntosh, General Manager.

    (a) Get a telegram form from a post office, complete it according to the instructions given above, and work out the cost.
    (b) Write a suitable letter confirming the telegram.

14. Explain the meaning of the following words and phrases:
    (a) a subscriber (referring to the telephone),
    (b) a switchboard,
    (c) an extension,
    (d) an internal telephone,
    (e) the engaged tone,
    (f) STD,
    (g) a personal call.

15. Under what circumstances might you wish to make use of:
    (a) the Transferred Charge Call service,
    (b) the Alarm Call service.

16. Consult your local telephone directory and find out the codes which must be dialled in your area to obtain the following connections:
    (a) a trunk call,

(*b*) the time,

(*c*) the principal events of the day in London,

(*d*) the same information in French, Spanish, German and Italian,

(*e*) the Test Match score,

(*f*) the road weather conditions,

(*g*) the local weather forecast (if available in your area),

(*h*) a telephone call to Europe.

17. Consult the *Post Office Guide* and find out the following information:

(*a*) the cost of a 3 minute call to Belgium,

(*b*) the cost of a 3 minute call to Greece,

(*c*) the cost of a 4 minute call to Sicily,

(*d*) the cost of a 3 minute Sunday call to Canada,

(*e*) the cost of a weekday call to New York,

(*f*) the local time in Jamaica when it is 12 noon British Standard Time in London

18. Why do you think the telephone section of the *Post Office Guide* includes a list of local times in countries abroad?

19. Draw up a set of instructions for the correct use of the telephone for a junior in your office.

20. Write brief notes on the following:

circulation slip	distribution stamp
routing slip	NOO
FIO	routing methods

21. When is a telephone message pad used? What details should appear on it in addition to the actual message?

22. Describe fully the following Post Office Services:

(*a*) Telex.

(*b*) Business Reply.

(*c*) Freefone.

State the advantages of using them and the types of businesses which would find them most useful. (RSA, OP, I)

23. What are the main points to note in taking down a telephone message in the office? How would you deal with an urgent telephone message after you had taken it down?

(RSA, OP, I)

24. (a) Draw up a list of instructions for the guidance of junior office staff on the use of the telephone.
    (b) Draft a suitable press advertisement for a telephone switchboard operator in your firm.   (RSA, OP, II)

25. (a) What is the meaning of the letters STD?
    (b) How is the cost of such a call calculated?
    (c) How does this cost compare with the cost of calls connected by the operator?   (RSA, OP, I)

26. (a) For what purpose is a memorandum used?
    (b) What are the main parts of a memorandum form?
    (c) Give an example of a distribution list.   (RSA, OP, I)

27. Explain the following details featured on a Company's headed notepaper:

    452 2233 (STD Code 061)
    Telex 23721
    Cables MANCUNIAN STOCKPORT

    In what circumstances would you use these methods of communication?   (RSA, OP, II)

28. (a) A newcomer to your office says she is unfamiliar with the STD telephone service. State the main distinctive features of STD which you would point out to her and draw up a list of 'Do's and Don't's' for her guidance.
    (b) Write a short explanatory paragraph on each of these:
        (i) the 'yellow pages'
        (ii) an ADC call.   (RSA, OP, I)

29. Explain the following terms and state when each service would be used:
    (a) a 'reverse charge call';
    (b) STD;
    (c) ISD;
    (d) credit card calls.   (RSA, OP, I)

30. (a) List the essential features, other than the subject content, of a business letter.
    (b) Name the two International sizes of paper most widely used in business offices, and give one example of the work for which you would use each size.

31. What are the main points to bear in mind when dialling an international telephone number? Name two other ways in

which a message can be sent overseas using Post Office facilities. (RSA, OP, I)

32. Explain some of the important uses made of the teleprinter in offices. (RSA, OP, I)

33. (a) Your employer is concerned because a number of incoming messages received by telephone have not been dealt with efficiently.
    (i) Draft a telephone message form which could be used on all occasions when the person required is not available.
    (ii) What would you do if a telephone caller would not leave a message?
    (b) What is the Post Office Telex System and what are the advantages of using it? (RSA, OP, II)

34. Explain the following telephone services and indicate the circumstances under which each might be used:
    (a) Fixed-time calls.
    (b) Telephone credit cards.
    (c) Telephone-answering machines.
    (d) Transferred charge calls. (RSA, OP, II)

35. Using the telegram form below, draft a suitable telegram

Counter No.						Serial No.
Office Stamp		♔ POST OFFICE **INLAND TELEGRAM** FOR POSTAGE STAMPS			Chargeable words	Sent at/By
					Charge	Circulation
	Prefix	Handed in	Service Instructions		Actual Words	
If you wish to pay for a reply insert **RP here**	TO	BLOCK LETTERS THROUGHOUT PLEASE				

The particulars on the back of this form should be completed.

FRONT

*NAME AND ADDRESS OF SENDER
and telephone number (if any)

*NOTE. These particulars will not be telegraphed unless included in the message overleaf.

BACK

Reproduced by permission of H.M. Postmaster-General

from the following information:
To: Mr Nigel Smith, of Smith, Son & Nephew, 13 Minster Road, Warrington. Telegraphic address—THIMS WARRINGTON.
FROM: Mr Jonathan Briggs, of Briggs Limited, 20 Queen Street, London, S.W.1.
Mr Briggs has arranged to meet Mr Smith in his office in Warrington at 2.30 pm, on Wednesday the 1st July, but unfortunately he has been delayed on business in Dublin. He will however, be flying in to Ringway Airport on Thursday the 2nd July, flight number BE 1234, due to arrive at 11.30 am, and he would like Mr Smith to meet him in the arrival lounge at the Airport. (RSA, OP, I)

Chapter 6

Commercial Documents

As we learnt in Chapter 1, the purpose of all businesses is to make a profit. The profit is derived from the difference between the cost price and the selling price of the articles sold; or, in the case of businesses which provide services (e.g. builders', hairdressers', banks), from the difference between the cost of providing the service and the price the client pays for it.

The complete process of buying and selling an article is known as a transaction. During the course of a transaction much information has to be transmitted between the buyer and the seller. Special forms have become the accepted means of communicating this information, and many of the forms subsequently become part of the business records of the firm.

We shall now study (a) the series of forms needed to initiate and complete a business transaction, and (b) how these forms are used as records.

(a) DOCUMENTS USED FOR A BUSINESS TRANSACTION

1. **The enquiry.** An enquiry is sent by the person wishing to make the purchase to the likely suppliers. It will describe the goods required, state the quantities and specify a delivery date. Enquiries can be made by post or by telephone.

2. **The quotation.** A quotation is sent in reply to an enquiry and states the goods available, the current prices and delivery dates. A printed catalogue or price list is frequently sent with the quotation.

Tenders, specifications and estimates are special kinds of quotations usually sent by firms in reply to an enquiry for certain work to be carried out, e.g. building a garage, erecting a block of flats or decorating a room. The word *tender* is mainly used for the quotations of competing firms who are endeavouring to obtain a particular order or contract, such as the building of a school for a local council.

The prices quoted may be subject to certain discounts:

TRADE DISCOUNT. This is a discount allowed to firms in the same trade, or by one manufacturer to others or by manufacturers to wholesalers or by wholesalers to retailers; it is usually given for bulk purchasing to encourage customers to buy in large quantities. Before the discount has been deducted, the price is known as the *gross price*. The discount is usually calculated as a percentage of the gross price. When it has been deducted, the price is called the *net price* or *trade price*.

CASH DISCOUNT. This is an allowance to encourage prompt payment and may be given in addition to trade discount; it is calculated as a percentage of the net trade price. After the cash discount has been deducted, the price is called the *net cash price*.

Before placing an order the purchaser must also consider whether the prices quoted include the cost of transport and whether an allowance is made if the containers are returned to the supplier in good condition. The following expressions are used to describe these conditions:

CARRIAGE PAID. The cost of carrying the goods is included in the price quoted; carriage to the purchaser's place of business is paid by the supplier.

CARRIAGE FORWARD. The quoted price does not include the cost of carriage; that is, the purchaser must pay the cost of carrying the goods.

EX WORKS or EX WAREHOUSE. The cost of the goods only; the purchaser must arrange and pay for transport and delivery.

FOR (FREE ON RAIL). The supplier pays carriage to the nearest railway station and the purchaser pays for carriage by rail and delivery to his own place of business.

FOB (FREE ON BOARD). The supplier pays carriage, dock dues and handling charges for stowing the goods on a ship and the purchaser pays sea freight and importing charges (dock dues, customs duty, carriage from port of disembarkation to his place of business).

RETURNABLE EMPTIES. Some goods are packed in expensive wooden crates or metal drums or other structures. If the cost of the containers is included in the price, there is usually an allowance made when they are returned to the supplier in good condition.

3. **The order.** When the quotations or estimates have been received the purchaser has to decide with which firm he will place the order.   He will consider the quality, price and delivery date offered.   The order will be sent to the selected supplier and will state the goods required, the catalogue or quoted price and the reference numbers.   The purchaser will keep a copy of the order so that he knows what he has ordered.

The procedure following the receipt of the order by the supplier will depend upon the internal organisation of the firm.

A very common practice is for the order to be typed upon a set of similar documents, which are then distributed to the various departments concerned with the transaction.   A *packing* and *despatch note* will be sent to the department responsible for the actual packing and despatch of the articles.   Sometimes the despatch note is then sent to the purchaser so that he knows the goods are on their way, or a *delivery note* or an *advice note* may be included in the set.

A delivery note is used when the goods are sent by the firm's own transport.   The van driver is given two copies; one copy is handed to the customer with the goods, the other copy is signed by the customer and given back to the driver.

An advice note or despatch note is sent by post to the customer to tell him (a) that the goods have been despatched and (b) the way they have been sent, either by post or rail or by road. Sometimes a *consignment note* is also required; this document lists details and weights of the goods consigned, gives the name and address of the supplier (the consignor), the name and address of the customer (the consignee) and the date of despatch, and states whether the consignment should be conveyed by passenger train, goods train, by road on British Rail lorries, or by road by a transport contractor.

The top copy of the set of documents is known as the invoice. A copy of the invoice will be retained in the invoice department as a record of what is owed to them by various purchasers. Note that apart from the consignment note, which is usually provided by the carriers, all these documents can be produced from one typing.   In the illustration on page 69 you can see a typewriter producing sets of documents.   Each copy is taken on a different coloured paper for easier routing to the appropriate departments.

4. The invoice. The invoice lists the goods purchased and tells the purchaser how much he owes the supplier. The invoice may also state the way the goods have been sent, e.g. by rail, road or post. Details of discounts available will also be included. When the goods have been received the purchaser will check them against the invoice to make sure that the quantities and quality are correct.

A VAT invoice (officially referred to as a *tax invoice*), that is, an invoice for taxable supplies of goods or services sold by a registered taxable supplier to a taxable customer, must show:

(1) Number and date of issue.
(2) Date on which the goods were supplied i.e. *the tax point.*
(3) Supplier's name, address and VAT registration number.
(4) Customer's name and address.
(5) Type of supply, e.g. whether it is a sale, a credit sale, hire, lease or rental.
(6) Description of goods.
(7) Rate of trade discount offered if any.
(8) Quantity and amount payable, excluding VAT for each item.
(9) Total amount payable, excluding VAT
(10) Rate and amount of VAT charged—VAT is calculated on 9 above. Where special terms are offered for prompt payment (i.e. less 2½% within one month from date of invoice) this additional discount is deducted before the VAT is calculated (see p. 211). If the purchaser pays within the time given he deducts the 2½% when he pays (see p. 213). If he fails to pay within the time given he will owe VAT on the 2½% deducted by his supplier on the original invoice.
(11) Total amount payable including VAT.

The supplier must keep copies of all the tax invoices he issues. However, for amounts not exceeding £10 including VAT, a *less detailed tax invoice* may be issued which need show only items 2, 3 and 6 above, the total amount payable including VAT and the amount of VAT in force. Copies of these invoices need not be kept by the supplier but if the customer is registered as a taxable person, the invoices must be kept so that the tax paid can be calculated and reclaimed from HM Customs and Excise. Less detailed invoices usually carry the words *Inc.VAT 8%*, or *8% VAT included* or *Price inc. 8% VAT*.

5. The debit note. This is similar to the invoice; it also tells the purchaser how much he owes the supplier. Debit notes are used to make adjustments. For instance, if the supplier has undercharged on the invoice he will send a debit note for the difference.   Debit notes in respect of taxable supplies should show the same information as a tax invoice.

6. **The credit note.**   Credit notes are usually printed and typed in red, so that they will not be confused with invoices and debit notes.   They are issued when the seller owes the purchaser some money and are usually deducted from the invoice before it is paid.   Credit notes would be issued by a seller to correct an overcharge, or to allow for the return of faulty goods, or empty crates and containers which had been returned and for which the purchaser had paid.   A credit note relating to goods for which a tax invoice was issued must show, in addition to items 1, 3, 4 and 6 from the invoice (see above), the reason for the credit, e.g. 'Returned goods', the quantity and amount credited for each supply, the total amount credited excluding VAT, and the rate and amount of VAT credited.   The credit note should show the number and date of the original tax invoice, if possible.

7. **A pro forma invoice** is similar to a quotation.   If the quotation comprises a long list of items with discount allowances it may be more convenient to type it on a pro forma invoice form, which shows the purchaser how the invoice will be written out if he decides to buy the goods.   Pro forma invoices are also sent with goods despatched 'on approval' or on a 'sale or return' basis.   Pro forma invoices for taxable goods should show the rate of tax to be charged and indicate clearly whether the price quoted is inclusive or exclusive of VAT.

8. **The despatch note**.   The despatch note is sent to the department responsible for the packing and despatch of the articles.   If the goods are being sent by a form of transport not owned by the supplier, such as post, railway or road transport contractor, the despatch note is posted to the purchaser to inform him that the goods have been sent.   When the goods are being transported by British Rail or an outside transport contractor a consignment note may be required.

9. **The consignment note.**   This document serves as a contract between the sender (the consignor) and the transport company (the carrier).   The carrier signs the consignment note when he receives the goods (the consignment) for transport. The consignment note is supplied by the carrier, for example, British Rail.   It gives details of the consignment, the name and

address of the consignor, the name and address of the person or firm receiving the goods (the consignee) and the date of despatch.

If the goods are sent at carrier's risk, the carrier pays for any damage or loss caused during transit. A much cheaper way of sending goods by outside transport is at owner's risk, but as the term suggests, the carrier would not have to pay for loss or damage.

10. **The delivery note.** When a firm is using its own transport for delivering goods, the driver of the van or lorry is given two copies of the delivery note. When he delivers the goods, he gives both copies to the purchaser. The purchaser checks the goods against the delivery note and if they are correct, he signs one copy and gives it back to the driver. His signature is the acceptance of the goods. The driver takes the signed copy back to the supplier where it will form the basis of the invoice. The customer keeps the other copy of the delivery note for his records.

11. **Goods received note.** When the goods arrive at the purchaser's stockroom, the storekeeper writes the details on a goods received note or in a goods received book. He puts down the date of receipt, the name of the supplier, the quantity and type of goods received and the order number. This information on the goods received note is checked against the order to ensure that what was ordered has been received and at the same time that what has been received was ordered.

12. **The statement of account.** The invoices sent to each customer are recorded on his ledger card or on his page in the sales ledger. At the end of each month or other agreed period a copy of the entries is made on a statement of account, which tells the purchaser the total sum owing for the period. The statement will show:

    a) The balance brought forward from the previous month (*Account Rendered*).
    b) The net amount of each invoice sent during the month.
    c) The net amount of credit notes.
    d) The amount of cash received from and cash discount allowed to the purchaser.
    e) The balance owing at the end of the month.

(*contd. page 219*)

margaret mansfield
The Wool Centre
High Street, Banfield, Essex, BA6 7EF
(Registered Office) tel. 45 58491

Company Registration No. 123456
VAT No. 000000

Ref. MM/PWS   4 September 1976

Sales Manager
Yorkshire Knitting Wool Co Ltd
Dale House
LEEDS
LE2 4SE

Dear Sir

I have received enquiries from several of my customers for
your 'Alpine' and 'Modale' knitting wools.

Will you please send me copies of your catalogue and current
price list, and let me know which colours are available from
stock.

As this is my first enquiry with you, you may wish to take
up references. My bank is the National Bank Ltd, Banfield.

Yours faithfully

Margaret Mansfield

Margaret Mansfield

QUOTATION (REPLY TO ENQUIRY)

YORKSHIRE KNITTING WOOL Co. Ltd.

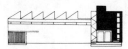

Company Registration No. 999999
VAT No. 000001

Dale House, Leeds, LE2 4SE
Telephone 0532 46301
(Registered Office)

Managing Director: M. F. Beckwith

Our ref. KWR/TSC
Your ref. MM/PWS

5 September 1976

Miss Margaret Mansfield
The Wool Centre
High Street
BANFIELD
Essex
BA6 7EF

Dear Madam

Thank you for your letter dated 4 September. We have
pleasure in enclosing a copy of our latest catalogue
and current price list.

'Alpine' and 'Modale' knitting wools are available in
all colours shown on the shade card attached and can be
supplied from stock.

Orders are dealt with promptly, and we can promise
delivery within four days of receipt of your order.
Orders over £10 are sent carriage paid and a discount
of $2\frac{1}{2}\%$ is available on accounts settled within one
month of date of invoice.

Yours faithfully
for YORKSHIRE KNITTING WOOL CO LTD

K W Rolands
Sales Manager

Encs

213

margaret mansfield
The Wool Centre
High Street, Banfield, Essex, BA6 7EF
(Registered Office)
tel. 45 58491

Company Registration No. 123456
VAT No. 000000

TO .Yorkshire Knitting Wool Co Ltd .   Account No. 32 2789 00

Dale House, LEEDS, LE2 4SE . . .

DATE .8 September 1976

PLEASE SUPPLY THE FOLLOWING GOODS:

CAT. NO.	QUANTITY	DETAILS	PRICE
245	10 x 50 g balls	'Alpine' Wool – White	32p per 50 g ball
246	10 x 50 g balls	'Alpine' Wool – Black	32p per 50 g ball
249	10 x 50 g balls	'Alpine' Wool – Blue	32p per 50 g ball
250	10 x 50 g balls	'Alpine' Wool – Red	32p per 50 g ball
251	10 x 50 g balls	'Alpine' Wool – Green	32p per 50 g ball
263	10 x 50 g balls	'Modale' Wool – Black	35p per 50 g ball
264	10 x 50 g balls	'Modale' Wool – Blue	35p per 50 g ball
265	10 x 50 g balls	'Modale' Wool – Green	35p per 50 g ball
725	1 dozen	Instruction leaflets	75p per dozen
728	1 dozen	Instruction leaflets	75p per dozen
730	1 dozen	Instruction leaflets	75p per dozen

DELIVERY .Immediate. . . . .

SIGNED *M Mansfield* . . . . .

214

INVOICE

YORKSHIRE KNITTING WOOL Co. Ltd.

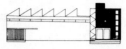

Company Registration No. 999999
VAT No. 000001

Dale House, Leeds, LE2 4SE
Telephone 0532 46301
(Registered Office)

Managing Director: M. F. Beckwith

TO Miss M Mansfield
. . . .
The Wool Centre
. . . .
High Street
. . . .
Banfield, ESSEX
. . . .

INVOICE NO. 447

DATE . 11 September 1976

Account No. 32 2789 00   Discount 4%

CAT NO	DESCRIPTION	QUANTITY	PRICE £	GROSS AMOUNT £	DISC. VALUE £	NET VALUE £	VAT RATE	VAT AMOUNT
245	'Alpine' – White	10 x 50g balls	0.32	3.20	0.13	3.07	8%	
246	'Alpine' – Black	10 x 50g balls	0.32	3.20	0.13	3.07	8%	
249	'Alpine' – Blue	10 x 50g balls	0.32	3.20	0.13	3.07	8%	
250	'Alpine' – Red	10 x 50g balls	0.32	3.20	0.13	3.07	8%	
251	'Alpine' – Green	10 x 50g balls	0.32	3.20	0.13	3.07	8%	
263	'Modale' – Black	10 x 50g balls	0.35	3.50	0.14	3.36	8%	
264	'Modale' – Blue	10 x 50g balls	0.35	3.50	0.14	3.36	8%	
265	'Modale' – Green	10 x 50g balls	0.35	3.50	0.14	3.36	8%	
725	Instruction leaflets	1 dozen	0.75	0.75	0.03	0.72	0%	
728	Instruction leaflets	1 dozen	0.75	0.75	0.03	0.72	0%	
730	Instruction leaflets	1 dozen	0.75	0.75	0.03	0.72	0%	
				TOTAL	GOODS	27.59		1.98*
				TOTAL	VAT	1.98*		
					TOTAL	29.57		

TERMS Less 2½ per cent within one month from date of invoice

Despatched by passenger train. Carriage paid.

*This is calculated on the Net Value of taxable items
less further discount for prompt payment (2½%)

215

YORKSHIRE KNITTING WOOL Co. Ltd.

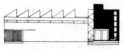

Company Registration No. 999999
VAT No. 000001

Dale House, Leeds, LE2 4SE
Telephone 0532 46301
(Registered Office)

Managing Director: M.F. Beckwith

TO Miss M Mansfield
The Wool Centre
High Street
Banfield ESSEX

STATEMENT

TERMS 2½% one month

DATE 30 September 1976

DATE	REFERENCE	DEBIT	CREDIT	BALANCE
1976 11 Sept	To goods Your Order No.221	29.57		£29.57

THIS STATEMENT SHOWS THE POSITION OF YOUR ACCOUNT AT
THE ABOVE DATE. PAYMENTS RECEIVED AFTER THIS DATE ARE
NOT INCLUDED.

THE LAST AMOUNT
IN THIS COLUMN IS
THE AMOUNT DUE

E & OE.

LETTER ENCLOSING CHEQUE

margaret mansfield
The Wool Centre
High Street, Banfield, Essex, BA6 7EF
(Registered Office)
tel. 45 58491

Company Registration No. 123456
VAT No. 000000

Ref. MM/PWS

2 October 1976

Accounts Department
Yorkshire Knitting Co Ltd
Dale House
LEEDS
LE2 4SE

Dear Sirs

I have pleasure in enclosing cheque for £28.88 in payment
of your account dated 30 September, made up as follows:

Your statement	£29.57
Less 2½ per cent	0.69
	£28.88

Yours faithfully

Margaret Mansfield

Margaret Mansfield

---

2 October 19 76   00-00-00

◥ National Westminster Bank Limited
Anytown Branch
41 High Street, Anytown, Berks

y *Yorkshire knitting Wool Co Ltd*   or order

Twenty eight pounds 88p   £28-88

SPECIMEN

Margaret Mansfield

⑈"000000"⑈ 00⑈0000⑊

THE BUSINESS DOCUMENTS INVOLVED IN A TRANSACTION

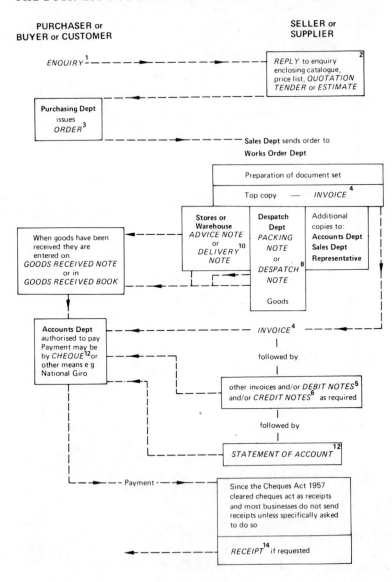

PURCHASER or BUYER or CUSTOMER

SELLER or SUPPLIER

ENQUIRY 1 ————————→ *REPLY* to enquiry enclosing catalogue, price list, *QUOTATION TENDER* or *ESTIMATE* 2

Purchasing Dept issues *ORDER* 3

Sales Dept sends order to Works Order Dept

Preparation of document set

Top copy — *INVOICE* 4

Stores or Warehouse *ADVICE NOTE* or *DELIVERY* 10 *NOTE*

Despatch Dept *PACKING NOTE* or *DESPATCH* 8 *NOTE*

Additional copies to: **Accounts Dept Sales Dept Representative**

When goods have been received they are entered on *GOODS RECEIVED NOTE* or in *GOODS RECEIVED BOOK*

Goods

Accounts Dept authorised to pay Payment may be by *CHEQUE* 12 or other means e g National Giro

INVOICE 4

followed by

other invoices and/or *DEBIT NOTES* 5 and/or *CREDIT NOTES* 6 as required

followed by

STATEMENT OF ACCOUNT 12

Payment

Since the Cheques Act 1957 cleared cheques act as receipts and most businesses do not send receipts unless specifically asked to do so

RECEIPT 14 if requested

The numbers refer to sections of the text on pp 219-222.

13. **The cheque.** Most firms make payments for goods they purchase by bank cheque. The cheque is considered to be the equivalent of cash for the amount written on it. A full discussion of cheques and their use is on pages 232 to 242.

14. **The receipt.** Formerly the payment of an account was always acknowledged by a receipt. Nowadays few firms send receipts. Since the Cheques Act was passed in 1957, the cheque itself, when it has been paid into a creditor's account, and returned to the drawer, acts as a receipt.

The following series of documents cover the purchase of goods by the owner of a wool-shop. The owner of the shop, Margaret Mansfield, is the *purchaser* of the goods. The *supplier* is the Yorkshire Knitting Wool Co., Ltd. The *goods* are the various items which have been ordered.

OVERSEAS TRADE

The documents we have studied in this chapter are used in the Home Trade, that is, the buying and selling of goods within the United Kingdom.

The sale of goods to a purchaser overseas (the export trade) and the buying of goods from a supplier overseas (the import trade) are two branches of what is known as Overseas Trade.

Overseas trading transactions require different sets of documents to cover the sending of the goods by sea or air, the regulations of the dock and harbour authorities, and the payment of customs and excise duties. Other documents are needed to transfer the payment for the goods from buyer to seller.

The study of importing and exporting, and the documents used in overseas trade, are covered in Book 5.

(b) DOCUMENTS USED AS RECORDS

1. **The enquiry.** When a firm wants to purchase goods, it may make enquiries to several likely suppliers to find the lowest price available or the earliest delivery date. Finding out the names of these suppliers may have involved research in classified telephone directories and specialised magazines.

The next time the goods are wanted the supplier who was selected for his price or delivery date may not be able to offer the same terms or service and the enquiries may have to be repeated. If records of the first enquiries have been kept, time and effort are saved when enquiring the second time as the names and addresses of the suppliers can easily be located.

In the case of written enquiries, a carbon copy of each letter should be filed under a heading for the goods, stationery or knitting needles, for example. If telephone enquiries are made, a record of the name, address and telephone number of each supplier should be recorded and put in a file under the type of goods.

2. **The quotation.** Printed catalogues or price lists sent in reply to an enquiry should be kept as the firm may want to refer to them at a later date for information about other goods made by the supplier.

Catalogues are often too bulky to put in a file and they may have to be stored on a shelf or rack. If a label is attached to each shelf, the required catalogues are easier to find.

Price lists and thin catalogues may be stored in files under the name of the type of goods.

3. **The order.** It is usual to keep carbon copies in date order, as a record of what has been ordered. When the goods have been received they are marked off against the items on the carbon copies of the original orders. This is particularly important in businesses placing large orders covering many items, as it is not unusual for some items to be delivered at different times from others. Reference to the marked-off copies will always tell you what items are outstanding—that is, those items which have been ordered but which have not yet been delivered. For example, schools frequently order several sets of text-books on one order. Sometimes one particular text-book will not be available as it is being reprinted. In such a case you would write 'Re-printing' against the appropriate entry. When you were asked whether the book had been delivered you would refer to the folder containing the carbon copies of orders and be able to give the required information.

4. **The invoice.** You will remember that invoices tell the purchaser the price, quantity and description of the goods he has bought. The invoice must be checked against the order given and the actual goods received. The details from the invoices will be entered in the financial records of the firm, which may take the form of ledgers and journals or manual or machine accounting loose-leaf forms or cards. In more ad-

vanced systems this information is already stored on magnetic tape.

From these records the following information will be available:

1) The total amount spent by the firm in any given period.
2) The total amount paid to an individual supplier.
3) The total amount spent by one department of the firm.

An analysis of the invoices for text-books in a school office, for example, would tell you how much had been spent on books by the English Department, the Languages Department and all the other departments.

Here is another example. A shipping company buys very large quantities of food for the ships in its fleet. The company will need to know not only the total amount owing to each supplier at the end of each month but also the amount to be charged to the accounts of each separate ship. Therefore the invoices will first be listed under the individual suppliers and then re-sorted and listed under the name of each vessel.

5. **The debit note.** Since a debit note is a request for payment, it must be kept for the financial records of a firm. If an invoice has undercharged a purchaser and a debit has not been issued by the supplier for the extra amount, the debit note should be attached to the invoice to which it refers. The amount on the debit note can then be transferred to the firm's accounts records with the amount on the invoice to show the actual sum paid.

6. **The credit note.** Credit notes, which are printed in red, are sent to a buyer when the supplier owes him money. They are usually issued for returned goods (that is those which were unsatisfactory or damaged when received), or for what are known as 'returnable empties'. Containers such as crates and bottles are charged for when the goods are delivered, but if they are returned in good condition the supplier will issue a credit note for the value of the returned empties. The credit notes, therefore, form a record of the allowances which may be set against the totalled invoices for each supplier when payment is made at the end of the month.

7. **The pro forma invoice.** The pro forma invoice must be kept until the invoice or statement of account reaches the purchaser. If the purchaser wishes to query anything on the

221

statement or invoice, he has the supplier's list of the goods and terms typed on the pro forma invoice.

8. **The statement of account.** If the purchaser buys goods on credit, at the end of the period of credit, usually the end of the month, he receives the statement of account which itemises all the goods bought, the money owed for each and the total amount owed. The accounts department pays the amount owed and keeps the statement as a record of the transaction. The details of payment on the statement are entered in the accounts ledger or other form of accounts records.

9. **The cheque.** After the cheque has been paid into the supplier's bank account and returned to the purchaser through his bank, the cheque can be considered as a receipt for the payment. Since it is a receipt, the cheque should be kept by the purchaser as proof that payment was made in case any query arises. Since the date on the cheque is the day on which the purchaser paid the supplier, the cheque also acts as a record of the date of payment.

10. **The receipt.** If the supplier sends the purchaser a receipt for payment, the purchaser should keep the receipt as proof of payment in the same way as the cancelled cheque is kept.

EXERCISES

1. Explain the following words and phrases:
   (*a*) a transaction,
   (*b*) a tender,
   (*c*) a discount,
   (*d*) a consignment,
   (*e*) a pro forma invoice,
   (*f*) a credit note,
   (*g*) Home trade,
   (*h*) Overseas trade.
2. Make out sets of documents (on the typewriter, if possible) to cover the following transactions:
   (*a*) the purchase of office stationery supplies by the Standard Insurance Co., Ltd. from Office Supplies, Ltd.
   (*b*) the purchase of setting lotions, shampoos, pins, etc., by a hairdressing salon, Henri, from the Hamilton Trading Co., Ltd.

(c) the purchase of stock by the Manor Cycle Stores, Ltd., from British Bicycle Accessories, Ltd.

3. Study the following document, then answer the questions below:

STATEMENT

ROYSTON & CO. LTD.
94 Royal Avenue, W.1.
Tel. 01–493 7432

R. L. Fisher, Esq.,   **1st August, 1976**
17 Courtland Road,
N.4.
A/c 4/F/91

Date	Balance from previous month	Dept.	Purchases	Amount due
	£		£	£
1 Jul. 69	6.60			6.60
10 Jul. 69		H'ware	7.40	
16 Jul. 69		Mill'y	3.20	
22 Jul. 69		F'ture	11.35	21.95
				£28.55
Terms: Strictly net				

(a) What is the name of the customer?
(b) What is the name of the firm?
(c) What is the reference number of the account?
(d) What is the date of the statement?
(e) How much did the customer owe at the beginning of the month?
(f) How much did the customer spend during the month?
(g) How much did the customer spend in each department?
(h) What was the total amount due at the end of the month?
(i) What is the meaning of 'Terms: Strictly net'?

4. Explain the following terms and abbreviations:

carriage paid ex Works
trade price   net cash price
FOR   FOB

5. Explain the following terms and their importance when a purchasing officer is considering a supplier's quoted prices.

    a) trade discount   c) carriage forward
    b) cash discount   d) carriage paid

6. (*a*) State one difference between trade discount and cash discount.

   (*b*) Make out the receipt which you would give to a man who has just bought an old filing cabinet from your firm for £4.00.   (RSA, OP, I)

7. You work in the central purchasing office of a Local Authority. The various departments of that Authority inform your office of the supplies which they need, using a requisition form, and your office then places orders for the supplies.

    Draft: *a*) a requisition form for use by the departments, and

            b) an order form for use by the central purchasing office.   (RSA, OP, II)

8. Your company wishes to sell goods in the following ways:
   a) on credit;
   b) by COD;
   c) against cash with order.

    Outline three suitable office routines—one for each of the above methods—from the time when an order is received until the times when goods are despatched and payment is made.   (RSA, OP, II)

9. What is the importance of a cash discount in a business transaction?   (RSA, OP, I)

10. The purchasing department of a firm wishes to order a large quantity of a new item which it has not obtained previously. Describe the office procedures which will be followed and the documents which will be involved up to the stage when the firm pays for the items obtained.

11. Following the visit of a sales representative, your firm is about to purchase a new photo-copier. Write a short paragraph on each of the business documents involved in this transaction. (The usual procedure in your office is monthly settlement of all accounts.)   (RSA, OP, I)

12. (*a*) On the Credit Note Form below enter the following details:

On the 24th June Browning & Co., 13 Lake Street, Grasmere, Westmorland, returned to Burke & Co., 14 High Street, Dublin, the following, by B. & C. Steamship Co., vessel 'Brigand':

6 crates at 14p. each;
120 bottles at 8p. each;
6 bottles of Whisky (damaged) at £2·90 each;
3 small bottles of Whisky (sent in error) at 75p. each.

(*b*) How does this Credit Note affect the account of Browning & Co. with Burke and Co.?

(*c*) Give THREE reasons for which a Credit Note might be sent out. (RSA, OP, I)

BURKE & CO.,		*Ref. No.:* CN/133		
14 HIGH STREET				
DUBLIN				
CREDIT NOTE				

13. (a) You have been asked by your firm, 'Office-Equip', to order today the goods listed below from Camm and Co. Ltd., Wholesalers, of Barton Road, Sandling, Hants. Use the form below to make out the order and have it ready for the signature of your Purchasing Officer. The firm's account number with Camm and Co. Ltd. is X553, and the stock reference is F. 118.

Goods required:

½ gross 'Westline' pencils, 2B @ 5s. per dozen; ½ gross do. HB @ 5s. per dozen; ½ gross do. 2H @ 5s. per dozen; (all less 10%); 1 gross 'Motoway' ball-point pens @ 12s. per dozen (nett); 2 dozen 'Abso' ball-point erasers @ 4s. 6d. per dozen (less 10%).

(b) How would your Purchasing Officer obtain information about the prices offered by firms other than Camm and Co. Ltd.? (State *three* sources of such information.)

(c) The prices offered by these firms would no doubt interest him when making future orders. State *three* other factors which might influence his choice.

(RSA, OP, I)

ORDER

Tel. Townlea 4579	Date	Order No.

"OFFICE-EQUIP", Holtam Street, TOWNLEA, Berks.

CUSTOMER ACCOUNT No.	Our Stock Ref.

To:

Please Supply and Deliver:

Qty.	Description	Price

NO DELIVERIES ACCEPTED UNLESS AGAINST OUR OFFICIAL ORDER. PLEASE QUOTE ORDER NO. AND DATE.	Signed
	Purchasing Officer

14. The following transactions took place between Mr Thomas Grey of 13 High Street, London, EC, and The Regional Supply Co Ltd of St Peter's Circus, Bigtown.

Note: All goods supplied to Thomas Grey during the month of April are subject to a Trade Discount of 20%. The figures given below are the catalogue prices.

1971

1st April	Balance owing by Thomas Grey £69.32
7th April	Goods supplied by the Regional Supply Co £80.15 (Invoice No. X.2314)
12th April	Some of the goods supplied on 7th April (catalogue price £10.50) returned by Thomas Grey and he was sent Credit Note R.423
14th April	Twenty items supplied by the Regional Supply Co at £5.35 each (Invoice No. X.3160)
23rd April	Fifty items supplied by the Regional Supply Co at 80p each (Invoice No. X.4214)
26th April	Thomas Grey returned packing cases and was allowed £10 (Credit Note No. R.501)
28th April	Thomas Grey paid by cheque the balance owing on 1st April, 1971

a) Enter the above transactions in the Statement on the next page. Complete the Statement and show the balance owing on 30th April, 1971.

b) Using the form on the next page make out a cheque for the signature of Mr Thomas Grey in settlement of the sum owing by him to the Regional Supply Co Ltd on 30th April, less $2\frac{1}{2}$% Cash Discount. The payment is made on 4th May.

c) What is the purpose of the magnetic characters at the foot of the cheque? (RSA, OP, II)

227

THE REGIONAL SUPPLY CO. LTD.
St. Peter's Circus,
Bigtown
Tel. Bigtown 4431

STATEMENT

Date:

DATE	TRANSACTION	DOCUMENT NO.	DEBIT	CREDIT	BALANCE

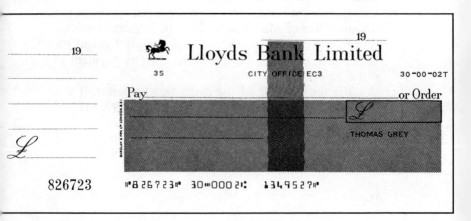

Chapter 7

Methods of Payment

IN the transaction described in Chapter 6 the goods were paid for by cheque. While the cheque is the most common form of payment between firms, other methods of payment are available through the banking system and the post office. Each form of payment has advantages and disadvantages and the wise firm or individual chooses the method of payment that is the most suitable for each transaction.

(a) PAYMENT THROUGH THE BANKING SYSTEM

Banks provide a wide range of facilities to help their customers to make payments. Individuals or businesses can open a bank account and use the many services of the bank to make payments.

Bank Cashiers behind bullet-proof glass screens

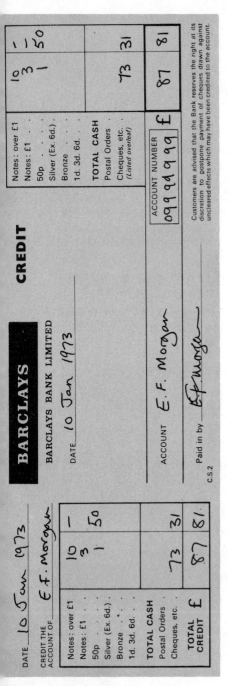

BARCLAYS   **CREDIT**

BARCLAYS BANK LIMITED

DATE 10 Jan 1973

Notes: over £1	10	
Notes: £1	3	
50p	1	50
Silver (Ex. 6d.)		
Bronze		
1d. 3d. 6d.		
TOTAL CASH		
Postal Orders		
Cheques, etc. *(Listed overleaf)*	73	31
£	87	81

ACCOUNT NUMBER

09 99999

ACCOUNT *E. F. Morgan*

Paid in by _E F Morgan_

C.S.2

Customers are advised that the Bank reserves the right at its discretion to postpone payment of cheques drawn against uncleared effects which may have been credited to the account.

DATE 10 Jan 1973

CREDIT THE ACCOUNT OF _E. F. Morgan_

Notes: over £1	10	
Notes: £1	3	
50p	1	50
Silver (Ex. 6d.)		
Bronze		
1d. 3d. 6d.		
TOTAL CASH		
Postal Orders		
Cheques, etc.	73	31
TOTAL CREDIT £	87	81.

230

Cheques etc.

Onion Publishers	54	75
U.D.C.	10	46
Excelsior Prod.	8	10
TOTAL CARRIED OVERLEAF £	73	31

A paying-in slip.

TYPES OF ACCOUNT

Banks offer two types of accounts: one type for saving money and one for making payments. *Deposit accounts* and *savings accounts* are for saving and the money in these accounts earns interest. *Current accounts* do not normally earn interest, but the money in these accounts can be paid out through the banking system to settle debts. The *budget account* works like a current account but it is used in special circumstances (see pp. 242–243).

PAYING MONEY INTO A CURRENT ACCOUNT

A customer pays money or cheques into his current account by filling in a *paying-in slip* or *credit slip*. The completed form and the money and/or cheques are handed to the cashier at the customer's branch and the customer's account is credited with the amount. A *credit* is money added to, that is credited to, an account.

If a customer wishes to pay into his account at a time when he cannot reach his own branch, he can do so by completing a *Bank Giro Credit form* (see page 245). The bank receiving the money and/or cheques will send the form to its head office who will pass it on to the customer's own branch where the amount will be credited to his account. This method of paying money into an account is known as *Credit Transfer 1*.

BANK STATEMENT

Each customer receives a statement from the bank which shows all the transactions that have gone through the customer's account. The date is the day on which the transaction took place within the bank, not the date on which the cheque was written. *Debits* are sums of money deducted from the customer's account which have been paid to a creditor or with-

---

When a bank customer pays money into a current account, he completes a paying-in slip (opposite). Each bank designs its own paying-in slips but they all contain the same information: the date, the name of the account-holder and the number of the account, the cash (listed in denominations) and the cheques being paid in. Details of the cheques being paid in are usually listed on the back of the paying-in slip. The person who is paying in the amount signs the form in the space provided. The cashier or teller stamps and initials the paying-in form and counterfoil, and then detaches the counterfoil and passes it back to the person who has signed the paying-in form. The counterfoil may be kept as a record of the transaction.

A. SPECIMEN

Date	Detail	Debits	Credits	Balance when overdrawn marked DR
1972	BALANCE FORWARD			373.92
9FEB	78739	1.CC		372.92
11FEB	CASH/CHEQUES		129.85	502.77
22FEB	CR. TRANSFER		29.15	531.92

BG Bank Giro Credit	DV Dividend	Account No 09999999	Statement No 12
DD Direct Debit	SO Standing Order		

A bank statement. Against the date '9 FEB' is the number 78739 in the 'Detail' column; what does this number indicate? How are the abbreviations at the bottom of the statement used?

drawn by the customer. *Credits* are sums paid into the account either by the account holder himself or by another person. The *balance* is the amount left in the account.

Banks usually send out statements every six months but a customer can arrange to receive a statement as often as he wishes. Most banks no longer send the used cheques, called *cancelled cheques*, with the statement unless an account holder specifically instructs them to do so. They are, however, filed by the bank in case it is necessary to double check that a certain amount was drawn by a payee.

THE CHEQUE AS A METHOD OF PAYMENT

A cheque represents the amount of money written on it and is considered in law to be the same as cash. The cheque is a form of instruction to the bank to take money out of the current account of the person writing the cheque, called *the drawer*, and

232

A crossed cheque and counterfoil. *1. Date. 2. Printed numbers. 3. Payee and drawer. 4. The amount. 5. The counterfoil.*

to credit that amount to the account of the person receiving the cheque who is called *the payee*. The clerical processes which take place (within a branch of a bank, between the branch and the head office, and between the branches and head offices of different banks) to effect and record this transfer of money from one account to another are discussed under 'Clearing a cheque' on pp. 235–6.

Cheques can be used in several ways. A cheque can be given or sent to a creditor to settle a bill; or the drawer can take money out of his own account by cashing a cheque; or the drawer can give the payee a cheque that the payee can cash.

CHEQUE FORMS

Legally cheques can be written on anything and there is a true story of a man who wrote a cheque on a cow and took the cow to the bank for payment. However, most cheques are written on the official cheque forms which are issued in cheque books to all bank customers who have current accounts. The bank prints the customer's name and account number on each cheque in the book. Cheques printed in this way have become known as 'personalised cheques' and the banks prefer customers to use their own cheques rather than the blank unidentified 'cheque forms' which some large shops have available for a customer who says, 'Yes, I'd like to buy that, but unfortunately I haven't my cheque book with me today'.

PARTS OF A CHEQUE

Each part of a cheque has a purpose and each part must be filled in correctly for the cheque to be valid.

1. *Date*. The date on the top is usually the day on which the cheque is written. Cheques are valid for six months after the date on the cheque. If a cheque is presented for payment after six months have elapsed, the bank sends it back to the drawer who must change the date on the cheque or issue another one before payment is made. (See AMENDING A CHEQUE on page 235.)

Post-dated cheques. In certain circumstances a person may wish to post-date a cheque, that is write the date of some time in the future in the space provided. The payee cannot pay the cheque into his account or present the cheque for payment until the day written on the cheque.

2. *Printed numbers*. The printed number next to the date or just above it and the other printed numbers at the bottom of the cheques are codes which have a meaning for the bank and make handling cheques easier. The number in the top right-hand corner is the code number for the drawer's branch.

The numbers at the bottom of the cheque are printed in magnetic ink so that they can be read by a computer. The number on the left is the number of the cheque. The middle one is the branch code number again, and the drawer's account number is on the right.

3. *Payee and drawer*. The payee's name, either a person or a firm, is written on the first line after 'Pay'. The printed name and the signature are those of the drawer.

4. *The amount*. The amount must be written in figures in the box provided. The number of pounds is written in letters on

A cheque for 'five pounds only'. What is the name of the payee? What is the code number of the bank? What is the number of the cheque and what is the drawer's account number?

---

1   60-90-01

National Westminster Bank Limited ↻

Anytown Branch   9 February 19 73
41 High Street, Anytown, Berks

Pay Marion P Lartes   or order

five pounds only   £5

                A. SPECIMEN

             A. Specimen

⑈123456⑈ 60⑈9001⑊ 99999999⑈

Cheques Drawn					
Cheque No.	Date	Payee	Amount		
123456	9 Feb	Marion P Lanter	5	—	
123457	12 Feb	Evans + Hooper	6	45	
Notes					

A record page from a cheque book.

the second and third lines and the number of pence is written after in figures. If the cheque is in pounds and no pence, it is wise to write 'only' after the number of pounds on the second line, to prevent someone adding to it.

5. *The counterfoil.* As soon as he has written a cheque the drawer should fill in the counterfoil. Cheque counterfoils provide a record of the cheques that have been written. By checking his counterfoils the drawer can keep track of his total debits between statements. Some customers find it more convenient to use a smaller cheque book which has a record page interleaved between each set of five cheques and no counterfoils. The customer should enter the details of each cheque he writes on the record page.

AMENDING A CHEQUE

After it has been completed, a cheque can be amended only by the drawer. He simply crosses out (erasing invalidates the cheque) the part he wants to change, writes the amendment next to it and initials the alteration. This method may be used to change the date of a cheque presented more than six months after it was written. However, it is always safer to write out another cheque and destroy the original one.

CLEARING A CHEQUE

Clearing a cheque means passing it through the banking system so that the payee's account is credited and the drawer's account debited for the amount of the cheque. To explain the system of clearing a cheque we will use the example of a cheque

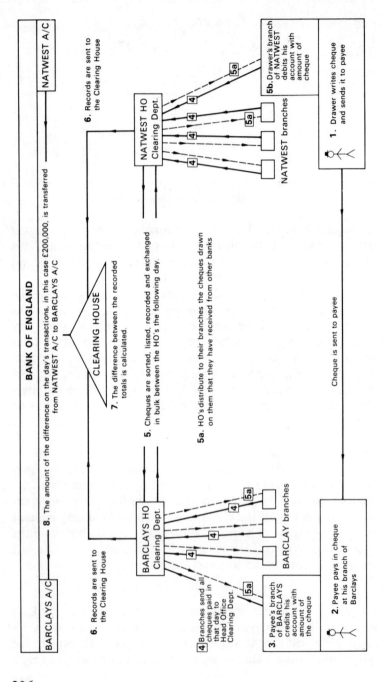

BANK OF ENGLAND

BARCLAYS A/C

NATWEST A/C

8. The amount of the difference on the day's transactions, in this case £200,000, is transferred from NATWEST A/C to BARCLAYS A/C

6. Records are sent to the Clearing House

CLEARING HOUSE

7. The difference between the recorded totals is calculated.

5. Cheques are sorted, listed, recorded and exchanged in bulk between the HO's the following day.

5a. HO's distribute to their branches the cheques drawn on them that they have received from other banks

6. Records are sent to the Clearing House

NATWEST HO Clearing Dept.

NATWEST branches

5a

5b. Drawer's branch of NATWEST debits his account with amount of cheque

1. Drawer writes cheque and sends it to payee

BARCLAYS HO Clearing Dept.

BARCLAY branches

4. Branches send all cheques paid in that day to Head Office Clearing Dept.

3. Payee's branch of BARCLAYS credits his account with amount of the cheque

2. Payee pays in cheque at his branch of Barclays

Cheque is sent to payee

236

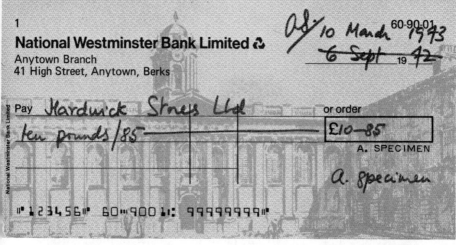

1

National Westminster Bank Limited ↻

Anytown Branch
41 High Street, Anytown, Berks

60-90-01

10 March 1973

~~6 Sept 19 72~~

Pay *Hardwick Stores Ltd*   or order

ten pounds /85   £10—85

A. SPECIMEN

a. specimen

⑈123456⑈ 60⑈9001⑉ 99999999⑈

This is an example of a cheque written on 6 September 1972 for £10.85 made payable to Hardwick Stores Ltd. For some reason the cheque was not presented for payment within the six month period allowed, so the drawer was asked to amend the date. He did this by changing the date to 10 March 1973 and initialling the alteration.

drawn on the National Westminster Bank (where the drawer has his account) in favour of a payee with his account at Barclays Bank.

When the payee pays in the cheque at his branch, it is credited to his account. The cheque is sent together with all the other cheques paid in that day, to the Clearing Department at Barclays head office. (In addition to this system, each bank has its own branch clearing—cheques drawn on different branches of the same bank are settled between those branches—and some towns have local clearing, but finally all cheques are sent to the Clearing Department of the bank's head office.) The Clearing

---

How a cheque is cleared. 1. The drawer writes a cheque and sends it to the payee. 2. The payee pays in the cheque at his branch of Barclays. 3. The payee's branch of Barclays credits his account with the amount of the cheque. 4. The branches send all cheques paid in that day to their Head Office Clearing Departments. 5. The clearing departments of the banks' head offices sort, list and record the cheques; the actual cheques are exchanged in bulk the following day. (5a. The Head Offices distribute to their branches the cheques drawn on them that they have received from other banks. 5b. The drawer's branch of NATWEST debits his account with the amount of the cheque.) 6. The clearing departments of the banks' head offices send the records to the Clearing House. 7. At the Clearing House the difference between the recorded totals is calculated to find out how much money one bank owes the other. 8. The amount of the difference on the day's transactions, in this case £200,000, is transferred from National Westminster Bank's account at the Bank of England to Barclays Bank's account at the Bank of England.

237

Department makes a list of all the cheques that come in that day and puts this record on microfilm. The cheque is then sent to the Clearing Department at the head office of National Westminster with all the other cheques drawn on the National Westminster. All the cheques are then sent back to the branches on which they are drawn (where they are filed, as explained on page 232), but the records are sent to the Clearing House, a building in Lombard Street in the City of London.

The Clearing House is the place where all the member banks, called Clearing Banks, meet to exchange records of cheques and to arrange the transfer of money to pay for these cheques. All the large British banks are Clearing Banks.

Because a payment by cheque is the transfer of money from the drawer's account to the payee's account, the bank on which the cheque is drawn, National Westminster, must transfer the amount of the cheque to the bank of the payee, Barclays. However, since millions of cheques are cleared every day, a separate transfer is not made for every individual cheque. Barclays adds up the total amount it is owed by National Westminster from cheques paid to Barclays and drawn on National Westminster that day. National Westminster adds up the total owed to it by Barclays from cheques paid into National Westminster and drawn on Barclays that day. For example, National Westminster may owe Barclays £1 million and Barclays may owe National Westminster £800,000. The difference between these totals for the day is the actual amount that is transferred, in this case £200,000, from National Westminster to Barclays. The transfer is made between the banks' accounts at the Bank of England.

Cheques drawn on different branches of the same bank are cleared within the branch clearing system of the bank. If the payee's branch and the drawer's branch are in the same locality outside London, the cheque may be cleared under local arrangements. All other cheques are sent to the Clearing Department at the banks' head offices in London to be cleared through the Clearing House.

USING A CHEQUE FOR PAYMENT

The cheque is a safe and simple method for individuals or firms to pay for goods and services. Cheques are safe to send through the post because the cheque can be used only by the

238

payee unless it has been endorsed, that is the payee has signed his name on the back. There are safeguards if a cheque is lost or stolen. (See SAFEGUARDS FOR A CHEQUE below.)

Many firms pay their employees by cheque to avoid keeping large sums of money in the firm. If a firm asks to have its cancelled cheques returned with its statement, they serve as a receipt for the firm's records.

WITHDRAWING MONEY WITH A CHEQUE

If a bank customer wants to draw money out of his current account, he can write a cheque to himself. This is called *cashing a cheque*. On the first line he writes 'cash' or 'self' instead of the name of a payee. He can cash cheques at his own bank branch or at another branch where he has previously made an arrangement. (See also CHEQUE CARDS on page 247).

A person draws money out of his current account by writing a cheque to himself. He writes 'Cash' or 'Self' after the word 'Pay' and 'uncrosses' the crossing by writing 'Please pay cash' between the crossing lines and signing the instruction. The cheque must be endorsed, that is signed, on the back as well.

SAFEGUARDS FOR A CHEQUE

Since a cheque represents money, certain safeguards are used to protect the bank, the drawer and the payee.

Specimen signature. When a person opens a current account he gives the branch a specimen signature. To prevent forged cheques the branch can check the signature on each cheque against the specimen before debiting the drawer's account.

A crossed cheque.

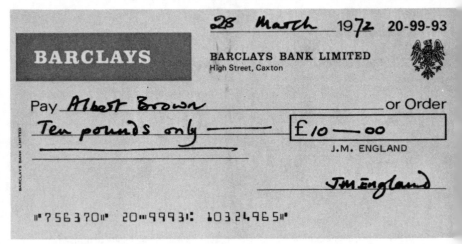

An open cheque.

A crossed cheque cannot be cashed (unless it is 'uncrossed' and made out to 'Cash' or 'Self') but must be paid into a bank account or into the Post Office Giro or the National Savings Bank. If the payee endorses the crossed cheque it can be paid into someone else's account. An open cheque becomes a crossed cheque if the drawer puts two vertical lines on the cheque.

Crossed and open cheques. The two vertical lines on a cheque indicate that it is a *crossed cheque.* A crossed cheque cannot be cashed but must be paid into a bank account or into the Post Office Giro or the National Savings Bank. If the payee endorses the crossed cheque it can be paid into someone else's

240

account.   Even if crossed cheques are lost or stolen, no one can cash them; therefore, only crossed cheques should be sent by post.

An *open cheque*, a cheque without the vertical lines, can be cashed if the payee *endorses* it by signing his name on the back. However, the cheque must be cashed at the branch where the drawer has his account unless a special arrangement has been made at another branch.   This is a safeguard for the bank and also for the drawer.   If the drawer has not enough money in his account to cover the cheque, the branch can refuse to cash it.   The branch also has an opportunity to check the signature on the cheque against the drawer's specimen signature.

A crossed cheque can be opened if the drawer signs his name between the vertical lines, and an open cheque can be crossed if the drawer puts two vertical lines on the cheque.

Forms of crossing.   The two vertical lines across a cheque, with or without the words '& Co.', are classified as a *general crossing.   Special crossings* may stipulate that the cheque should be paid into an account at a specified branch of a bank, or into a specified account.   The name of the bank, e.g. 'Midland Bank Ltd. Solihull', or the name of the account, e.g. 'a/c Payee only' or 'Motor Fund a/c', is written between the two parallel lines of the crossing.*   Another form of special crossing acts as a safeguard against fraud by stipulating the maximum amount payable; for example, the words 'Under £5' written between the lines of the crossing would prevent a cheque for £4 being altered to £40 or £400.

---

* 'The two remarks "account payee only" and "not negotiable" are added to cheques as additional safeguards, in case cheques fall into wrong hands.   The phrases do not mean exactly what they seem to mean: "account payee only" sounds as if that cheque could only be paid into the named payee's account, and the words "not negotiable" seem to indicate that this cheque cannot be passed to anyone else.   This is not the case.   Both these cheques can in fact be paid into anyone's bank account, but the words "account payee only" will cause the collecting bank to look with extreme suspicion and exercise great care if the person paying in the cheque is not the named payee.   The words "not negotiable" mean that if the cheque gets into the wrong hands anyone to whom it is given has no right to the money for which it stands.'   Basic Business Studies Book 1, Commerce, Swift, Stanwell and Warson, Edward Arnold (Publishers) Ltd.

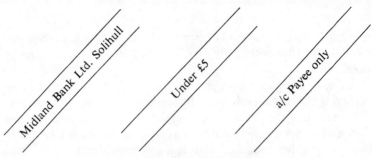

Examples of special crossings.

Stopping a cheque. If a cheque has been lost or stolen, the drawer can instruct his branch to stop the cheque. When a crossed cheque that is stopped arrives at the drawer's branch it is returned unpaid to the payee's branch. The drawer's account is not debited. If an open cheque is stopped, the drawer's branch will refuse to cash it.

An account holder can notify his branch to stop a cheque by telephone in the first instance but this must be confirmed in writing. The branch should be notified immediately when a completed cheque or a cheque book is lost or stolen so that it can put a stop on the cheque or cheques immediately.

Dishonoured cheques. When a drawer writes a cheque for more than the balance in his account, his branch will refuse the cheque and it will be returned to the payee's branch marked 'R/D' (refer to drawer); it is then up to the payee to contact the drawer and get the money he is owed. Cheques marked 'R/D' are known as 'dishonoured cheques' and are said 'to bounce'. It is illegal to bounce cheques.

OVERDRAFTS

Some firms and individuals arrange to have an *overdraft* with their bank. This means that the bank pays for cheques that would normally bounce up to an agreed amount. In effect, a customer with an overdraft is borrowing money from the bank and the customer is charged interest on the amount of his overdraft.

BUDGET ACCOUNTS

As most people have large bills to pay at certain times of the year, the banks have a system called the *Budget Account* which, as its name suggests, helps customers to budget. The budget

National Westminster Bank Limited

Budget Account

Schedule of Estimated Annual Commitments

Nature of Payment	Estimated Maximum Annual Expenditure			Month(s) when payment(s) become due
	£	s	d	
General Rates and Water Rate				
Telephone				
Electricity				
Gas				
Fuel (including Oil and Coal)				
School Fees				
Life Insurance				
House and Contents Insurance				
Car Insurance				
Car Licence				
Season Ticket				
Television and/or Radio Licences				
Holidays				
Annual Subscriptions				
Clothing				
Christmas Expenses				
Total Estimated Annual Expenditure	£			
Add: Service Charge of £6 to cover first £200; thereafter £1 per £50 of expenditure or any part thereof	£			
N. B. Minimum charge £6				
Add: Savings	£			
Total	£			
Amount, hereby authorised, of monthly transfer from Current Account, being 1/12th of the				
Total	£			

Date_____   Signature_____

NWB 1406-13-10:69   Signature_____

A Budget Account form. The Budget Account holder totals his expected annual expenditure on necessary items, such as electricity, clothes, rates and car licence. To this is added a charge for operating the account. The final total is divided by 12 and each month this amount is transferred from the customer's current account to his budget account.

243

account holder totals his expected annual expenditure on necessary items, such as electricity, clothes, rates and car licence. To this total is added a charge for operating the account. The final total is divided by 12 and each month this amount is transferred from the customer's current account to the budget account.

The customer has a separate cheque book for his budget account and he can pay his bills when they arrive with the cheques as he would with a çurrent account. The budget account holder can make a payment that overdraws his account so long as that payment is not more than one-quarter of the annual total expenditure. No interest is charged on budget account overdrafts as this is covered by the service charge.

BANK GIRO

The Bank Giro is the credit clearing system which transfers money from one account to another. (The National Giro operated by the Post Office is discussed on pp. 257–264.) The system of credit clearing follows the same procedure as clearing a cheque: the account of the person making the transfer is debited for the amount involved which is credited to the payee. Like cheque clearing, credit clearing is transacted through the Clearing House (see page 238).

CREDIT TRANSFERS 1 AND 2

In the section on PAYING MONEY INTO A CURRENT ACCOUNT we explained the method of crediting an account through the Bank Giro known as *Credit Transfer 1*.

Another method of payment using the Bank Giro is *Credit Transfer 2*. This system enables a customer to have any number of amounts transferred by issuing one cheque. Many firms use this method to pay their employees. All the payments are listed on a sheet showing the employees' branches and code numbers, and a credit slip is made out for each one. The firm writes one cheque for the total amount. The list of payments to be made, the slips and the cheque are sent or handed to the firm's own branch who then distribute the credits to the banks to which they are addressed.

The credit transfer system can also be used by a bank customer to instruct his branch to transfer money from his account to another account at any other bank. A non-customer, that

244

A Bank Giro credit form with counterfoil.

is a person without a bank account, can also pay money through the Bank Giro credit transfer system; he hands in the amount of cash, completes a form and pays a small charge. The charge for the service is 2p which is less than the cost of obtaining a money or postal order and mailing it in a stamped envelope.

STANDING ORDERS

When an account holder wants to make a regular credit transfer, for example for the annual payment of a club subscription or the monthly payment of rent, he can arrange for a *Banker's Order* or *Standing Order*. He completes and signs a standing order form or writes a letter to the bank branch. The form or the letter gives the bank the payee's account number and branch, the amount to be transferred and the dates on which the payments should be made. The bank makes the credit transfers on the correct dates without further instructions. A customer can stop the standing order at any time.

A standing order form. Forms for standing orders are usually supplied by the firm or organisation to whom the money is to be paid. Instructions for standing orders may also be made by letter from the customer to his bank branch.

paying by Bankers' Order, please return this page intact to the RAC at the address shown overleaf

BANKERS' ORDER in favour of **THE ROYAL AUTOMOBILE CLUB**

NAME OF MEMBER'S BANK..

BRANCH ADDRESS ....

ease pay **NOW** the sum of £ .... to NATIONAL WESTMINSTER BANK LTD., 1 St. James's Square, S.W.1.
ode No. 60-00-09 quoting A/c No. 13381989

d **ANNUALLY** thereafter on........................ until further notice the sum of £
oting A/c No. 13381997

ll Name ....

              (BLOCK LETTERS)

To the Remitting Bank: Please quote the undermentioned reference **on your CREDIT TRANSFER SLIP**

Member's Signature........................

Member's Bank A/c No........................

Date ....

—/ /—/—

DIRECT DEBIT

Some organisations, such as insurance companies and building societies, which had large numbers of customers paying by standing orders are now using the *direct debit system* which is a variation of the Standing Order System. The effect for the client of the insurance company is the same: an amount is debited from his account at regular intervals and paid to the insurance company's account. However, direct debits save clerical work for the banks.

The client of the insurance company signs a *direct debit authority* and fills in his bank account number, his branch, the amount to be debited from his account and the dates for the debits, for example, the first of every month. The client sends the completed form to the insurance company which sends it with the direct debit authorities from all its other clients to its bank branch. The insurance company's branch adds up the amounts that all the clients are due to pay to the insurance company on the first of every month. This total is the total amount the insurance company should receive from its clients on the first of every month, that is, the total amount to be credited to the insurance company's account. The total is recorded and the individual direct debits are sent to each client's bank branch, where they are accepted as authorisations to debit the nominated accounts.

On the first of every month the insurance company's branch makes one credit to the insurance company's account; that credit is the total of the amounts paid by all the clients. The branch then sends out debit notes (which are instructions to debit an account through the clearing system) to the branch of each client who signed a direct debit authority.

Direct Debit Authority form.

STANDING ORDER DIRECT DEBIT AUTHORITY

Name and address of Bank Branch:

....

....

....

I/We ....

....

authorise you with effect from ....and until further notice in writing to charge to my/our account

with you, on or about the ....day of every month at the instance of the ABBEY NATIONAL BUILDING SOCIETY

by direct debit the sum of £............(Amount in words ....pounds)

S.A.Y.E. ACCOUNT NUMBER.. Signature ....

When a client's branch receives the debit note, the client's account is debited for the amount. The authorisation for this debit is the direct debit authority which is held by the client's branch. The client can terminate the direct debit at any time.

TRADERS' CREDITS

The system of traders' credits is available to anyone, whether or not he is an account holder. An account holder gives the bank a list of his creditors and the amount owed to each one. He writes out a cheque for the total amount. The bank debits his account for the sum on the cheque and makes credit transfers for the correct amount to each creditor's account. Someone without a bank account can give the bank cash for the total amount plus a service charge and the bank makes credit transfers to the creditors.

Traders' credits can be used by anyone. Some firms with a large number of bills to pay find it more economical to negotiate a fee for the bank to make their payments instead of employing staff to write out cheques and envelopes and paying for postage.

CHEQUE CARDS

In recent years the banks have introduced credit cards and cheque cards to make it easier for customers to pay for goods. The cheque cards, which have a specimen signature, act as a form of identification for the customer. When a customer writes a cheque using his cheque card, the person receiving the cheque writes the number of the card on the back of the cheque. The bank guarantees to honour that cheque and pay the payee, even if the cheque would have bounced in normal circumstances. This guarantee is only on sums up to £30. With a cheque card a customer can cash cheques at any bank or buy goods and the bank cashing the cheque or the person selling the goods knows he will get his money providing the cheque has been drawn in accordance with the instructions issued with cheque cards.

CREDIT CARDS

The Barclaycard issued by Barclays Bank and the Access credit card issued by Lloyds, Midland and National Westminster Banks are credit cards. The Barclaycard and the Access card replace cash or cheques when used at a shop or restaurant that accepts them. The holder shows his card and

A cheque Card (front and back).

Barclaycard.

National Westminster Bank Limited

Branch

Sorting Code
Customer's Name
Batch/Serial No.

Customer's Personal Code Number *	654321

* Customers are requested to keep a careful record
of this number.
It should not be written on the cashcard.

24-hour cashcard and envelope.

the shop takes down the details.   Bills are sent to Barclaycard or Access headquarters who then issue statements to each customer showing what he owes.   Large sums can be paid off in instalments, as a form of loan, but interest is charged.

CASHCARD

Another bank service to customers is the 24-hour cashcard. With this card, a customer can go to a dispenser outside a bank and get £10 in cash any time of the day or night.   Each customer has a code number which is not printed on the card but is indicated by a series of holes that can be 'read' by the machine in the dispenser.   The customer puts his card in the dispenser and taps out his number on a set of buttons.   If he has tapped the right number, £10 drops out in a plastic packet.   The card disappears into the dispenser and it is sent back to the customer's bank where the £10 is deducted from his account.   The code number is not printed on the card in case it is lost or stolen. Without the number, no one can use the card.   If the wrong number is tapped out on the buttons, the dispenser will reject the card.   The customer has three chances to tap out the correct number.   After the third attempt, the machine keeps the card.

Cashcard dispenser.

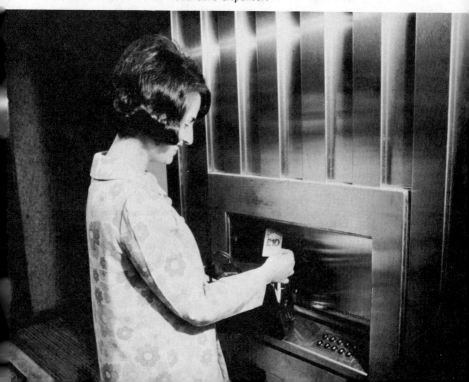

Large firms usually encourage all their employees to open bank accounts as this simplifies the payment of salaries and wages. As banks do not open on Saturday mornings and as they are closed by the time you leave the office in the evening,* you will probably find it convenient to open an account at a bank near your office rather than near your home. If you apply to open an account with your company's bank at the branch which keeps your company's account, the fact that you are a member of staff will serve as an introduction.

If you work for a medium-sized or small firm you may be paid by cheque or cash. In either case, it would be wise to open a bank account into which you can pay your salary. When you have chosen the bank and the branch where you would like to have your account, you should visit the bank branch and tell one of the cashiers at the counter that you wish to open an account. The manager or one of his assistants will then interview you and ask you one or two questions about where you work and what type of account you wish to open. If you have not been introduced to the bank by your employer, the bank manager may ask you to give the names of one or two referees who will confirm your suitability to be an account-holder at the bank. You will then be asked to give a specimen signature (see page 239). You will have to decide exactly how you are going to sign your name (either your initials followed by your surname, or your first and/or second names in full followed by your surname) and you must keep to that version whenever you sign your cheques.

When the bank has received the replies from your referees and the manager is assured of your suitability to be a customer of his branch, you will be asked to call at the bank to collect your cheque book, or it may be sent to you through the post. The possession of a cheque book is a responsibility, so remember the following points:

1. Keep your cheque book with you or in a safe place.
2. Do not put your signature on the cover.
3. Never give blank cheques to strangers.
4. If you lose your cheque book, let the bank know *at once*,

---

* Some bank branches are introducing a system whereby they open for business in the early evening once a week, say from 4.30 pm to 6.30 pm.

by telephoning, and then in writing, and they will 'stop' the cheques concerned.

5. When writing a cheque, use ink. Begin writing as far as possible over on the left-hand side, and do not leave spaces into which unauthorised words could be put.

6. Initial any alterations.

7. Always use the same signature as the one you gave when you opened the account.

8. Fill in the counterfoils or record page so that you can check your own record of spending against your Bank Statement.

When you receive your bank statement, it will seldom agree with your own record of the balance of your account; or, to put it another way, the final balance shown in the statement is rarely the current balance by the time you receive it. The reason for this is that the bank statement will not include records of transactions that have taken place since the last entry on it, which will of course have been made before the statement was posted from the bank. During those few days you may have written some cheques which have not yet been debited; or some cheques paid in to your account may not have been credited; or some bank charges* may have been debited to your account which you have not included in your own figures; or you may have forgotten to debit your records with some standing orders which the bank has deducted from your account.

When you have checked the figures on your bank statement with the counterfoils of your own receipts and payments, you should prepare a *Bank Reconciliation Statement*, that is a statement which adjusts the balance shown in the bank statement to the current balance, by entering those transactions which have taken place since the last item on the statement.

1. List the cheques outstanding, that is those which have not yet been presented for payment.

2. List credits outstanding, that is sums paid into the bank but not yet credited.

3. Enter as debits any banker's or standing orders or bank charges (ledger fees), and add any receipts such as salary credits received by the bank direct.

* For making the services of a current account available to customers, the banks may make a quarterly or half-yearly charge, known as *bank charges* or *ledger fees*.

251

Then prepare a Bank Reconciliation Statement in the following way:

BANK RECONCILIATION STATEMENT
4 January 1977

		£	£
Balance as shown on Bank Statement dated 31/12/76.			156.75
Deduct Cheques drawn but not presented			
456123 Carters Ltd		5.25	
456124 B.W. Read		2.50	
Standing order: Regal Insurance Co		10.00	
Charges		2.00	19.75
			137.00
Add Salary NBC			82.80
Balance			219.80

A Bank Reconciliation Statement adjusts the balance shown in the Bank Statement to the current balance by entering those transactions which have taken place since the last item on the statement.

OTHER BANKING FACILITIES

In addition to providing the various means for payment and for drawing cash which we have just described, banks provide many other facilities for their customers.

Night safe. A customer may make an arrangement with the bank which allows him to use the night safe. This is built into the outside wall of the bank. The bank gives the customer a pouch which has two keys; one key is held by the customer, the other is kept in the bank vault in a sealed envelope.

The customer fills in a paying-in slip or paying-in book in the usual way and puts it in the pouch with the money he wants to

252

The night safe is built into the outside wall of the bank.

The customer locks the pouch and puts it into the night safe.

bank. Then he locks the pouch and puts it into the night safe. The next day, during normal banking hours, the customer goes to the bank and collects the pouch and the counterfoil of the paying-in slip or the paying-in book. This service is of great use to shopkeepers and other businessmen who are unable to pay-in during normal banking hours yet do not wish to keep large sums of money on their premises overnight.

Loans and overdraft facilities. Customers can borrow money from their banks and also overdraw—that is, draw money in excess of the balance in their current accounts—if they have previously obtained the permission of the bank manager. A bridging loan is a special type of bank loan usually granted to a customer who is selling a house or flat and buying another one. If a person is being pressed to complete the purchase of a new house before he has received payment for the property he is selling, the bank will usually give him a loan to bridge the period between the sale of one house and the purchase of another. The charge for a bridging loan is usually three or four per cent above the bank's base rate, that is, the minimum lending rate.

Traveller's cheques. Banks sell traveller's cheques and foreign currency to customers who are going abroad either on holiday or on business. Traveller's cheques are issued in denominations of £2, £5, £10, £20 and £50. It is important to make a note of the numbers on traveller's cheques as soon as they are bought in case they are lost or stolen. The list of numbers should, of course, be kept separately from the cheques. If traveller's cheques are mislaid, the issuing bank must be informed immediately so that 'cashing' by unauthorised persons can be stopped.

Overseas trade. Banks assist their customers with references and exchange control formalities, and provide information on trade statistics, licensing regulations, foreign markets and economic conditions.

Advice and information. Advice on insurance, income tax, investment, Trusts and Wills, is available from all the leading banks. A customer's bank will hold his Will and act as executor.

MONEY SHOPS

One of the most recent developments in banking services is the money shop. Money shops are open six days a week during

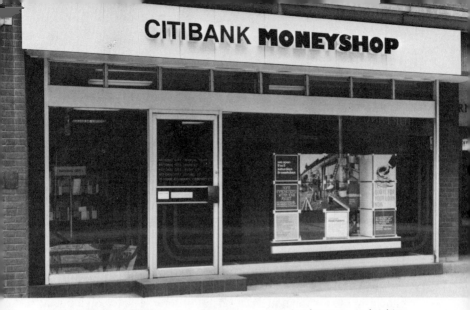

A CITIBANK MONEYSHOP, one of the most recent developments in banking services.

normal shopping hours and provide many banking facilities. Some money shops offer only personal loans, savings and insurance facilities; others provide comprehensive banking and financial services.

The main appeal of money shops is their personal loan service, but the banking facilities offered by some of them are designed to extend banking methods of payment to a greater number of people.

The current accounts available at some money shops work like those at banks. Account-holders have cheque books for making payments and cheques pass through the bank clearing system with one of the clearing banks acting as the money shop's agent. Statements are sent to account-holders at regular intervals and standing orders are available for paying regular amounts, such as rent, mortgage payments or club subscriptions. Although overdraft facilities are not available, customers are offered a variety of personal loan plans.

(b) PAYMENT THROUGH THE POST OFFICE

The Post Office provides facilities for making payments in Britain and overseas through postal and money orders and the National Giro. Anyone can go into any post office and buy a

255

postal or money order.   Anyone aged 15 or over or any business can open a National Giro account with the deposit of £1.

POSTAL ORDERS

For sums up to £21.22½ it is cheaper to send a postal order than a money order; a money order may be obtained for any sum not exceeding £50.

Postal orders are available for amounts from 5p to £1 and for £2, £3, £4 and £5.   If you wish to send a postal order for a sum for which none is available, not more than two stamps may be stuck on the postal order to complete the required amount. For example, if you wished to send someone 9½p you would buy a 7½p postal order and stick on a 2p stamp.

When you buy a postal order you must pay a fee.   This is the charge made for the issue of a postal order.   The fee on a postal order of 5p to £1 in value is 2½p, and on a £2, £3, £4 or £5 order it is 5p.

Reproduced by permission of the Post Office

To complete a postal order, fill in the name of the payee in the space provided and the office of payment.   If you do not know the post office most convenient to the payee, fill in the name of the town or district where the payee lives.   The order may then be cashed at any post office in the place named.

You should also complete the counterfoil which is provided on every postal order.   When you have filled in the name of the payee, the date sent, the office of payment, etc., tear off the counterfoil and keep it with the correspondence covering the despatch of the postal order.

Postal orders may be 'crossed', like cheques. 'Crossed' postal orders may only be paid into a bank account.

An 'uncrossed' postal order may be cashed at a post office. Before payment is made the payee must sign his name in the space provided. This is a form of receipt.

INLAND MONEY ORDER

An inland money order is used to send any sum of money (not exceeding £50) to a specified person. Payment is made at the post office stated on the money order. An issuing fee is also charged on money orders, and they may be 'crossed' like postal orders and cheques.

An Inland money order request form.

An application form, supplied by the post office, for the purchase of a money order must be completed. When you hand in the completed form together with the total amount due (the sum you wish to send to the payee plus the issuing fee), the clerk at the post office will give you the money order which you can then send to the payee. At the same time the post office issuing the order will advise the paying office that a money order for the sum stated will be presented for payment within a few days; a money order may, however, be presented at any time up to six months from the end of the month of issue.

INLAND TELEGRAPH MONEY ORDER

An Inland Telegraph Money Order enables money to be sent to a specified payee by telegraph. Application must be made

257

on the same form that is used for a money order, and the words 'By Telegraph' must be written across the completed form. In addition to the fee the following charges must be paid:

1. The cost of the telegram of advice.
2. A fee per word for any private message sent with the order.

When you send a telegraph money order you will be given a certificate of issue.

OVERSEAS MONEY ORDER

Overseas money orders may be used to send money to some foreign countries. The *Post Office Guide* gives full particulars of those countries to which money orders may be sent, and the maximum amount which may be transmitted. A special application form must be used. The issuing fee charged is higher than that on an inland money order. Money orders may also be sent by telegraph to some countries.

Applications to remit money orders to countries outside the Scheduled Territories (formerly known as the Sterling Area) must be made on form P2229H, where the purpose of the remittance must be stated. The form is obtainable at any money order office, where it may be ascertained which countries are outside the Scheduled Territories. The Scheduled Territories are those countries, which, although they may have their own currencies for day-to-day purposes, use British currency as a common factor in overseas trading, to measure the value of goods and services bought and sold. About half the trade of the world is done in sterling.

THE NATIONAL GIRO

The word Giro comes from the Greek *guros* meaning wheel and describes the circular way the Giro system passes money around from one person or firm to another. A form of the Giro system began in Austria in 1883 and since then it has spread throughout the Western hemisphere and is now operating in most European countries and in many parts of Africa and Asia.

The National Giro is the Post Office banking service which provides a fast and economic means of collecting money and making payments within the United Kingdom and to many other countries. The National Giro Centre at Bootle in

258

Lancashire keeps records of all Giro accounts; it has large computers and the most modern accounting and data processing machines. Some Giro transactions may be carried out over the counter at post offices but the debiting and crediting of accounts is done at the National Giro Centre.

Types of account. The National Giro offers two types of account: the *private account* for individuals and the *business account* for large organisations. Giro accounts like current accounts in banks are intended for making payments and no interest is paid on deposits. Application forms for Giro accounts are available at any post office.

Giro statement. Business account holders receive a statement through the post from the National Giro Centre every day. The statement shows the state of the account on the day it is prepared: the opening balance; each debit to the account and the total debit; each credit and the total credit; the balance after the day's transactions. There is usually no charge for daily statements.

Private account holders receive a statement every time money is credited to their accounts or after every ten debits, or every three months if there were no credits or fewer than ten debits during that period. These statements are free.

Stationery. Each Giro account holder has personalised forms for Giro transactions. Giro transfer forms, deposit forms and cheques are printed with the account holder's name, address and account number. The account holder may also buy 20 postage-paid envelopes for 10p which are printed with the address of the National Giro Centre. Since most forms have to be posted to the National Giro Centre, this saves the

TEMENT OF ACCOUNT
ber 58 627 3966   27FEB71

National Giro
Bootle
Lancs

CK 393433
Serial 9

mary		Transactions		£
ous balance 20FEB71	£52.17		DEBITS	
debits	49.88	24FEB S 2143211 BLDG SOC		19.35
credits	32.53	26FEB S 1769281 ANY UDC		4.00
nt balance 27FEB71	£34.82	27FEB S 3173962 FPLY INS		5.00
		27FEB T 1031234 B GAS BD		11.50
		27FEB P 0016 OUTPAYMENT		10.00
		FEES		0.03
		27FEB	CREDITS	
THE VISITOR		D SELF		5.25
GIRO EXHIBITION		T 4286237 PAY		27.28
ANYTOWN				

A Automatic   I Inpayment   T Giro transfer
 debit transfer P Payment   for further information
D Deposit   S Standing order see overleaf

GIRO STATEMENT HELPS YOU TO KEEP A SIMPLE CHECK ON YOUR EXPENDITURE
U GET ONE EVERY TIME AN AMOUNT IS PAID INTO, OR WHENEVER 10 PAYMENTS
VE BEEN MADE FROM YOUR ACCOUNT

customer writing out an envelope and covers the cost of postage for $\frac{1}{2}$p per envelope.

Account holder paying money into his own account.   Account holders make deposits to their own accounts by paying money in at any of the 22 000 post offices in the United Kingdom or by sending bank cheques payable to them to the National Giro Centre.   In both cases the account holder fills in a personalised deposit form with the amount and gives it in or sends it with the deposit.

Account holder paying another account holder.   A person who has a Giro account uses a transfer to pay another Giro account holder.   The person paying the money fills in his personalised transfer form with the amount of money to be transferred and

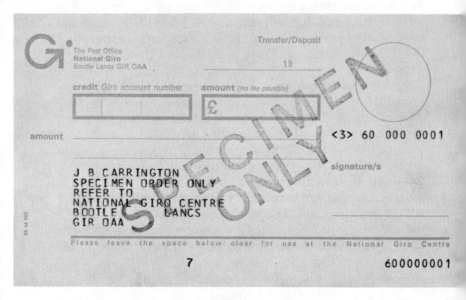

the account number of the payee.   A message for the payee can be written on the back of the transfer form.   The completed form is sent in a postage-paid envelope to the National Giro Centre where the amount is debited from the account of the person making the transfer and credited to the account of the payee.   The transfer form is sent to the payee with the statement showing the credit to his account.

Low balance charge.   The account holder is not charged for making a transfer unless he has to pay a low balance charge.

This charge of 5p is deducted from any account that has an opening balance of less than £30 on the day the account is debited.

Standing order. If an account holder wants to pay another account holder a fixed sum of money at regular intervals he can arrange for a standing order. He fills in a standing order form giving the details of the amount to be paid, the dates of the payments, his account number and the account number of the payee. This form is sent to the National Giro Centre where his account is debited for the amount and the payee's account credited on the specified dates without further instructions. This service is free unless a low balance charge has to be applied on the day the debit is made.

Giro standing orders can only be made within the Giro system. A Giro account holder cannot make out a standing order to someone who does not have a Giro account. Money cannot be transferred from a Giro account to a bank account except in one instance: a Giro account holder can make one transfer a month from his Giro account to his own bank account.

Automatic debit transfers. A Giro account holder can pay varying amounts on fixed or variable dates to another account holder by an automatic debit transfer. For example, a Giro account holder with a charge account at a department store may arrange to pay the store by automatic debit transfers, although the amounts vary and his visits to the store are irregular.

The account holder signs an authorisation form and sends it to the store. The store sends the form to the National Giro Centre. After that the National Giro Centre will act at any time it is instructed by the store by making a transfer from the customer's account to the store's account for any amount specified by the store.

To safeguard the customer the store must agree that the National Giro Centre can reverse any transfer of money if the customer disputes the amount. In addition the store agrees to make up any loss to Giro through misuse of the automatic debit transfer system.

The customer receives a statement from Giro after every debit transfer is made. Both the statement and the transfer are free.

Person without a Giro account paying an account holder. A

261

.... 19.........
Giro account number

the Post Office
National Giro
Bootle Lancs GIR OAA

credit ....

Giro account number

.... 19.........

amount

£

£ amount

The Giro Inpayment Service is subject
to the conditions which are set out
in the Post Office Guide, a copy of
which may be seen at any Post Office.

Name and address of payer ....

signature ....

The space below this line must be left clear for machine processing at the National Giro Centre

person who does not have a Giro account can pay money to a Giro account holder in two ways. If the person paying the money wants to pay in cash and if he knows the Giro account number of the payee, he can pay in the money at any post office using an Inpayment Form for a small charge; or he can send a bank cheque to the payee who then sends the cheque to the National Giro Centre with a deposit form. A person without a Giro account should not send bank cheques directly to the National Giro Centre even if he knows the payee's account number.

When a Giro account holder sends a bank cheque to the National Giro Centre there is a three day waiting period before the cheque is credited to his account so that the cheque can be cleared through the bank clearing system (see pp. 235–238 for information on the bank clearing system).

Agent deposit service. Some firms have branches, representatives or salesmen in different parts of the country who receive cash from customers. Under the agent deposit service all the salesmen of a firm can deposit money at their local post offices for credit to the firm's Giro account. If a firm uses this service the salesmen depositing money do not have to pay the usual inpayment charge. The firm's fee for the service is negotiated with the Post Office. If there are large sums of cash to be deposited, a post office van will pick up the money and take it to the post office for an extra fee.

Giro cheques. The Giro cheque may be used like a bank cheque, although Giro account holders can pay each other by transfer. All Giro cheques are open but the drawer should

cross the cheque himself before he sends it or gives it to a person without a Giro account.

Account holder paying a person without a Giro account. When a Giro account-holder uses the Giro system to pay someone without a Giro account, he writes out a personalised Giro cheque and crosses it. The payee can pay the Giro cheque into his bank account or endorse the cheque, that is sign it on the back, for someone else to pay into his bank or Giro account. A small charge is made to the Giro account holder when a Giro cheque is debited to his account.

The Giro system cannot be used to settle a transaction if neither party is a Giro account-holder.

Withdrawing up to £20 by cashing a cheque. Giro account-holders may withdraw up to £20 from their accounts by cashing one of their personalised open cheques at one of two post offices nominated for the purpose when they opened their accounts. The account-holder has a Giro card with a specimen of his signature which he presents with the cheque at the post office counter. The cheque is sent to the National Giro Centre where the account is debited for the amount on the cheque.

No overdraft facilities. Giro account-holders are not allowed overdraft facilities. If a Giro account-holder makes a transfer for an amount greater than his balance, the transfer is refused.

The rules about cashing cheques are designed to prevent accounts being overdrawn. Account-holders are allowed to cash cheques at only two nominated post offices so that the

National Giro Centre can easily order cheques to be refused if the account-holder has no money in his account. As a further safeguard, account-holders may cash cheques on alternate days only. This allows the National Giro Centre time to inform the nominated post offices if the account-holder has emptied his account with the last cheque he has cashed.

If an account-holder overdraws his account by cashing a £19 cheque when he has a balance of only £17, for example, the National Giro Centre writes to the account-holder to warn him not to overdraw again. If the account-holder does overdraw again, his account is closed unless there are exceptional circumstances.

Authenticated cheques. In certain circumstances listed below an account-holder must have a cheque authenticated by the National Giro Centre before he can cash it or send it to the payee. Authentication means that the amount on the cheque is debited to the drawer's account before the cheque is cashed by the drawer or given to the payee to cash. This is another safeguard to prevent overdrawing. The drawer is charged 10p for each authenticated cheque.

The circumstances where authentication is needed are:

1. When the account holder wants to cash one of his own cheques for more than £20 (but less than £50) at one of the two nominated post offices.
2. When the account-holder wants to cash a cheque at a post office other than the two nominated ones.
3. When the account-holder wants to send or give the payee an open cheque that the payee can cash. If the open cheque is for more than £50, the drawer must nominate the post office where the cheque should be cashed.

Pre-authenticated cheques. Business account-holders can arrange to have pre-authenticated Giro cheques. These are cheques that have already been authenticated and they may be cashed at any post office by the payee. Pre-authenticated cheques are used to pay employees working away from the firm's offices or to pay company pensions. This enables company pensions to be collected at the same time as state pensions.

International Giro. Firms and individuals in Britain can make or receive payments through Giro to or from any other country operating a Giro system. These countries are Austria, Belgium, Denmark, Finland, France, Italy, Japan, Luxemburg,

Netherlands, Norway, Sweden, Switzerland and West Germany. Outpayments can be made to any country in the world, subject to Exchange Control regulations.

Giro Gold Card. National Giro offers approved account holders extended cheque cashing facilities which are similar to the cheque card available to bank customers. The Giro Gold Card enables an approved customer to cash cheques for amounts up to £30 on every other day at any post office in the United Kingdom.

EXERCISES

1. Explain the following terms: (*a*) a counterfoil, (*b*) issuing fee, (*c*) payee, (*d*) per cent per annum, (*e*) the National Giro.

2. Whilst on holiday in the Black Forest you borrowed £2 from a German friend. When you returned home you wished to repay the debt. How could you send the money if your friend had no bank account?

3. What is the quickest way to send £2 from London to Birmingham?

4. What are the advantages of having a Savings Bank Ordinary Account?

5. You have been given £5 as a birthday present and wish to invest it at the post office. Which of the methods of investment would you choose and why?

6. Explain the following terms and expressions:

budget account	drawer
current account	traders' credits
authenticated cheque	agent deposit scheme

crossed cheque	paying-in slip
standing order	clearing house
night safe	24-hour cashcard

7. Explain the difference between a standing order and a direct debit or automatic debit transfer. What advantages does a standing order offer a firm? Why would a firm supplying stationery be glad if its customers used direct debit transfers for payment?

8. In addition to facilities for making payments and drawing cash, what other services do banks offer their customers?

9. Explain the differences between:
   (a) a post-dated cheque;
   (b) a stale cheque;
   (c) a dishonoured cheque.

10. Describe THREE services offered by the banks to the business-man.

11. For what purposes are the following methods of payment used:
    (a) postal order; (b) standing order; (c) credit transfer; (d) credit card? (RSA, OP, I)

12. In what circumstances would you use the following banking services?
    (a) Current Account; (b) Deposit Account; (c) Standing Order; (d) Overdraft. (RSA, OP, I)

13. Explain the meaning of the following and the purposes for which they are used in banking:
    (a) Credit Transfer; (b) Bank Statement; (c) Cash Dispenser; (d) Banker's Card. (RSA, OP, I)

14. Explain how the Post Office Giro operates and indicate how the service which it offers differs from that provided by a Joint Stock Bank. (RSA, OP, II)

15. (a) You have just received your firm's Bank Statement made up to 30th April, 1976, and you notice that it quotes a credit balance of £970·45 whereas the balance in your firm's cash book was £860·32 on that date. When the previous Bank Statement (made up to 31st March, 1976)

266

had been received, the credit balance at the bank was £903·26 as against the firm's cash book balance of £1064·50.

Explain ways in which these two differences could have occurred. (RSA, OP, II)

16. A Yorkshire firm wishes to send wages to an employee working on an Isle of Man site. Choose
   (*a*) two of the methods offered by the Post Office, and
   (*b*) two methods offered by the commercial banks for transferring money, and indicate the strongest and weakest feature of each method. (RSA, OP, I)

17. Enter the following particulars on the Credit Form below: £27·50 to be paid by you into the account of Mr. N. Norfolk who banks at the Cathedral Branch of Barclays Bank, York. The Code Number is 13-93-16.
   5 £5 notes;
   2 £1 notes;
   1 50p piece. (RSA, OP, I)

18. (*a*) The morning post contains the following remittances:

Sender	Method of Payment	Amount
		£
J. Smith Ltd.	Cheque	4·62
R. Peters	Cheque	6·50
P. South & Co.	Cheque	5·60
M. Rayner	P.O.	1·50

R. Jones	Registered Mail	
	(five £1 notes)	5·00
The Albright Co. Ltd.	Cheque	41·31
R. Smith	M.O.	4·48

In addition, the following payments are made in cash at the main office:

Paid by: | *Money paid:*
J. Brown | Three £1 notes, two 10p coins, one 5p coin.

R. Smith | One £5 note, two £1 notes, one 50p coin, and four pennies

S. Wilson | One £5 note, and four 10p coins.

Prepare a paying-in slip for all the above receipts to be paid into the bank.
The Company for whom you work is Western Designs Ltd. Their Account Number is 1093706.

(*b*) Explain briefly the following bank services and state the circumstances in which they would be used:

  (i) Night Safe facilities.

  (ii) Standing Orders as a method of payment.

(RSA, OP, II)

19. Messrs Briggs and Smith are small retailers with a banking account at the Midland Bank Ltd (High Street, Spelford Branch). They recently obtained a private loan of £500 from a Mr T Grey and the cheque sent by Mr Grey is reproduced below. Briggs and Smith are repaying the loan (with interest) by 24 monthly instalments of £25·50, due on

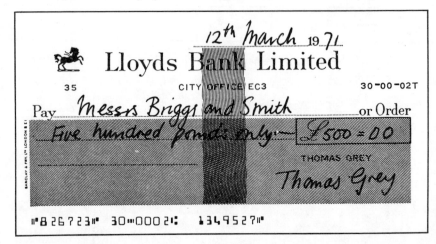

the 15th day of each calendar month. The first payment was made on 15th April, 1971.

All monthly payments due to date have been made by cheque. However, Briggs and Smith wish to arrange for all future payments to be made from their current account by a Banker's Standing Order.

(*a*) Complete the Standing Order Form below.

(*b*) What advantage (i) for Briggs and Smith (ii) for Mr Grey, will arise from this changed method of payment?

(*c*) Mr Grey has a Post Office Giro account. Briggs and Smith have no such account, but, if they wished to make their monthly payments through the Post Office Giro, what action should they take? (RSA, OP, II)

BANKER'S ORDER FORM

Standing Order

TO **Midland Bank Limited**

Branch _____

Date _____

Please make payments and debit my/our _____ account in accordance with the following details, to:

Bank _____

Branch _____

Sorting code number _____

For account of _____

Account number, if any _____

Reference number, if any _____

Amount £ [   ]

Payments to be made _____ weekly/monthly/quarterly/half-yearly/annually*

Date of first payment _____

Date of final payment _____

This order cancels the existing one* for £ _____

*Delete as appropriate

Chapter 8

Filing

(a) DEFINITION

What is filing? Filing is the storing of letters, records, carbon copies and documents in folders, binders, drawers and cabinets especially designed for the purpose.

Why is it done? Firstly, to keep the papers in safe custody; secondly, to keep them clean; thirdly, to keep the office tidy; and fourthly, and most important, so that the papers may be produced without delay whenever they are required. The efficiency of any filing system is judged by the speed with which papers can be found—a good filing system is a quick.finding system.

Whose job is it? As we learned in Chapter I, some very large firms employ many full-time clerks in a Central Filing Department which is responsible for the safe-keeping of all the files for the whole firm. In other firms, some departments store the current papers in the department and pass the completed files to the Central Filing Department at the end of each year. Within each department the filing will almost certainly be part of the typist's or shorthand-typist's duties, although the head of the department or the office manager will be responsible for the selection of equipment and methods best suited to the particular firm's business. In addition to this, many executives keep a set of confidential files which will be looked after by a private secretary.

When should it be done? In most offices there is a tray labelled 'Filing' in which can be placed any papers to be filed. This tray should be cleared once a day preferably first thing in the morning. Many typists find it convenient to file the previous day's correspondence while the post is being read and before they are called in to take dictation (or while the letters are being recorded on a dictating machine).

270

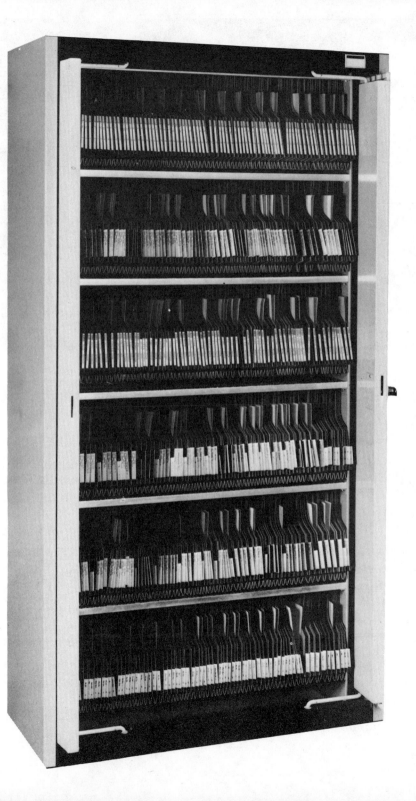

On page 267 is an example of files stored laterally in a cupboard. The files themselves are hung on racks. The photograph above shows a drawer in which the files are placed in a concertina of outer folders.

(b) EQUIPMENT

A 'file' is a collection of letters or documents dealing with one person or topic and placed together in a manilla card folder. Files may be stored either:

    (a) in drawers; or

    (b) on shelves, or cupboards (lateral filing).

The photographs show these two methods. The lateral method is often used today as a means of saving space. Notice that the lateral filing unit is fitted with a shutter which protects the files from dust and enables the whole unit to be locked.

In both the drawer and lateral systems the files (or folders) are either:

    (a) stood on their backs (or spines); or

    (b) hung from frames or rails, either separately or in a 'concertina' of outer folders, which are *not* removed when the papers are wanted.

272

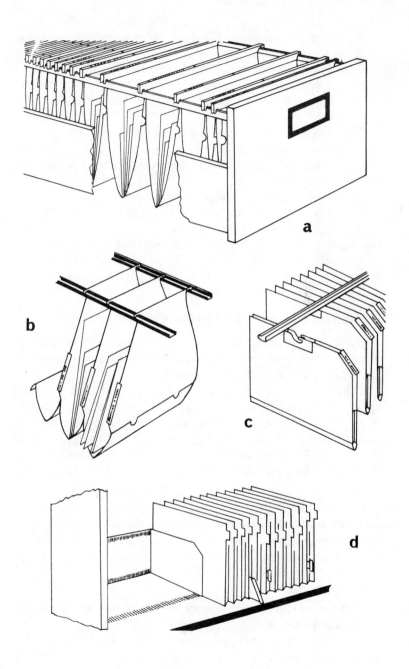

The diagrams on page 273 show three suspended and one standing filing system.

- (*a*) Files hanging from a frame in a drawer, making use of a concertina of outer folders. The outer folders are joined by metal slides on which are fixed the index tabs.
- (*b*) Files in a concertina of outer covers hanging from a frame which can be placed in a cupboard. Here the index tabs are fixed at the side because the files are inserted sideways.
- (*c*) Files hanging separately from a centre rail.
- (*d*) Files standing on their spines in shelves. This method can also be used in drawers.

For ease of reference, files are often subdivided alphabetically, numerically, regionally or by subjects. These divisions are marked by guide cards, usually coloured and easily identified.

(c) METHODS OF CLASSIFICATION

We must now study what are usually called 'the methods of filing'; these are really the various methods of classification, or the order in which the files are placed.

The basis of all classification is the alphabet; and when we speak of *alphabetical order* we mean the order in which the words in a dictionary, or names in a telephone directory, are arranged; even the so-called Numerical System depends upon an alphabetical index. Here are some rules which must be borne in mind when files and cards are being arranged in alphabetical order.

1. File according to the initial letter of the surname and each subsequent letter, e.g.

> Parker, E. H.
> Parkinson, M. W.
> Parsons, N. V.
> Partridge, S. O.

2. If the surnames are the same, file according to initials, e.g.

> Chapman, B. D.
> Chapman, C. M.
> Chapman, C. P.
> Chapman, H. A.

3. Ignore titles, but include these on the flap or tab of the folder, e.g.

Price, F. G.
Price, Dr. H. J.
Price, Col. P. R.
Price, R. W. (Mrs.)
Price, Capt. T. D.

4. 'Nothing' comes before 'something'—a surname alone precedes a surname with an initial; and a surname with an initial precedes a surname with a first name. e.g.

Wilkinson
Wilkinson, H. J.
Wilkinson, N. E.
Wilkinson, Albert J.
Wilkinson, Alfred H.
Wilkinson, Alfred John

This rule, common in offices, deviates from the order in most telephone directories, where initials and names are sorted together, alphabetically.

5. Consider the surname prefix as part of the surname, and treat names beginning with M', Mc and Mac as if they were all spelt MAC—that is, file according to the first letter of the next syllable, e.g.

De Gruchy, M. N.
De Haan, A. R.
De Havilland Aircraft Co., Ltd.
De Hems Restaurant
De La Motte, Mrs. C.

McAdam, B. D.
MacAdam, F. P.
McAllister, S. W.
Macalpine, Mrs. D.
McAlpine, R. T.
MacAlpine, Harold W.

6. Ignore 'The', '& Co.' when filing names of firms and companies, e.g.

Metal & Alloys Welding Works, Ltd.
Metal Box Co., Ltd., The
Metal Containers, Ltd.

Metcalfe & Mulligan, Ltd.
Metropolitan Carriage Co., Ltd., The
Metropolitan Water Board.

7. File names consisting of initials, before whole words, e.g.
A.A. Duplicating Co., Ltd.
A.B.C. Valet Service
A.J.P. Gown Manufacturers
A-Z Enquiry Services Ltd., The
Aaronson, Mrs. E.
Abbey Court Hotel

8. File all names with the prefixes 'St.' or 'Saint' under SAINT, e.g.

St. Agatha's School
Saint Catherine Press Ltd.
St. Pancras Hospital

9. Treat any number in a name as if it were written in full, e.g.

51 Restaurant, The   (fifty-one)
 3 Arts Society, The   (three)

10. File government departments and ministries under the key word, e.g.
Health and Social Security, Department of
Supply, Ministry of
Overseas Development, Ministry of
Transport, Ministry of

11. Subdivide files for county councils into departments, e.g.
Greater London Council, Lettings Department
                     Staff Department
                     Welfare Department

12. Always file letters under the name of the firm, company or institution, and not under the name of the individual to whom you are writing.

CROSS-REFERENCING. Even if all these rules are followed, we are often faced with problems of arrangement. For example, would you file a folder for the Begum of Tunis under B, or under T—Tunis, Begum of?

When you have to make such a decision, it is wise to put a note in the section where the folder is NOT filed indicating where it will be found. This is called making a cross-reference. It is useful because:

- (*a*) you may not remember under which letter you filed the correspondence; and
- (*b*) if you are absent from the office, the cross-reference slip will assist anyone who needs the file.

If you decided to file letters from the Philippa Fawcett College under 'P', you would put a cross-reference note under 'F'.

```
        FAWCETT, PHILIPPA, COLLEGE

                    see

        PHILIPPA FAWCETT COLLEGE
```

A cross-reference slip

When a file is taken out of the office, it is a good plan to keep a register to show by whom it was borrowed, the department or office where the borrower works, and the date. This entry will be marked off when the file is returned. An 'OUT' card may be inserted in the place where the file is normally kept. Some 'OUT' cards, such as that shown below, have a frame into which can be fitted a card giving details of the location of the missing folder.

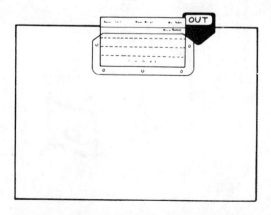

Date	File	Name	Returned
1976			
3 Mar.	Johnson + Parker Ltd	B. Stock, Sales Dept.	5/3/76
4 Mar.	The Ramsay Share Co.	A. Cousins, Personnel	
5 Mar.	Hyam, Mrs A.C.	Miss Keller, Management	5/3/76
6 Mar.	Bank of Scotland	D. Wilkes, Accounts	9/3/76

A page from a File Register

CLASSIFICATION BY NAME.   This is one of the commonest and simplest methods of classification.   A folder is labelled for each firm or individual with whom you correspond and the folders are arranged in alphabetical order.   In a small filing system the sections are separated by one guide card for each letter of the alphabet.   A larger filing system will require some subdivision between the letters, especially the letters B, C, H, S and W, as many more English names begin with these letters than, say, the letters Q and Y.   In the illustration below we can see the 'B' section subdivided into B–Be, Be–Bi, Bi–Bo, Bo–Br.

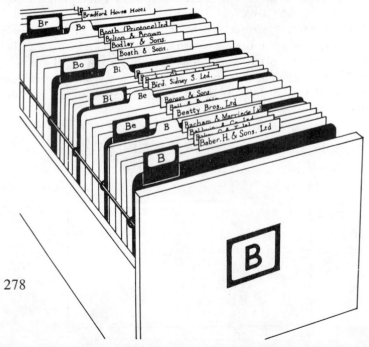

Sometimes the correspondence with one firm will be too small to justify the making out of a separate file. For this purpose a miscellaneous folder is made out for each letter of the alphabet and letters which have no files of their own can be filed in the miscellaneous folder. For example, if there were no file for Nash (Packaging) Ltd., letters from this firm could be filed in the 'N Miscellaneous' folder.

GEOGRAPHICAL CLASSIFICATION. Sometimes it is convenient to arrange files in alphabetical order according to their location, and then subdivide by name. In the illustration the main guides indicate counties, the subsidiary guide cards indicate towns and the individual folders for correspondents in each town are placed behind the appropriate guide cards.

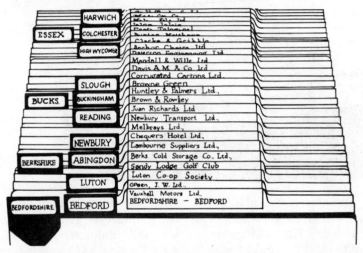

This method is frequently used by wholesale distributors who deal with many small firms. It is also used by gas and electricity companies, insurance companies, sales offices, mail-order firms, laundries and firms employing travellers.

A firm corresponding with agencies abroad often finds it more convenient to file under the name of the country and town, than under the name of the individual agent. Travel agents and shipping companies have agencies all over the world, and they nearly always file under the name of the port or town rather than under the name of the agent, which is often difficult to remember. Furthermore, the name of the agent may change

279

but the name of the town will remain the same. It is, for example, easier to look under 'T' for Teneriffe, than under 'M' for Miller y cia S.A., the Teneriffe agent.

CLASSIFICATION BY SUBJECT. Professional people such as architects, builders, engineers and lawyers often find it convenient to have a file relating to each project or case; subdivisions may be made for each particular aspect of the subject as in the file shown below. This method is also frequently used in personnel departments, and offices dealing with schools and colleges.

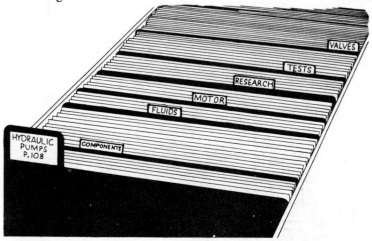

NUMERICAL CLASSIFICATION. Most large filing systems adopt numerical classification, where each folder is given a serial number. The folders are then placed in numerical order; folder 87,536 would be placed after folder 87,535 and before folder 87,537. Guide cards divide the folders into groups of ten.

An alphabetical index has to be used in conjunction with this system, because before we can locate a customer's file we must know the file number. Small index cards stating the name of each correspondent and his file number are kept in alphabetical order in a box-drawer. The usual size for these index cards is 125 mm by 75 mm, and they can be used to record other information, such as the address of the correspondent. A society or association might also record on the index cards whether the member had paid his subscription, whether he was a 'Town' or

280

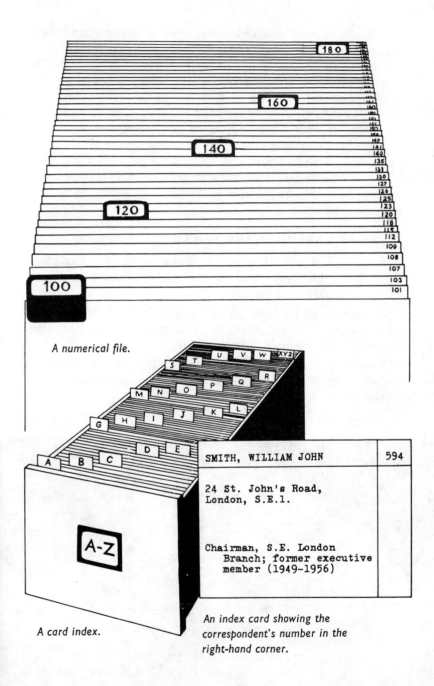

A numerical file.

A card index.

SMITH, WILLIAM JOHN	594
24 St. John's Road, London, S.E.1.	
Chairman, S.E. London Branch; former executive member (1949–1956)	

An index card showing the correspondent's number in the right-hand corner.

281

'Country' member and any other personal information which was relevant to his membership.

One important advantage of the numerical system is that it can be expanded indefinitely. A new correspondent will be allotted the next available number, his folder will be placed at the back of the existing folders, and an index card recording his name and number will be put in the card index.

A further advantage of this system is that the file number will be quoted on all correspondence; the filing clerk does not need to read the correspondence; as soon as he has read the reference number he knows the number of the folder in which the papers must be filed.

(d) SOME USEFUL FILING HINTS

1. Sort the papers into piles before you file them, so that each folder is handled only once. The photo below shows one **type** of sorter used for this purpose.

2. Remove paper clips. Single sheets are easily trapped **by** clips and pins. If it is necessary to attach carbon copies to the letters answered, staple them together.

3. Keep the correspondence in each folder in chronological (i.e. date) order. New material is always placed in the front of the file.

An Ambidex desk sorter.

4. If a folder becomes overcrowded, transfer the oldest material to a reserve file. Do not forget to make out a cross-reference slip for inclusion in the current folder.

5. Place papers 'squarely' in the folder so that they do not become creased. Projecting papers make a set of folders look untidy and inefficient, and may hide the tab or index flap.

6. Be consistent. If you once decide to file correspondence from the National Association of Distributors of Office Equipment under 'O'—Office Equipment, National Association of Distributors of, always file correspondence from that association under 'O'. Remember to put cross-reference slips under 'N' and 'D'.

7. Keep a record of all files on loan to other departments.

8. Before you go home in the evening, make sure the filing cabinet is locked, if this is the practice in your office.

(e) MICROFILMING

Many large firms and institutions, such as hospitals, avoid having valuable floor-space used for storing old files by microfilming their records. The original documents can be destroyed once they have been microfilmed and the small rolls of film or drawers of 'microfiches' take up very little storage space. Thousands of documents can be recorded on a 30 m roll of 16 mm film and stored in a 7·5 cm diameter container: more than 3000 pages of information can be recorded on a transparency 10×15 cm.

Microfilm may be stored in long or short lengths, or each individual frame can be mounted on a card. The smaller the unit of storage, the easier any particular frame will be found. When it is required to read the records, the microfilm is put into a reader, which may be a separate machine or may be incorporated in the microfilm camera. The reader projects and enlarges the microfilm negative so that it can be easily read.

The characteristic of modern microfilm is speed of retrieval; it is possible to select one from 999 999 frames in less than one minute.

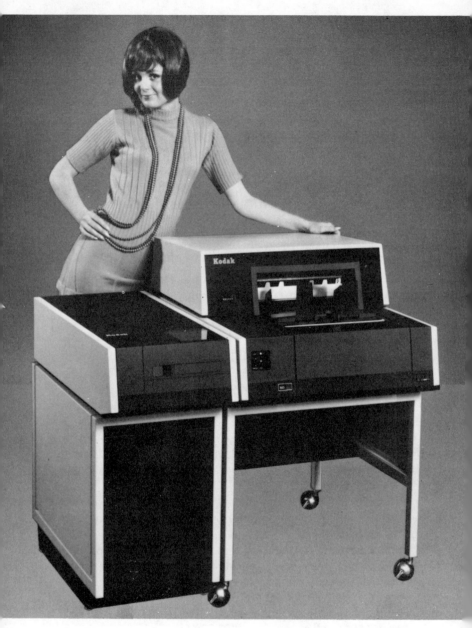

The Kodak Instamatic microfilm system. The unit on the right is the new Kodak 700 Microfilmer and beside it is the new Instamatic microfilm processor.

284

The RV-2 STARFILE Microfilmer model is especially well suited for microfilming legal documents and business and public records on 16 mm film. It can microfilm at speeds up to 60 documents per minute, compacting as many as 2600 legal-size documents on a 30 metre roll of 16 mm microfilm weighing only 170 grammes.

(f) COMPUTER OUTPUT MICROFILMING

Computer output microfilming (COM)* is the generation of microfilm from a computer, with no intermediate paper print-out.   It is an extremely efficient method of handling vast quantities of data.

Until the introduction of COM the output of a computer was

* COM—some writers define COM as 'computer originated microfilm'.

285

restricted to the speed of the output printer and occupied a considerable amount of space. COM enables computer output to be produced direct on microfilm; copies that can be read with the aid of a reader can be made as required. The latest microfilm reader-printer will produce a readable full-size copy of any selected microfilm frame simply by having the 'PRINT' button pressed when the required document is in view on the screen.

The Kodak KOM90 Computer Output Microfilmer converts computer-produced magnetic tape directly into human readable data on microfilm. The computer information on the magnetic tape is translated on to microfilm at rates of up to 90 000 characters per second.

A 3M Microfilm cartridge reader-printer.

(g) FOLLOW-UP FILING, REMINDER SYSTEMS AND TICKLER FILES

In every kind of business it is necessary to follow-up various operations. A sales representative, for example, needs to know which prospective customers he must visit again three or six months from the date of his original call. Similarly, letters which have not produced a reply within a reasonable period may have to be followed-up by a reminder. Yet another instance is when a telephone call fails to reach either the person required or someone authorised to speak on his behalf (because

287

of holidays or illness) and the caller must have some kind of reminder system so that he can telephone again at a later date.

Sometimes *desk diaries* or *desk calendars* form part of a reminder system. A note to make or to expect a phone call, or to check that some action has been taken, can be entered against the appropriate date in the desk diary.

Juni Juin Giugno June

11	Sonntag Dimanche Domenica Sunday	
12	Montag Lundi Lunedi Monday	Williams back from leave. Contact re overdraft.
13	Dienstag Mardi Martedi Tuesday	3·0 Marketing meeting
14	Mittwoch Mercredi Mercoledi Wednesday	Blake arriving from USA Expect phone call.
15	Donnerstag Jeudi Giovedi Thursday	12·30 lunch. Royal Hotel, Eric James.
16	Freitag Vendredi Venerdi Friday	Check that proofs of autumn Catalogue have gone back to printers.
17	Samstag Samedi Sabato Saturday	

Page from a desk diary.

A *tickler file* or *follow-up filing system* consists of 12 month guide cards and a set of 1–31 day guides for the current month.

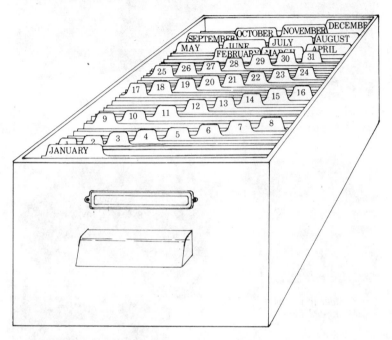

A follow-up or tickler filing system.

Documents for future action are filed immediately behind the guide cards bearing the dates of the days upon which the action must be taken. Follow-up files may also be used to store carbon copies of letters awaiting replies, so that if replies have not been received within a reasonable time, enquiries can be made to find out whether the original letters were safely delivered.

Another reminder system comprises the use of files or folders to keep copies of letters awaiting reply or documents relating to work in progress. The titles given to such folders vary from office to office; sometimes they are called *Bring-up Files* or *Pending Files*, or they may be labelled *Work in hand*, *Work in progress*, or *In abeyance*.

Sometimes two folders are kept: the one labelled 'PENDING' or 'IN ABEYANCE' will contain papers relating to matters which

289

A part-file.

An A–Z concertina file.

A buff folder in use as a
'Bring-up' file

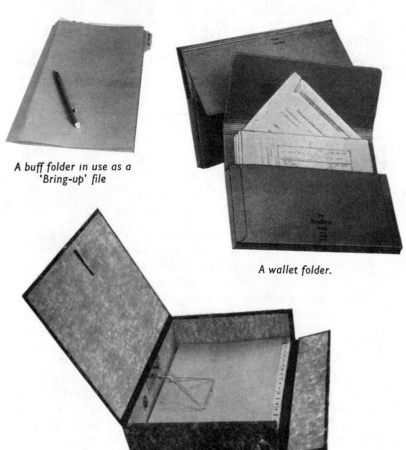

A wallet folder.

A spring-clip box file with set of A–Z dividers or index sheets.

290

are pending; the one labelled 'WORK IN HAND' will contain papers relating to work actually being done at any given point of time.

Despite this variety of titles and practices, the functions of such files and systems are similar: to keep in one place all the pieces of paper relating to work which is in the process of being performed. In some offices a date is hand-written on carbon copies indicating when a reply may be expected, or a remark such as 'Bring up in two weeks' is noted on the papers. With this type of office procedure, part of the daily routine is to look through the 'BRING-UP FILE' each morning and take whatever further steps are required since the various matters were last being dealt with.

(h) TRANSFER OF FILES

As the documents in a file gradually become out of date and as the files themselves become thicker with the continual addition of new material, most companies have a system for thinning-out files by transferring material from the *active files* to the *inactive files*. As their name implies, *active* files are those which are in daily use. *Inactive* or *storage files* are those which contain obsolete papers and the documents all businesses are obliged, by law, to preserve for a certain number of years.

Many companies find this division of files into active and inactive or storage suits their filing requirements. Some firms find it expedient to separate the most recent papers and most frequently used files from those which are less frequently referred to; under this system, all documents are transferred to *semi-active files* as soon as the transactions or events for which they were used have been completed.

Inactive files may be kept in boxes which are clearly labelled with the contents and dates, and stored in a basement or store-room. As we have already mentioned, many firms avoid using valuable space for storing old files by microfilming their records.

DOCUMENT DESTRUCTION

When the inactive material has been microfilmed or is no longer needed, the documents can be destroyed. Some companies burn old files in an incinerator; others dispose of their

* There are some statutory records which must not be destroyed. Documents which should be preserved and suggested periods of retention are listed in *The Disposal and Retention of Documents*, published by The Chartered Institute of Secretaries.

old files through waste-paper dealers but take the precaution of shredding the papers beforehand.

There are many different shredding machines available, ranging from a small model which will take single sheets of paper to large models which can shred complete files.

Document shredders. The model on the left is mobile and can reduce up to 22 sheets of multi-part continuous stationery to unreadable shreds at a rate of 98 feet per minute. Output is collected in disposable plastic bags. The model on the right disposes of single documents.

EXERCISES

1. Explain the following expressions:
   - (*a*) lateral filing,
   - (*b*) suspension filing,
   - (*c*) manilla folders,
   - (*d*) alphabetical order,

(e) 'nothing' comes before 'something',

(f) a cross-reference,

(g) an 'OUT' card,

(h) a miscellaneous folder,

(i) guide cards,

(j) chronological order.

2. Study the sketches of geographical and subject filing on pages 279 and 280 and suggest one disadvantage of each system.

3. Describe suitable systems of filing and classification for:

(a) The central records department of a large hospital. Each patient admitted to the hospital is allotted a case number.

(b) The national headquarters of a trade union.

(c) The owner of a small shop.

(d) An architect who designs houses for private clients.

(e) An architect employed by a county council to design schools and colleges.

(f) An international firm with branches in large cities all over the world.

(g) A bank (there will be correspondence with the head office, other branches, and with customers).

(h) The head office of a chain of shoe shops (there will be branches in every large town in the country; in some towns there will be more than one branch).

(i) A school office.

(j) A dentist.

4. Sketch guide cards and folders to illustrate any of your answers to question 3.

5. Draft some 'Hints on filing' for the guidance of junior staff in your department.

6. Type or write each of the names listed on a 125 mm by 75 mm card:

Mitchell Galleries Ltd.

The British Council

7-Up Bottling Co. (London), Ltd.

The T.B.T. Electric Co., Ltd.

Dr. J. B. Smythe

A. O'Brien
The General Building Society, Ltd.
National Council of Labour
Hotel Victoria
Elders & Fyffes Ltd.
The Premier Engineering Co., Ltd.
British European Airways
Mrs. Janet Smith
Dean and Wood, Ltd.
Smiths Motor Accessories Ltd.
British Association of Chemists
The Reliance Telephone Co., Ltd.
William Moss & Sons, Ltd.
Hoffman Chemicals Ltd.
National Association of Funeral Directors

7. Sort the cards you typed in exercise 6 into alphabetical order.

8. See how quickly you can find the following cards, which are amongst the twenty you have sorted into alphabetical order:
   Dr. J. B. Smythe
   William Moss & Sons, Ltd.
   British Association of Chemists
   Hoffman Chemicals Ltd.
   Hotel Victoria

9. Make up an address for each of the twenty cards and write or type it in the correct position.

10. Make out the necessary guide cards and sort the cards into geographical order.

11. Explain the following expressions:
    box files   active files
    semi-active files   inactive or storage files
    shredding   tickler files

12. Compare the advantages and disadvantages of microfilming with those of conventional filing.

13. You are starting a new filing system. What factors would you take into account in choosing the alphabetical, geographical, subject, or numerical methods of classification?

(RSA, OP, II)

14. (*a*) List the following names in alphabetical order for filing
or indexing:

Rev B P Smythe   Cynthia Melborne BA
Top Secretaries Ltd   Central Office of
Corporation of Manchester   Information
Dr J M Smith   Times Newspapers
Saltdean Provident   Ltd
  Industrial Co-operative   J K Littleton
  Society Ltd   The London Fur
                      Company

(*b*) If you were in charge of the Filing Department of a
large firm how would you make sure that:

(i) papers taken out of files could be traced and put
back in their correct places;

(ii) 'dead' files could always be found quickly and
easily? (RSA, OP, I)

15. (*a*) What is the difference between Centralised and De-
Centralised Filing?

(*b*) What are the advantages of Microfilming? In what
size of office would you expect this system to be used
and why?

(*c*) How would you file Plans or Blueprints? (RSA, OP, I)

16. (*a*) It is claimed by some people that a good filing system
for correspondence does not need a separate index.
Give your views on the truth or otherwise of this claim
and illustrate your answers by reference to the various
methods of filing.

(*b*) What method and equipment would you use for filing

(i) Sales ledger cards;

(ii) Stock record cards? (RSA, OP, II)

17. (*a*) Explain the operation of *either* geographical *or* alphabetical filing.

(*b*) Why do we use guide cards?

(*c*) Why is pre-sorting important before filing?

(RSA, OP, I)

18. What uses are made of the following items in filing:

guide cards   index cards
absent/out cards   transparent plastic folders
bring forward book   miscellaneous folder?

(RSA, OP, I)

19. What are the features of a centralised filing system and under what circumstances would this arrangement be preferable to departmental filing? (Include in your answer some reference to the ways in which space may be economised.) (RSA, OP, I)

20. Describe the methods of filing, type of equipment, and indexing (if any) which you would use for keeping any FOUR of the following:

(a) Invoices received from suppliers.
(b) Confidential staff records.
(c) Catalogues received from wholesalers.
(d) Minutes of meetings.
(e) Petty cash vouchers.
(f) Used stencils required for subsequent use.

(RSA, OP, II)

21. (a) Place the following names in the correct form and order for indexing:

Walter Jones & Co Ltd
The Beverley Mills Ltd
J Robert Skinner
Smith and Robinson
De La Rue and Co Ltd
Thomas Slater
The Borough Council of Bigtown
P R McGrath
Department of Employment and Productivity
Dr John Peters
F B O'Sullivan
20th Century Supplies Ltd

(b) Describe in detail two 'follow-up' systems which could be used to ensure that replies are received to letters sent from your office. (RSA, OP, II)

22. What effect is mechanisation having on filing procedures? Select any one procedure to illustrate your answer.

(RSA, OP, II)

23. (a) List below the following titles in alphabetical order and then number each file consecutively starting at 401.

Dictaphone Ltd   A B Dick Co Ltd
Twinlock Ltd   Addo Ltd

Roneo-Neopost Ltd
IBM United Kingdom Ltd
Rank Xerox Ltd
Muldivo Ltd
Gestetner Duplicators Ltd
The Reliance Telephone
  Co Ltd

Autoscan Ltd
Roneo Ltd
Automatic Punched
  Tape Ltd
Olympia Business
  Machines Co Ltd
Copycat Ltd

400	Miscellaneous	

(b) Explain the importance of correspondence references in filing.

(c) Explain what uses would be made of the miscellaneous file.   (RSA, OP, I)   (RSA, OP, I)

Chapter 9

Record-keeping

(a) INDEXING

In addition to the storage of papers and documents in files, every office needs a system of record-keeping. All businesses have to keep records of their accounts, but other kinds of records kept depend on the nature of the business. All businesses record the names and addresses of their customers or clients; schools keep records of pupils' names, addresses and dates of birth; dentists and doctors keep records of their patients; libraries keep records of all the books they own, as well as keeping separate records of the books on loan and when they should be returned; and some offices keep a record of all the letters received and also a record of letters despatched.

An *indexing system* is used for keeping most of these records. An *index* is an alphabetical list of subjects or names; some indexes (like the card index we mentioned in connection with Numerical Filing in the last chapter or the index at the back of a book) tell us where to find further information on the subject we have looked up. Other indexing systems give all the information needed on the actual *index card*; for example, the record cards a dentist keeps will state not only the name, address, age and National Health number of each patient but also the dates of appointments and brief notes of the treatment given and a chart of the mouth showing teeth which have been filled or extracted.

(b) EQUIPMENT

The card-index drawer is still one of the commonest types of equipment. A loose-leaf book is another type frequently used for accounts, ledger cards, bank statements and minutes. A third type is the visible card index. In this index system between fifty and sixty cards are held in a flat metal drawer which fits into a cabinet. The names on all the cards are immediately visible. The cabinet shown in the photograph opposite has fifteen drawers and will therefore hold over seven hundred and

fifty cards. The firms who manufacture these visible card systems will print cards specially designed to suit the requirements of a particular office.

One advantage of all these systems is that new cards are easily inserted and old cards may be withdrawn when no longer required. When loose-leaf books contain valuable or confidential records this may become a disadvantage as pages can be misplaced or lost. For this reason some loose-leaf books can be locked, and only the person holding the key can remove or insert pages. A further disadvantage of loose-leaf books is that the ring-holes sometimes get torn; when this happens the holes should be reinforced with linen washers.

An alternative to the card index drawer is the wheel. Here,

as the above drawing shows, index cards are stored on wheels which revolve and enable any card to be quickly located.

STRIP INDEXES. In a visible card index, only the edges of the cards appear, giving the appearance of a number of strips. A further development of the visible indexing is the strip index, which does in fact consist only of strips, giving information such as a mailing list, and is easily maintained in alphabetical order. These indexes are stored either in drawers or on stands as the ones shown in the photograph on p. 302.

PUNCHED INDEX CARDS. Sometimes it is necessary quickly to select from a number of index cards all those marked with the same item or items of information. A simple way is to punch

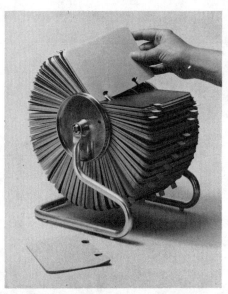

This illustration shows a wheel holding very small cards. It is called the 'Mini-Cardwheel' and is suitable for keeping records of addresses, membership, credit ratings. Various models are available, holding from 600 to 4 800 cards.

information instead of writing it on to a card. Holes are put in the appropriate sections to denote certain items such as department, age group, sex, etc. If you wish to pick out, for example, all the female employees in any one department, a rod is slid through all the punched holes for 'female' and another through the hole for the appropriate department. In one method, all the cards so punched are lifted: in another method, all the cards *except* the ones wanted are lifted clear, so that the required cards can be examined and listed. The photograph on p. 302 (bottom) illustrates this latter method.

SIGNALLING INFORMATION. On all indexes, including those on the top of files, information can be given by attaching coloured signals. This creates a pattern. You can see this pattern clearly in the photograph of the visible index cabinet on page 299. Similar colour signals can be arranged on a wall chart so that the up-to-date position of, say, sales can be seen at a glance. The wall chart illustrated on p. 303 consists of a perforated board. The coloured signals are placed in the

(Above) *Roneo Stripdex visible strip indexing.*

(Below) *The Paramount punched card sorting system.*

perforated holes. Similar boards exist which make use of pockets instead of holes.*

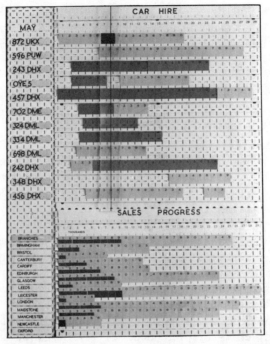

PUNCHED TAPE. You will remember from Chapter 3 that a number of machines, including typewriters, now punch a tape as well as performing their usual function. As the number of such machines increases, it may well be that punched tape will become 'common language' in many offices. In other words, the original information typed when an order is received will be automatically recorded on punched tape, and many subsequent operations such as despatch and labelling will be performed from the original tape. This tape in itself may be said to be a record, and it is certainly the medium from which many other types of record can be created.

MAGNETIC TAPE AND FILM. With the increased use of punched tape, punched cards and computers to process and deal with

* For more information on the use of wall charts and display material see Section (i), Visual Aids.

303

information in an office, there will follow a wider use of magnetic film on which to store records. These films, which may, for example, hold dated records of customers' accounts, will be stored in special types of containers, for use with computers. Instead of pieces of paper, files and cards, businesses will gradually be accustomed to records which cannot be looked up at present, but which will have to be interpreted or read by a computer, which will then print out the information required.

(c) MAIL RECORDS

INCOMING MAIL

In most businesses the mail is opened each morning in the Postal Department. If there is no Postal Department the mail will be sorted in a general office and distributed to the various departments. Letters addressed impersonally will be opened, but those addressed individually or marked 'Personal' or 'Private' will be sent to the addressee unopened. The clerks in charge of opening the post are frequently required to arrive an hour or half an hour before the official opening hour of the office, so that the post will be sorted and opened by the time the remainder of the staff arrive.

In some firms all incoming mail is recorded; in others only registered letters are recorded. A few large organisations photocopy all incoming mail. In firms where there is decentralised opening, departments may record their own mail, but as the recording consumes valuable time, this practice is rapidly going out of fashion.

A more common practice is for all mail to be date-stamped with the date of receipt. Sometimes a combined date and time stamp is used.

The person who opens the post must ensure that nothing is left inside the envelope before it is thrown away; any enclosures must be securely fixed to the letter.

Date	Sender	Subject	Attention	Replied

If you should work in an office where an Incoming Letter Book is still kept, the illustration on page 304 shows how it may be ruled.

the illustration on page 304 shows

OUTGOING MAIL

The recording of outgoing mail is another practice which is being abandoned by many firms.   Where it is still retained the procedure is as follows: two copies are made of each outgoing letter—one copy for the files, and one 'letter book' or 'office' copy.   The 'office' copies are retained in a loose-leaf file in date order and provide a record of every letter which has been sent out by the office.   As these copies are kept in chrono-logical order, that is the copies of each day's letters are sorted alphabetically, then punched and placed on top of the copy-letters of the preceding day, this file is often referred to as *'the chron file'* and the copies are called *'chron copies'*.   Another way of keeping the 'chron' or 'office' copies is to file them in a 'Letter Book', that is, a loose-leaf file with its own index. This index will be similar to a large address book with the pages tabbed alphabetically.   The copies in the letter book will be numbered and the index written up each day as in this example.

Date	No.	Addressee	Subject
3 Oct	12	Finlay & Co.	Order Outstanding
10 ,,	41	Fergusons	Price query
11 ,,	46	French Bros.	Complaint

Adherents to this practice claim these advantages for it:

(1) It provides a complete record of every letter despatched.

(2) Any letter may be found very quickly.

(3) All clerks can keep in touch with matters handled by other sections of the office.

(4) If the head of the department has been away from the office for a day or so, the letter book provides him with a concise progress report on any matters which have developed or any decisions taken during his absence.

305

Despite these so-called advantages very few firms keep letter books nowadays. Here are some of the reasons why they are no longer used:

(1) A letter book copy does not prove that a letter has been posted.

(2) If the filing system is efficient, the correspondence will be found immediately it is required; and the folders will contain not only copies of letters sent but also the original letters which have been answered.

(3) In a well-run office the clerks do not have to rely on reading through a letter book to find out what is going on in other sections.

(4) Nowadays it is often much quicker and cheaper to make a telephone call than to write a letter, so the letter book no longer provides a complete progress report as it did in the days when the telephone was less frequently used.

POSTAGE BOOK

As we have already mentioned, the outgoing mail in large firms is frequently franked by machine. Smaller firms need to keep a supply of stamps, and these are bought out of petty

Received		Date	Name	Address	Postage	
£		197–			£	
3	00	Nov. 4	Villiers	Liverpool		4
			Schmidt	Germany		10

Received		Date	Description	Postage	
£		197–		£	
3	00	Nov. 4	Letters		18
			Parcel		12
			Circulars		84

cash. Records of stamps bought and used may be kept in a Postage Book, and this is another job which frequently forms part of the duties of a typist, shorthand-typist or secretary. Sometimes the Postage Book is kept by a junior member of the male staff. Formerly a separate entry was made for each letter or packet despatched, but nowadays it is more usual to enter only the total for each day, except for the large amounts covering the despatch of circulars or parcels. Some firms require the Postage Book to be balanced every evening; others require this to be done every week. The illustrations opposite show first individual entries and secondly block entries in a post book.

(d) STOCK RECORDS

You have probably heard expressions like 'out-of-stock' and 'delivery ex-stock' and remarks like, 'I'm sorry, we don't keep that size in stock'. *Stock*, in all these examples, has the same general meaning—articles, items, goods or material kept in a special place, usually called a Stock-room or Store Room or just the Store or Stores, ready to be taken out when needed— although the nature of the stock, the purposes for which it is held and therefore the way it is controlled, differ in various types of organisations such as factories, shops and offices.

In factories there are usually two stores: one store keeps the items of raw material from which the end-product is manufactured, the other store keeps the finished articles ready to sell to the wholesaler or retailer. In shops *the stock* means all the things that are offered for sale, although shops usually have store-rooms or stock-rooms too where additional stock is stored before it is put on display in the sales areas. Offices, just like schools and colleges, keep stocks of stationery. In general then we can say that stock means goods that are stored until they are sold (in the case of manufacturing, wholesale and retail firms), or drawn out for use (in the case of raw materials, components or items of stationery).

By *stock records* we mean the ways in which additions to stock (that is, the arrival of new goods) and the issues from stock are recorded. From these two entries a third figure is obtained, that is the quantity or balance held of each item at any given time. Stock records are also used to make sure that stock levels are kept up so that no item is 'out of stock'. As all space in a factory or office building costs money, the space allocated for storage is necessarily limited; therefore, being over-stocked is nearly as serious as running out of stock.

The storing and handling of goods is known as *stock control*. There are various ways of controlling stock and the way used in any particular store depends largely on the items to be stored and the nature of the business. In a large factory, whenever items are delivered the storekeeper will complete a *Goods Received Note* or record the arrival in a *Goods Received Book*. When the items have been checked to make sure that the delivery is correct as regards the items ordered, the quantity and quality, and the condition, that is, that there are no broken or damaged goods, the goods are stored on shelves or racks or bins according to the nature of the articles. The storekeeper then transfers the information from the Goods Received Note or Book on to a *Stock Card* or *Bin Card* or *Stores Ledger*.

In offices the articles that are delivered are usually items of stationery and office sundries, such as boxes of staples and paper

Date	Supplier	Goods			Purchase Order No.	Received by	Inspected		Entered	
		Qty	Description	No. of packages			Date	Initials	Date	Initials
3 Sept.	Diggins T.	3 reams	A4 Headed	3	70-495	SJ	3 Sept.	SJ	4 Sept	BJP
4 Sept.	Webbs Ltd	15,000	¼" Staples	3	70-498	WF	4 Sept.	WF	4 Sept	BJP

An example of entries in a Goods Received Book in an office.

clips. The amount of clerical work involved in stores records in most offices is not enough to justify the appointment of a full-time storekeeper so responsibility for the stocks of stationery usually forms part of the responsibilities of one of the clerks or shorthand-typists or secretaries.

As we mentioned in Chapter 2, Reception, if the person whose job it is to receive parcels is temporarily unavailable, you may find yourself taking delivery of new stock and before signing for the goods you should make sure that what you are accepting has been ordered and that the order is complete and in good condition. A Goods Received Book is frequently suitable for recording the receipt of goods in an office. You can see a typical ruling on page 308. In a large store, each item is given a reference number and in factories it is usual to show this on the Goods Received Note, also the number of the rack or bin in which the item is stored.

The *stock card* or *stores ledger sheet* is a most important

	A4 Headed, airmail										
Stock ref. no.				Item A4 Headed, airmail							
Receipts				Issues				Balance in stock	On order		
Date	Qty	GR No.	Supplier	Date	Qty	Req. No.	Dept.		Date	Qty	Order No.	Supplier
6 Nov	Balance	B/F						6				
				10 Nov.	1	075	Personnel	5				
				15 Nov.	1	193	Marketing	4				
Maximum level: 6				Minimum level: 1					Re-order level: 3		

A stock card suitable for use in an office stationery store. Sometimes it is found to be more convenient to record the maximum, minimum and re-order levels at the top right-hand corner of the card. As the number of items kept in stock in this store is comparatively small, the items are not allocated a stock reference number. The cards are, therefore, kept in alphabetical order in a visible card index.

document. Each item has its own card which should be designed to show clearly all the records about the stock: the receipts, the issues, the quantity in stock and on order, as well as the maximum, minimum and re-order levels. Using the stock card illustrated on page 309 each of these records can be studied in detail.

Stock reference number. Many firms have a code number for each item they keep in stock. The cards can then be filed in a visible index in numerical order. When stock is received or issued, the appropriate card can be found by looking up the code number of the article and the new information is then recorded on the card. Although there is a space for a stock reference number on the card illustrated on page 305 no number has been given as this card is being used in a fairly small office stationery store which does not stock a very large number of items, so it is perfectly convenient to file the stock cards alphabetically.

Receipts. To keep accurate records of new stock the following information should be transferred from the Goods Received Note: the date of delivery, the quantity, the Invoice number or Goods Received Note number, and the name of the supplier. With all this information on the stock card, it is unnecessary to refer to the Goods Received Note or the invoice when re-ordering.

Issues. Records are kept of stock issued to make sure that supplies are not being wasted or used uneconomically. By glancing at the stock card it should be possible to see if one department is using an excess of a particular item, such as typewriter ribbons. Therefore, the Issues column shows the date, quantity, requisition number and the department. The requisition number refers to the number of the official requisition form. This requisition is usually signed or initialled by the head of a department or another senior person. It is the responsibility of that person to requisition the correct amount of stock required by his department.

Balance in stock. This column shows how much of an item or how many articles remain in stock after the receipts have been added to the previous balance and the issues have been subtracted. It is important to keep a careful eye on the balance in stock to ensure that it accords with the figures given for maximum, minimum and re-order levels.

On order. When the balance in stock has been reduced to the *re-order level* specified on the card, more stock will have to be ordered. The re-order level is determined by the time usually taken to deliver a new order and the rate at which the items are withdrawn from stock. The re-order level for, say, headed notepaper will be higher than for plain A4 bond typewriting paper becasue the supplier will almost certainly be able to deliver plain A4 bond immediately, whereas it will take time for the headed notepaper to be printed. The *minimum stock figure* is of course lower than the re-order figure and it is hoped that the new delivery will arrive before the minimum figure is reached. If stock is approaching the minimum level and the person responsible for the stores can foresee a possible sudden demand for the item, then the suppliers must be telephoned or contacted in the quickest possible way and urged to make sure that the goods are delivered in the shortest possible time. The essential information about the goods on order is listed in the ON ORDER column under the headings DATE, QUANTITY, ORDER NUMBER and SUPPLIER. The quantity on order plus the balance in stock should not exceed the maximum level listed as firms do not want to spend money on excess stock or to waste storage space.

Periodic stocktaking is carried out at regular intervals to ensure that the balances on the stock cards are accurate and to guard against pilfering or loss of stock. In large firms, such as multiple stores, stocktaking is sometimes done for a few items at a time over a longer period. This is called *continuous stocktaking* or *perpetual inventory*. In this case, a trained staff of stocktakers visits each branch to take stock and make investigations if the amount of stock differs from the balance recorded on the stock cards.

Most firms have an *annual stocktaking* or *inventory*, usually at the end of the year, which assesses the value of goods in stock. Each item is counted or weighed as the case may be, and the value is calculated; for example, if there are 100 pencils in stock and each costs 8p, then the value of pencils in stock is £8. The total of the value of all the items in stock is called the *closing stock*. The closing stock figure appears in the final accounts for the year that show the true profit a firm has made.

(e) WAGES RECORDS

RATES OF PAY

There are several different ways of calculating wages and salaries and in a large firm all of them may be used for various groups of employees. Each method of paying employees requires its own set of records which must be accurately kept and properly stored.

Piece rate. Employees who manufacture articles or components may be paid at a piece rate. This means that they are paid a certain amount for each article they make. The faster a worker is, the more he earns. The employer pays only for the actual work produced.

At the end of the week each employee completes a job card or piece work ticket by filling in the number of articles or pieces he has completed. This card is initialled by the supervisor and sent to the Wages and Salaries Department where it is used to calculate the employee's pay.

Time rates. Many workers in factories and others whose work is not in offices are paid by time rates. There is usually a rate set for each hour worked. Some workers receive a higher rate for overtime, that is, time worked beyond the normal working day. This system benefits the man who is willing to work long hours and who is punctual in arriving. If an employee arrives late, a proportion of his hourly rate is deducted from his pay. Deductions for lateness are usually calculated to the nearest quarter of the hourly rate; that is to say, if a man is five minutes late he will lose a quarter of an hour's pay—this is known colloquially as 'losing a quarter'; if he is twenty minutes late, he will lose half an hour's pay.

Each employee paid by time rates has a number that is written on his *time card*. At the beginning of each week the time cards are placed in a rack next to a special clock called a *time clock*. When the employee arrives for work he puts his card into the machine attached to the clock and the machine stamps the time on the card. When he leaves he follows the same procedure.

The stamped time cards are used for record-keeping in two ways. In the first place they act as a record of attendance. Many office workers who are not paid by time rates have to stamp time cards for this reason. Secondly, the time cards are used to calculate an employee's wages. At the end of each

312

week the time cards are sent to the Wages and Salaries Department where the number of hours worked by each employee is totalled. The total number of hours is multiplied by the rate per hour to find the employee's *gross pay*, that is his pay before deductions are made.

Commission. Many salesmen work on commission. They are paid a small basic salary or possibly no salary at all and when they sell an item they receive a percentage of its selling price. For example, if a salesman is on 10% commission and he sells an article worth £100, he receives £10 commission. A hardworking salesman who is good at selling makes more money on a system of commission than a salesman who does not work as hard or who has not the same selling ability. The employer probably sells more goods under this system, although part of the selling price goes to the salesmen.

In order to calculate the amount of commission to be paid to each salesman, the Wages and Salaries Department requires information about the number of items he has sold and their value. When the total value of the goods sold has been calculated, the commission can be worked out.

DEDUCTIONS FROM GROSS PAY

Gross pay is the amount each employee earns before deductions are made. The employer subtracts the deductions from the gross pay and arrives at the net pay, which is the amount the employee receives.

Income tax. Everyone who earns money is considered for income tax deductions. Most employees in this country pay their income tax under the PAYE (Pay As You Earn) scheme. Under this system an employee pays some of his yearly tax every time he is paid. The exact amount payable for each week is set out in a printed set of tax tables supplied to the employer by the Inland Revenue.

Every employee paid under the PAYE system is allocated a *code number* by the Inland Revenue. The code number is based on personal circumstances, such as marital status, the number of dependants or the amount being paid for a mortgage or life assurance policy. To obtain a code number an employee completes an Income Tax Return which is both a declaration of his income and a claim for the various allowances to which he is entitled. From this information the correct code number is ascertained and is communicated to the employee in the form of a Coding Notice.

The code number determines the amount of each person's allowance of tax-free pay. The employee does not receive his tax-free pay all at once. A certain amount is allowed every time the employee is paid and the rest of the gross pay is liable to tax. The tax-free pay allowance of some employees based on their code number is the same as, or more than, the gross pay they have earned up to that point in the tax year; this means they do not pay any income tax.

The tax year begins on 6 April and runs until 5 April of the next calendar year. After the end of every tax year, the employer gives each employee a P60 form which states how much he has earned during the tax year and how much tax has been deducted. This important form should be kept in case the employee wants to claim earnings-related social security benefits.

If an employee changes jobs during the tax year, his firm gives him a P45 form which states how much he has earned, how much tax he has paid, his code number and his National Insurance number. The employee gives the P45 form to the Wages Department of his new firm so that they have complete records for working out his future income tax deductions without any delay.

National Insurance. In accordance with the provisions of the Social Security Act 1973, which came into force on 6 April 1975, the former National Insurance Scheme including the Graduated Pensions Scheme has been replaced by a Basic Scheme. Under the new Basic Scheme, stamp cards for employees have been abolished and national insurance contributions are now collected with income tax under the PAYE procedure.

Every person over school-leaving age is liable to pay National Insurance contributions. The contributions are worked out as a percentage of a person's salary at either the Standard Rate or the Reduced Rate. The percentage will be reviewed annually by the Department of Health and Social Security and therefore may vary from year to year. For the 1975/76 tax year, the standard rate of Class I (Employed earners) contribution has been fixed at 5·5% and the reduced rate at

2% within the earnings limits of £572 to £3,588 per annum. The Standard Rate is paid by employees who are under pension age (65 men, 60 women) or who are under age 70 (men) or 65 (women) and have not retired.

The Reduced Rate is paid by widows and most married women, e.g. those who had previously chosen to pay at the reduced rate or who are now entitled to do so. Certain employees, such as those over retirement age or those earning less than a stipulated amount, have no liability to contribute. The employers' contributions, however, are at the same rate regardless of whether the employee is liable to pay at the standard or reduced rate, or is non-liable.

Employees who are entitled to pay at the reduced rate or who have no liability to contribute must obtain a certificate to that effect from the Department of Health and Social Security. Until the employee produces such a certificate, the employer must make deductions at the Standard Rate.

An employee may be credited with contributions for complete weeks of sickness or unemployment and should apply to the local Social Security Office in the case of sickness and the local Employment Exchange if unemployed. The employee does not have to pay contributions when they are credited to him.

Regular contributions entitle a person to claim benefits for sickness, unemployment and injury at work. Women may also claim benefits for maternity and widowhood. Other national insurance benefits include a retirement pension and a payment to the next-of-kin on the death of the contributor.

National insurance contributions are collected by employers with income tax under the PAYE procedure. Unless a firm has permission to keep its own type of tax records, national insurance and tax deductions must be recorded on Form P11, the official deduction card. It contains the following columns for recording national insurance contributions:

Column 1(a)—Total of Employee's and Employer's
                    Contributions
Column 1(b)—Employee's Basic Contributions

National insurance contributions are listed in Tables produced by the Department of Health and Social Security.

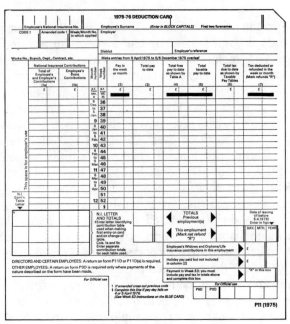

The two sides of form P11 (1975) Tax Deduction Card. National insurance contributions are recorded in columns 1(a) and 1(b).

316

Table A lists the Standard Rate Basic Contributions; Table B lists the Reduced Rate Contributions; and Table C lists the Employer's Contributions. Changes in National Insurance contribution rates are published in Leaflet NI 208 which is issued in advance of any alterations in rate and/or earnings limits. This leaflet, and other leaflets dealing with particular aspects of National Insurance (such as Leaflet NI 27A— National Insurance contributions for self-employed people with small earnings), can be obtained from local Social Security offices.

An employer is responsible for paying the whole cost of National Insurance contributions payable both by himself and his employees, but he may recover the employees' contributions only by deducting them from the employees' wages. National Insurance contributions and Income Tax collected are shown separately on Form P30 (Tax Remittance Card or Payslip); they must be paid to the Collector of Taxes within 14 days of the end of the month in which they are collected.

At the end of the tax year (5 April) the employer must complete the *Employer's Annual Declaration and Certificate* (Form P35) and send this to the Collector of Taxes together with all the Tax Deduction Cards (P11) or substitute documents, and any balance of tax and/or National Insurance contributions outstanding.

Voluntary deductions. Income tax and National Insurance contributions are set by law and employees must pay them. These are called *statutory deductions*.

Some firms offer their own employees certain benefits, such as company pension schemes and sports clubs, which are paid for by deductions from employees' pay. Sometimes the employees must contribute, while in other cases each employee chooses whether he wants the deductions made. The employer deducts voluntary contributions at the same time that statutory deductions are made from employees' pay.

FORMS USED TO CALCULATE WAGES AND DEDUCTIONS

All the records concerned with employee's pay are sent to the Wages and Salaries Department where the gross pay is calculated and the deductions are made. The amount of money left after statutory and voluntary deductions is the pay the employee receives, that is the net pay.

113. For employees who:
(1) are under pension age (65 men, 60 women); or
(2) are under age 70 (men) or 65 (women) and have *not* retired or are not treated as having retired for national insurance purposes; but excluding those married women or widows who are liable to pay basic contributions at the reduced rate – see Table B.

Monthly Table A	
Before using this table, please enter 'A' in the space provided on the deduction card/pay record. (See instructions).	**A**
STANDARD RATE BASIC CONTRIBUTIONS. FOR USE FROM 6 APRIL 1975.	

For men and women who have reached pension age (65 men, 60 women) and have retired, or are treated as having retired for national insurance purposes, see Table C.
If the exact gross pay figure is not shown in the table, use the next smaller figure shown.

Gross pay £	Total of employee's and employer's* contributions £	Employee's basic contribution £	Gross pay £	Total of employee's and employer's* contributions £	Employee's basic contribution £
47·67	6·77	2·66	97·00	13·72	5·39
49·00	7·00	2·75	99·00	14·00	5·50
51·00	7·28	2·86	101·00	14·28	5·61
53·00	7·56	2·97	103·00	14·56	5·72
55·00	7·84	3·08	105·00	14·84	5·83
57·00	8·12	3·19	107·00	15·12	5·94
59·00	8·40	3·30	109·00	15·40	6·05
61·00	8·68	3·41	111·00	15·68	6·16
63·00	8·96	3·52	113·00	15·96	6·27
65·00	9·24	3·63	115·00	16·24	6·38
67·00	9·52	3·74	117·00	16·52	6·49
69·00	9·80	3·85	119·00	16·80	6·60
71·00	10·08	3·96	121·00	17·08	6·71
73·00	10·36	4·07	123·00	17·36	6·82
75·00	10·64	4·18	125·00	17·64	6·93
77·00	10·92	4·29	127·00	17·92	7·04
79·00	11·20	4·40	129·00	18·20	7·15
81·00	11·48	4·51	131·00	18·48	7·26
83·00	11·76	4·62	133·00	18·76	7·37
85·00	12·04	4·73	135·00	19·04	7·48
87·00	12·32	4·84	137·00	19·32	7·59
89·00	12·60	4·95	139·00	19·60	7·70
91·00	12·88	5·06	141·00	19·88	7·81
93·00	13·16	5·17	143·00	20·16	7·92
95·00	13·44	5·28	145·00	20·44	8·03

*The employer's contributions included in this table are shown separately in Table C.

Monthly Table A showing the Standard Rate Basic Contributions for use from 6 April 1975.

318

The pay roll.   In a large firm the names of all the employees are listed on sheets called the pay roll.   In small firms a Wages Book is often used.   Next to each employee's name a member of the Wages and Salaries Department enters the number of hours worked or the number of pieces completed or the amount sold. He writes in the rate of pay or commission and calculates the gross pay.   The statutory and voluntary deductions are entered and subtracted from the gross pay to arrive at the net pay.   The employer's National Insurance and graduated pension contributions are also written on the pay roll.

The pay advice.   Each employee receives a slip called a pay advice with his wages or salary.   The Wages and Salaries department fills it in with information on hours or pieces completed or amount sold, rate of pay, gross pay, National Insurance contribution, graduated pension contribution, other deductions, net pay.

Some firms may have more headings on their pay advice forms, if they pay a different rate for overtime, for example.

Tax deduction card.   The Wages and Salaries Department also keeps an individual pay record for each employee called a tax deduction card.   The amount of income tax payable every week in the tax year (which runs from 6 April to 5 April of the following year) is worked out on the tax deduction card.

The employee's name and income tax code number and National Insurance number are entered at the top of the card.   The printed numbers on the left refer to weeks in the tax year.   Each time the employee is paid, a wages clerk fills in the line for that week.   Look at week 37 on the tax deduction card on page 320.

In the first column, 'Pay in the week or month', the clerk copied the employee's gross pay, £50·00, from the payroll. The next column is 'Total pay to date', the amount earned since the tax year began on 6 April.   The clerk added the week's pay to the total pay for week 36 and entered £1,850·00 which was the total pay to date for week 37.

The next column is 'Total free pay to date'.   Some tax free pay is allowed each week and the total free pay allowance in any week is given in Table A of the tax tables supplied by the Inland Revenue.   The clerk looked up the employee's code number under week 37 and filled in £960·15.   The difference between the total pay to date and the total free pay to date is the 'Total

319

TABLE A—FREE PAY

Code	Total free pay to date	Code	Total free pay to date	Code	Total free pay to date	Code	Total free pay to date	Code	Total free pay to date	Code	Total free pay to date	Code	Total free pay to date	Code	Total free pay to date
	£		£		£		£		£		£		£		£
0	NIL	51	370·00	101	725·20	151	1082·25	201	1437·45	251	1792·65	301	2149·70	351	2504·90
1	14·80	52	377·40	102	732·60	152	1089·65	202	1444·85	252	1800·05	302	2155·25	352	2512·30
2	22·20	53	384·80	103	740·00	153	1095·20	203	1452·25	253	1807·45	303	2162·65	353	2519·70
3	27·75	54	392·20	104	747·40	154	1102·60	204	1459·65	254	1814·85	304	2170·05	354	2525·25
4	35·15	55	397·75	105	754·80	155	1110·00	205	1465·20	255	1822·25	305	2177·45	355	2532·65
5	42·55														
6	49·95	56	405·15	106	762·20	156	1117·40	206	1472·60	256	1829·65	306	2184·85	356	2540·05
7	57·35	57	412·55	107	767·75	157	1124·80	207	1480·00	257	1835·20	307	2192·25	357	2547·45
8	64·75	58	419·95	108	775·15	158	1132·20	208	1487·40	258	1842·60	308	2199·65	358	2554·85
9	72·15	59	427·35	109	782·55	159	1137·75	209	1494·80	259	1850·00	309	2205·20	359	2562·25
10	77·70	60	434·75	110	789·95	160	1145·15	210	1502·20	260	1857·40	310	2212·60	360	2569·65
11	85·10	61	442·15	111	797·35	161	1152·55	211	1507·75	261	1864·80	311	2220·00		
12	92·50	62	447·70	112	804·75	162	1159·95	212	1515·15	262	1872·20	312	2227·40		
13	99·90	63	455·10	113	812·15	163	1167·35	213	1522·55	263	1877·75	313	2234·80		
14	107·30	64	462·50	114	817·70	164	1174·75	214	1529·95	264	1885·15	314	2242·20		
15	114·70	65	469·90	115	825·10	165	1182·15	215	1537·35	265	1892·55	315	2247·75		
16	120·25	66	477·30	116	832·50	166	1187·70	216	1544·75	266	1899·95	316	2255·15		
17	127·65	67	484·70	117	839·90	167	1195·10	217	1552·15	267	1907·35	317	2262·55		
18	135·05	68	490·25	118	847·30	168	1202·50	218	1557·70	268	1914·75	318	2269·95		
19	142·45	69	497·65	119	854·70	169	1209·90	219	1565·10	269	1922·15	319	2277·35		
20	149·85	70	505·05	120	860·25	170	1217·30	220	1572·50	270	1927·70	320	2284·75		
21	157·25	71	...·45	121	867·65	171	1224·70	221	1579·90	271	19?·10		2?2·15		

1975-76 DEDUCTION CARD

MF 06 24 59 C			
Employee's National Insurance No.			

Employee's Surname (Enter in BLOCK CAPITALS): CLIFFE
First two forenames: ERIC JAMES

CODE †	Amended code †	Week/Month No. in which applied	Employer
134 H			McDONALDS ENTERPRISES

District: SOUTH 1 Employer's reference 936/A 76

Works No., Branch, Dept., Contract, etc.

Make entries from 6 April 1975 to 5/6 December 1975 overleaf

Total of Employee's and Employer's Contributions (1a)	Employee's Basic Contributions (1b)	Month number	Week number	Pay in the week or month (2)	Total pay to date (3)	Total free pay to date as shown by Table A (4)	Total taxable pay to date (5)	Total tax due to date as shown by Taxable Pay Tables (6)	Tax deducted or refunded in the week or month (Mark refunds "R") (7)
£	£	B.F. from Mth. 8	B.F. from Wk. 35	£ 1750 00	£	£	£	£ 299 35	£
7 00	2 76	6 Dec. to 5 Jan.	36	50 00	1800 00	934 20	865 80	302 75	8 40
7 00	2 76		37	50 00	1850 00	960 15	889 85	311 15	8 40
		9	38						
			39						
7 00	2 76	6 Jan. to 5 Feb.	40	50 00	1900 00	1038 00	862 00	301 70	9 45 R
			41						
		10	42						
			43						
		6 Feb.	44						

320

taxable pay to date', £889·85, the total amount of pay on which tax is due.

By looking at tax Table B the clerk found the income tax due on the total taxable pay to be £311·15. Note that £311·15 is the 'Total tax due to date'. As the employee pays part of his income tax each week, he has paid most of the £311·15 in weeks 1 to 36. To find the amount of tax due in week 37, the clerk subtracted the total tax due in week 36 from £311·15. The difference, £8·40, is the tax deducted in week 37 and is written in the last column.

The lines for weeks 38 and 39 are blank because the employee was ill and unable to earn any wages. When the clerk filled in the line for week 40 he used the figures for week 37, the last week worked. Since the employee missed two weeks' wages, his total pay to date in week 40 increased by £50·00 to £1,900·00. The total free pay in week 40 was £1038·00. The total free pay subtracted from the total pay left total taxable pay of £862·00. The total tax due in week 40 was £301·70 which was lower than the tax due in week 37, £311·15. This means the employee paid more tax than was due and he received a refund marked with an R. The refund was £311·15 less £301·70 which is £9·45.

The employee's graduated National Insurance contribution is entered on the extreme left as this money is sent to the Collector of Taxes with the income tax.

After the end of the tax year (5 April) all employees' tax deduction cards must be sent to the Collector of Taxes with a covering certificate.

(f) PETTY CASH RECORDS

The paying out of petty cash and the keeping of the Petty Cash Book often form part of the duties of a junior member of the office staff, as the amounts of money handled are very small (hence the name 'petty'). A shorthand-typist may be responsible for the petty cash in a large general office; a secretary will certainly keep an account of the petty cash drawn by her principal.

The actual cash must be kept in a cash box which should be put in a locked drawer. The money will be used for paying out small sums such as local travelling expenses, postage, stationery, etc. When petty cash is paid out to other members of the office, a voucher should be obtained; other payments should be supported by receipted bills; in the case of postage, the amounts can be checked against the postage book.

Petty cash can be dealt with in two ways:

(1) A round sum of, say, £10 is advanced by the cashier, and when this is nearly spent a similar sum is advanced.

(2) The sum which it is estimated will cover the week (or month) is advanced. At the end of the period the petty cash book is checked and a further sum exactly equal to that spent is advanced; the sum advanced added to the cash in hand will equal the petty cash at the beginning of the period, so the petty cashier will always start the week (or month) with the same amount. This is called the Imprest System.

You will see from the illustration how a Petty Cash Book may be ruled. In the example, the imprest is £5 per week.

Cash		Date	Particulars	Fol.	Amount		Postage		Travel		Sundries	
£.		197-			£		£.		£.		£.	
5	00	May 1	To Balance									
		„ 1	By Stamps		2	00	2	00				
		„ 2	„ Fares	9		20				20		
		„ 3	„ Sealing Wax	10		75						75
		„ 3	„ Tea	11		18						18
		„ 4	„ Stamps	1		00	1	00				
		„ 5	„ Milk	12		38						38
		„ 31	To Cash									
4	51				4	51	3	00		20	1	31
			By Balance c/d		5	00						
9	51				9	51						
5	00	June 1	To Balance b/d									

Dr.   Petty Cash Book   Cr.

(g) CREDIT AND PAYMENT RECORDS

Credit buying has become part of the modern way of life. When goods are bought on credit they do not have to be paid for immediately. The customer may pay at the end of the month, as with a *charge account* at a shop, or he may pay part of the price each month or week. These payments are called *instalments*.

HIRE PURCHASE

Many firms that sell expensive consumer goods, such as refrigerators and televisions, offer their customers a hire purchase arrangement. Under a hire purchase agreement, the customer 'hires' the item while he pays the agreed number of hiring charges, which are usually on a monthly basis. After paying the hiring charges, the customer is given an option to buy the item for a small charge, usually another month's payment.

An application form to open a charge account (a monthly account) at a retail store.

REQUEST FOR MONTHLY ACCOUNT

NAME AND ADDRESS (BLOCKS)·	Initially I/WE we may require credit up to a Maximum of
	Please tick ► £25 / £50 / £100 / £250 / or £ (other sum)
	TRADE REFERENCE (A shop or service where you already have an account)
Please write your name as you wish it to appear on your account e.g. JOHN W. COX Esq. MARY BROWN , M.B.E. MR. and MRS. J.P. SMITH / TEL. No:	I/We also wish the undermentioned to be able to charge purchases on this account (Full name in Blocks) Mr. Mrs. Miss
BUSINESS OR PROFESSION / BUSINESS TEL. No:	I/WE UNDERSTAND AND AGREE THAT THIS ACCOUNT WILL BE FOR MONTHLY SETTLEMENT.
PREVIOUS ADDRESS (If you have resided at the above address for less than 2 years)	Signature(s) Date................ Age (If under 18)
	FOR OFFICE USE ISSUED BY: DATE: REG. No:
ANY OTHER ADDRESS FROM WHICH ACCOUNT MAY BE OPERATED	SPECIMEN OF MY/OUR SIGNATURE(S) AND OF ANY OTHER USERS OF THIS ACCOUNT:-
NAME AND BRANCH ADDRESS OF PERSONAL BANKERS (Vistitors to U.K. and recent arrivals: See note)	

Although the customer has the use of the article from the first payment, he does not own it. The seller is legally the owner until the customer takes up the option to buy. If the customer stops paying the monthly hiring charges, the seller can take back the goods, although there are legal safeguards for the customer.

Careful and complete records about every hire purchase transaction must be kept. Each customer's records must include the number of the hire purchase agreement, the details of the item, the hire price, the number and amount of the hiring charge and the date each payment is due. The receipt of each instalment must be noted in the customer's records. Overdue payments may necessitate a reminder letter. The date of the letter is important and must be noted as most companies give their customers time to react to the reminder before taking further action.

MAIL ORDER

Buying through the post is popular with many people who live away from towns or who cannot get to shops easily or who prefer shopping at home to wandering around crowded shops.

Mail order firms advertise their goods in magazines and newspapers or produce illustrated catalogues. Because the mail order customer does not see the actual item he is ordering, goods have to be sent on approval in the first instance. The customer is allowed a few days in which to decide whether he wants the item. If he decides to keep it, he posts his payment to the firm or arranges to pay in instalments. If he does not want the item he posts it back to the firm.

Firms that sell expensive items by catalogue have to decide whether a customer can be trusted to pay all the instalments. A customer who can be trusted may act as agent for the firm. The customer is not employed by the firm, but he is given a discount on goods he buys and on goods his friends order through him.

A large mail order firm must keep detailed and accurate records on the goods that have been sent on approval or sold, and on the instalments that are paid by the customers. Since many customers pay weekly instalments over a long period, records must always be up to date and correct. A customer who has kept up with all his instalments would not be pleased to receive a reminder about an overdue payment that has actually already been made.

CREDIT CONTROL

A firm dealing with credit selling must be able to trust its customers to pay what they owe. Of course, not all customers continue their payments and the firms have legal safeguards. However, legal action is costly, long and unpleasant. Large firms selling on hire purchase or by mail order try to avoid legal actions by choosing customers who can be trusted with credit. Deciding who can be allowed credit and how much they can be allowed is called *credit control*.

One method of deciding whether a customer is worthy of credit is to take up references with the customer's bank or with another firm who has sold the customer goods on credit.

A customer who is worthy of credit is said to have a good *credit rating*. A firm can discover whether a customer has a good credit rating or a bad credit rating by inquiring at a *credit reference bureau*. The business of the credit reference bureau is to supply firms with information on the credit rating of customers. From this information and the references of a customer, the firm has to decide if the customer is worthy of credit, and if he is, how much credit he can be allowed.

(h) VAT (VALUE ADDED TAX) RECORDS

On 1 April 1973 Purchase Tax and Selective Employment Tax were replaced by Value Added Tax. VAT is a tax on sales turnover; it starts with the manufacturer or first supplier in a chain of sales and ends with the ultimate consumer of the goods or services. The government department responsible for the collection of VAT is HM Customs and Excise. In order to comply with the VAT regulations, every trader whose turnover in taxable supplies of goods and/or services exceeds £5,000* a year must:

1 keep copies of all documents concerning the taxable aspects of every transaction for at least three years—this means the retention of documents such as invoices, credit and debit notes but not, of course, documents like packing or delivery

* It is estimated that nearly two million traders are concerned with VAT, compared with 70,000 who were concerned with Purchase Tax.

notes; the records may be stored in any form including storage on microfilm or in a computer;

2 be able to produce for visiting Customs and Excise officials documentary evidence of

  (*a*) outputs (sales)—there is a list of ten items (such as name of supplier, date of supply) which 'must be clearly shown' for every taxable supply to 'another taxable person', and

  (*b*) inputs (purchases)—six details of each transaction must be recorded;

3 return a form, VAT 100, showing total input tax and total output tax for each tax period (normally three months).

The introduction of VAT legislation has meant that not only must businesses keep detailed records of every taxable transaction, but also that the information must be stored in such form that it can be speedily retrieved when needed, e.g. when required by a visiting Customs and Excise official. Traders have, therefore, had to redesign their invoices to provide space for the entering of VAT rates, amounts and registration numbers; they have also had to improve their record-keeping systems to make sure that an office copy of an invoice can be retrieved within seconds. All VAT records and related documents e.g. trading accounts, profit and loss accounts and balance sheets, must be kept (by law) for three years from the last date to which they refer.

(*i*) VISUAL AIDS

Although information stored in files may be arranged in an orderly way, it has to be retrieved before it can be used. For example, if the sales manager of a soap powder manufacturer wanted to know Mr Brown's sales figures for the previous month, he would probably ask his secretary to look up the information in the files. If the sales manager wanted to know the previous month's sales figures of three of his salesmen, Brown, Jones and Smith, in order to find out who sold the most, the secretary would have to look up three items of information.

Retrieving information from files is time-consuming and therefore costly but it is, of course, necessary to the smooth-

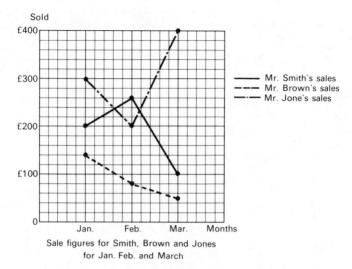

Sale figures for Smith, Brown and Jones
for Jan. Feb. and March

running of a firm. In some cases time and money can be saved by using charts or other visual ways of recording and displaying information. If the sales manager has a chart on the wall of his office showing the sales figures of Brown, Smith and Jones, he could find out and compare the previous month's sales figures at a glance. Display materials, such as wall charts, which present statistics and other information, are called visual aids.

USES

The main purpose of visual aids in business is quick reference. Figures on a wall chart or graph can be seen at a glance. When figures for several months or years are on one chart, the businessman can see the upward or downward trend and use this information for estimating future requirements or forecasting probable results.

Visual aids also make information easier to understand. A list of figures can be overwhelming but an attractive visual display makes them easier to understand and digest.

A common use for visual aids is to record progress. A progress chart is designed for a particular job of work with headings for each stage of the job. As the employee completes a stage, he marks it on the chart. The secretary or the publicity officer of a dress manufacturer designed this progress chart

327

Name	Invitation sent	Accepted	Rejected	Hotel reservation needed	Hotel reservation made	Hotel information mailed
Miss Wall	▭		▭			
Miss Carter	▭	▭				
Mlle Dupont	▭	▭		▭	▭	
Frau Wurot	▭	▭		▭	▭	▭
Miss Benson	▭		▭			

A progress chart.

for her part in arranging a fashion show for British and European journalists.

When a stage is completed, the secretary puts a coloured marker against the name of the journalist in the correct column. She may use different coloured markers: Invitations Accepted may be marked in red and Invitations Declined in blue. The markers must be kept up to date or the chart is useless.

The chart gives an overall picture of the amount of work completed and the work still to be done. It also allows the secretary or her boss to find out quickly if one part of the job has been done. For example, when Mlle Dupont, a French journalist, telephones to ask if her hotel reservation has been made, the publicity officer can answer her after a quick look at the chart. If the reservation was made but there is no marker under Hotel Information Mailed, the publicity officer can remind his secretary to complete that stage.

DIFFERENT TYPES OF CHARTS

The two examples above show that there are different ways of presenting information in visual form. The type of visual aid used depends on the information to be portrayed. The graph showing sales figures would not have been suitable for the publicity officer's progress chart, and the signalled information on the progress chart could not be used to show statistics of sales.

When visual aids are used, the type should be chosen that is most suitable for the material to be presented. In some cases, more than one method may be suitable, while in others, there is only one possible type.

Design. When the type of visual aid has been chosen, it should be designed to show clearly the information intended for display. Every chart or graph should have a clear title. The scale should suit the information: if the chart is showing profits in thousands of pounds, it is bad design to have a division for every £10. If necessary a key should be provided to explain the chart. A chart that is confusing or difficult to read is useless.

Line graphs. Line graphs are ideal for displaying statistical information where there are two elements in the statistics, such as number of people per acre, profits each month, sales for the year, the temperature each day. The vertical line or axis on the left has a scale that increases upwards for one of the factors and the horizontal axis at the bottom has a scale increasing towards

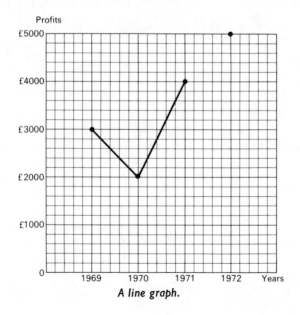

A line graph.

the right for the other factor. Each axis must be clearly labelled.

If a firm uses a line graph to show its profits each year, the vertical axis is marked off in thousands of pounds and the horizontal axis in years.

The profit for each year is marked by a point on the graph. Since graph paper has lines printed on it at regular intervals, £3000 profit for 1969 is plotted by following the lines for £3000 and 1969 until they meet. Each year the point for the profit is plotted. The line joining the points shows the movement of the profits up or down.

Since line graphs are simple to design and easy to read, they are frequently used to display statistics in business, science, sociology, economics and many other fields. Businesses can use line graphs to show profits, losses, sales, exports, imports, costs, new orders and many other statistics.

Multi-line graphs. In the graph of sales figures below two sets of points were plotted and two different lines drawn. This is called a multi-line graph as more than one line is used. With multi-line graphs comparisons between different sets of figures can be made.

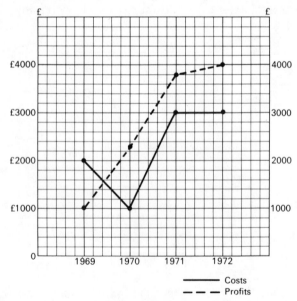

A multi-line graph.

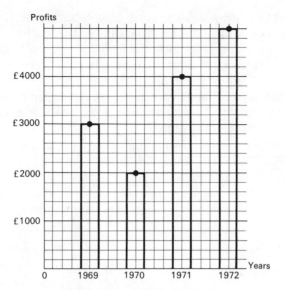

Yearly profits of Zed Products Ltd.

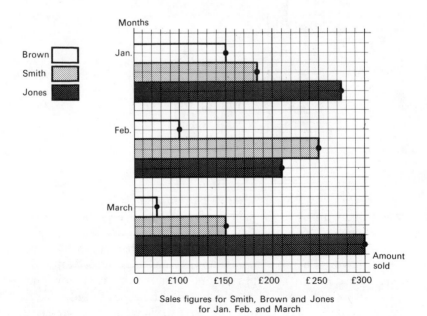

Sales figures for Smith, Brown and Jones
for Jan. Feb. and March

Examples of bar graphs.

331

On a multi-line graph each line must be **drawn** differently so that they can be distinguished easily and so that the lines will not be confused if they cross each other. The lines can be drawn in different colours or in different ways. In either case a key must be provided that clearly explains the meaning of each line.

Another type of multi-line graph has two different scales on the vertical axis. The second scale is shown on a vertical axis on the right side of the graph.

Bar graphs. The information shown on line graphs and multi-line graphs can often be displayed equally well in bar graphs. The axes (plural of axis) are drawn in the same way. After the points have been plotted a bar is drawn from the bottom axis to the point. The bars can be vertical or horizontal.

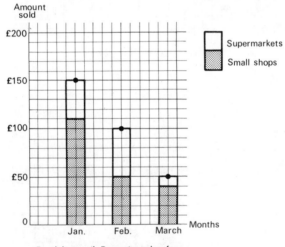

Breakdown of Brown's sales for
Jan. Feb. and March

There are some cases where a bar graph must be used instead of a line graph. If the sales manager wanted a graph to show how much of Mr Brown's sales were made to supermarkets and how much to small shops, he would use a bar graph like the one above. Each bar represents the total sales for each month but the different shadings within each bar indicate how the sales were divided. Two colours could have been used.

Pie graphs. Pie graphs are used to show how a whole is divided. For example, in the pie graph on page 333, the circle

332

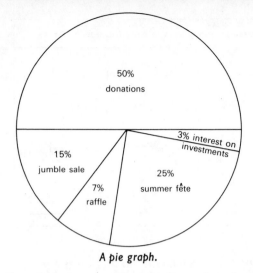

A *pie graph.*

represents the whole income of a charity and each section is a percentage of the income. The size of each segment should correspond to the percentage it represents: the section for 50 per cent, for example, should be half the circle.

Typewritten tables. Statistical information is very often displayed in typewritten tabular form. Clear headings must be

Representative	January Units	February Units	March Units
Arkwright	78	157	75
Barnes	312	501	301
Bartholomew	255	454	250
Beavers	237	566	325
Bell	59	120	75
Clive	346	406	300
Dent	45	98	53

Representative	January £	February £	March £
Arkwright	6.24	12.56	6.00
Barnes	24.96	40.08	24.08
Bartholomew	20.40	36.32	20.00
Beavers	18.96	45.28	26.00
Bell	4.72	9.60	6.00
Clive	27.68	32.48	24.00
Dent	3.60	7.84	4.31

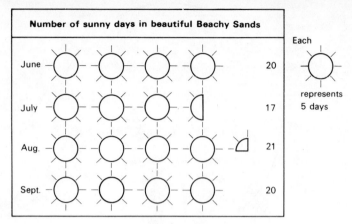

Number of sunny days in beautiful Beachy Sands

June		20
July		17
Aug.		21
Sept.		20

Each ☼ represents 5 days

A pictogram.

typed at the top of each column and on the left side. In some cases lines are drawn on the table to make it easier to read.

If there is a large number of figures to be displayed, type-written tables are simpler to read than multi-line graphs or bar graphs. If the sales manager wants a chart of the sales figures of the firm's 100 salesmen, a typewritten table would have to be used as a graph with 100 lines would be very difficult to read.

Symbols or pictograms, and picture charts. The use of symbols to represent figures on a chart makes an attractive display. For the sake of accuracy, the figure represented should be written next to the symbol. Symbol charts would be used for advertising or publicity purposes rather than for day-to-day business information.

A picture chart.

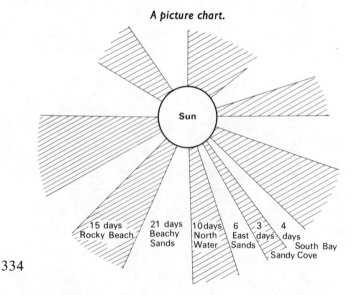

Another attractive method of displaying statistics is a picture chart. Picture charts are an ideal way of presenting a few statistics in posters, advertisements and illustrations in magazines.

Visual control boards. The secretary's progress chart to the fashion show arrangements on page 328 is one sort of visual control board. Several types of visual control boards are made, but the basic principle is the same. The board has spaces at the top and side for headings to be inserted. Coloured markers can be placed on the board in holes, slots, channels or held on magnetically or by other methods of adhesion. The markers can be added, taken off or moved about to show changes in the situation from day to day.

Besides being used as progress charts, visual control boards are ideal for showing amounts of stock, statistics that change rapidly, the position of personnel within a firm or at branches, movement of stock or products from one department to another or one branch to another and any other information that is likely to change.

EXERCISES

1. Explain the following words and expressions:

   axis   visual aid
   visual control board   graph paper
   multi-line graph   pie graph

2. Design a line graph to show the yearly expenditure of the Well-Made Products Company on stationery. Plot these figures on the graph. 1968: £350; 1969: £200; 1970: £300; 1971: £400; 1972: £450.

3. Your chief is ordering envelopes, pencils, carbon paper and manilla files from four different suppliers. Design a progress chart of the visual control board type to follow the progress of these orders. The heading on the top should be the documents used for each part of the transactions. Each heading will be filled in for each item when that document has been sent or received.

4. Explain the following terms and expressions:

   mail order   goods sent on approval
   credit rating   credit control
   instalments   option to buy

5. What circumstances should a firm consider before deciding to give a customer credit? How can the firm find information about the customer's credit-worthiness?

6. The following is a Sales Record of assistants working in the Fabric Department of a large store.

Assistant	Mon	Tues	Wed	Thurs	Fri	Sat	Totals
	£	£	£	£	£	£	£
Miss Jones	15.75	16.34	17.62	13.21	19.23	23.62	105·77
Miss Dunn	16.30	17.23	18.34	12.05	20.40	35.70	G
Mrs Cook	14.24	16.32	15.21	11.46	18.32	25.65	H
Miss Cooper	13.16	15.21	16.57	11.82	19.64	28.90	I
Miss Wright	17.90	18.60	19.62	12.34	20.40	32.75	J
Totals	£A	£B	£C	£D	£E	£F	£K

(a) Write down the letters A–K underneath each other, and enter each total against the appropriate letter.
(b) Why are the sales on Thursday lower than those on any other day?
(c) Which assistant sold most?
(d) Which assistant had the highest daily average?
(e) Which assistant sold least?

7. Several methods are used for determining the weekly wage of employees, including: (i) time rates, (ii) piece rates, (iii) commission.
(a) Describe each of the above three methods and, in each case, indicate the type(s) of worker for whom the method would normally be used.
(b) Mention the advantages of each method.
(c) What records must be kept under each separate method in order to provide information from which the wages can be calculated? (RSA, OP, II)

8. (a) Explain two methods of paying wages or salaries to employees.
(b) Describe two deductions made from wages or salaries before payment. (RSA, OP, I)

9. The manufacturing company for which you work employs about 100 sales representatives. Each is provided with a

car and, between them, the representatives cover the whole of Great Britain and Ireland. It is decided to start a card-index system recording details of the cars used by the representatives, the mileage each covers, repairs and maintenance, and other relevant details.

(*a*) Explain what type of equipment might be used for such records and give reasons for your choice.

(*b*) How might you ensure that all relevant information was obtained for entering in the records? (RSA, OP, II)

10. You work in the head office of a large company which has five branch offices. The company has engaged twelve trainee sales executives and, during the six months beginning on 1st August, 1971, it is proposed that each trainee will spend one month in each branch office and one month in head office.

(*a*) Design a visual control board or chart suitable for recording the locations of all the trainees during the six-month period, and fill in details showing the possible locations of each trainee throughout that six-month period (assuming that two trainees will be in each branch and two at head office at any one time).

(*b*) What information do you consider that Branch Managers should send to the Company's Personnel Officer about each trainee at the end of each month.
(RSA, OP, II)

11. (*a*) A firm receives an order from a customer who has no credit account with that firm and does not enclose any payment with his order. What action should be taken by the firm?

(*b*) What records about customers would you expect a firm's credit control department to keep? What would the firm do if one of its customers had not yet settled an account which was several months overdue?
(RSA, OP, II)

12. Your firm has decided to set up a small branch office and it is agreed that the branch office should have a certain amount of petty cash provided by head office on the imprest system. What action should be taken by head office to start the petty cash account at the branch office? Subsequently what records and documents should be kept at the branch office

and what information should the branch office supply to head office?

(RSA, OP, II)

13. (a) Draw up a stationery stock record card suitable for note pads and make entries for the following:

Maximum stock: 4 gross   Minimum stock: $\frac{1}{2}$ gross

1.6.70   Balance in stock: 160
8.6.70   Issued 50 note pads to buying department
18.6.70   Issued 60 note pads to sales department
22.6.70   Bought 3 gross note pads from J R Brown Ltd
30.6.70   Issued 40 note pads to drawing office
3.7.70   Issued 20 note pads to spares department

(b) Why is it necessary to keep such stock records and what is the purpose of showing the maximum and minimum stocks? (RSA, OP, II)

14. (a) What documents should a man produce when he changes his employment?
(b) What information about him should his new employer record at that time and during his employment:
(i) for the purpose of preparing wages, and
(ii) for inclusion in general personnel records?

(RSA, OP, II)

15. Give the meaning of each of the following abbreviations, or terms, and state briefly when each one is used:
PAYE   CODE NUMBER   P.45
TAX TABLES   FREE PAY   (RSA, OP, I)

16. (a) Describe the purpose of:
(i) a Pay Roll;
(ii) a Pay Advice (for the employee);
(iii) an Employee's Individual Pay Record.
(b) A small firm intends to use a Manifold Posting Board for the preparation of wages documents. Give a brief explanation of this method.
(c) What are Graduated Pension Contributions and by whom are they paid? (RSA, OP, II)

17. (a) Office sundries include such items as typewriter ribbons and pencil erasers. List four others.
(b) Name the books and equipment necessary for the efficient operation of a petty cash system.

(c) Make out the Petty Cash Voucher below, referring to the sum of 62½p paid for window cleaning in the office this week. (RSA, OP, I)

```
┌─────────────────────────────────────────────────────┐
│                                    No. ...............│
│              PETTY CASH VOUCHER                       │
│   Expenditure authorised by .......................   │
│      For What Required              £                 │
│                                                       │
│                                                       │
│                                   _____    │
│                                   ════════════════    │
│                  Signature ..........................  │
│                       Date ..........................  │
│                                                       │
└─────────────────────────────────────────────────────┘
```

18. The clock card of an employee, J Ayres, is shown opposite. He is paid at the rate of 40p. per hour for a 40-hour week and time-and-a-quarter for the next six hours. After that he is paid time-and-a-half for work on week-days and double-time for work on Sundays. **Note:** The official starting time (Monday to Friday) is 8.00 a.m. The employees are allowed 3 minutes' grace without deduction.
    (a) Complete the card down to and including the figure for total hours.
    (b) Calculate the total gross wages for the week.
    (c) What compulsory deductions will be made by the employer?
    (d) List the items of machine equipment which you would expect to be used to calculate wages and to prepare wages sheets by a company which has a large pay-roll but which does not have access to an electronic computer or punched card equipment. (RSA, OP, II)

NAME J.Ayres							
NO. 83				WEEK ENDING 3rd. May, 1970			

DAY		IN	OUT	IN	OUT	IN	OUT	TOTAL
M	AM	8.00						
	PM		12.30	1.30	5.30			
Tu	AM	8.01						
	PM		12.30	1.30	5.30	6.00	8.00	
W	AM	7.58						
	PM		12.15	1.30	5.30	6.00	9.00	
T	AM	8.02						
	PM		12.30	1.30	6.30			
F	AM	8.00						
	PM		12.00	1.00	5.30			
S	AM	7.30						
	PM		12.15					
Su	AM	9.00						
	PM		1.00					
						TOTAL HOURS		

(b) Total Gross Wages: ....

(c) ....

....

(d) ....

....

....

19. On 1st April, 1971, the central stores of G Smith & Co Ltd, High Street, Welbridge, had 48 reams of A4 lined paper in stock. During the month of April, 1971, the following issues were made:

5th April	Sales Department	10 reams
7th April	Planning Department	6 reams
9th April	Publicity Department	8 reams
15th April	Accounts Department	10 reams
26th April	General Office	8 reams

The maximum stock level is 100 reams and the minimum

stock level is 25 reams. On the appropriate date an order for a further supply was placed with G Roberts Ltd, 15 Low Road, Welbridge, and this supply was received five days later.

(a) Using a form of your own design, make out the order for the further supply of stationery mentioned above.

(b) What is the purpose of stocktaking? (RSA, OP, II)

20. (a) Make the following entries for A4 bond paper on the stationery card below.

Max. stock 200 reams   Min. stock 40 reams   1970

March 3 Balance in stock 120

7 issued 10 rms. to Sales Dept. Reqn. No. 746

12   ,,   14   ,,   to Chief Buyer's Dept. Reqn. No. 861

14 delivery 50 rms. from Spipacks Papers invoice 27754

(b) Enter the balances in the end column after each transaction.

(c) Describe briefly the main reasons for having a stock control system for stationery in an office. (RSA, OP, I)

STATIONERY STOCK CARD							
Item				Maximum Stock:			
....				Minimum Stock:			
Date	Receipts			Issues			Balance in Stock
	Quantity Received	Invoice No.	Supplier	Quantity Issued	Requisition No.	Department	

21. Explain the following terms or expressions:

National Insurance card   employee's code number

flat rate contribution   net pay

piece rate   pay advice

P60 form   total gross pay to date

22. Explain how graduated pension contributions are paid and the amount that is paid.

23. Give arguments for and against using an Incoming Mail register in an office.

24. You are employed as assistant to the Chief Clerk of a department which consists of the head of the department, the Chief Clerk, six assistant clerks, two shorthand-typists and a secretary who works mainly for the departmental head. The Chief Clerk asks you to draw up a holiday rota chart and to indicate on it the holiday arrangements for all the staff in the department. Each person is allowed three weeks holiday but may take only two weeks consecutively. The head of the department is taking the first two weeks in August and the last week in October. Two of the assistants clerks are married with young families and want to take their leave during the school holidays if possible. One shorthand-typist is a winter sports enthusiast.

Draw up a suitable chart and block in the periods each employee will be away on leave. (Assume that you have had the opportunity to discuss the arrangements with each member of the department and that suitable dates have been agreed.)

Chapter 10

Reference Books

IT is often said that a knowledgeable person is not a person who knows a lot of facts, but a person who knows where to find the facts when they are required. The term 'General Knowledge' is used to describe the sort of information which an educated person is expected to have at his finger-tips. No one is expected to learn by heart the detailed information which is contained in some reference books—it is sufficient to know to which books reference should be made.

For example, to know the London termini for northbound trains would be classed as General Knowledge. To learn by heart the times of the trains would be a foolish waste of time and mental energy; but a well-informed person is expected:

    (*a*) to know what reference book contains this information; and

    (*b*) to be able to extract the required information quickly and accurately.

As a well-informed citizen and as a competent employee in the business world you should be familiar with the nature of the information available in the following reference books.

SPELLING AND USAGE

The Concise Oxford Dictionary. Remember that in addition to telling you how to spell words, a dictionary also tells you:

    (*a*) the plural of the word, if it is an exception to the general rule,

    (*b*) the pronunciation of the word,

    (*c*) the part of speech,

    (*d*) the derivation,

    (*e*) the prepositions which must follow certain words,

    (*f*) the meaning,

    (*g*) if the word is slang, vulgar or old-fashioned.

Modern English Usage, by H. W. Fowler, is generally accepted to be the standard work of reference on English usage. By 'usage' we mean the customary practice of the best writers and speakers. Whenever you are not sure which of two words to use (e.g. 'dreamt' or 'dreamed') or when you cannot remember some point of grammar (such as whether 'each of them is' or 'each of them are' is correct), refer to Fowler's *M.E.U.* and you will usually find a ruling on the question.

An A.B.C. of English Usage, by H. A. Treble and G. H. Vallins, is a very similar book to *Modern English Usage*. The decisions on usage are mostly taken from Fowler, but the language is simpler and the reasoning easier to understand. From the point of view of the office worker who wants a quick decision on correct usage, the book by Treble and Vallins is more practical; Fowler, however, is more satisfying, as he gives reasoned explanations in addition to decisions. Compare the entries under 'lay, lie' in each of the two books, and the articles on the word 'naive'.

Roget's Thesaurus of English Words and Phrases, arranges words in groups according to their meanings. Each page is printed in two columns; one column lists synonyms, the other lists antonyms. To use the book you must first look up the word in question in the index. The number against the word refers you to the section in which the word occurs. In that section you will find all the other words and phrases used in English which have a similar meaning; and in the adjacent column you will find lists of words with opposite meanings.

Usage and Abusage, is one of many books written by Eric Partridge. The ground covered is similar to Fowler's *M.E.U.* but the subjects are treated from a different angle. The author has a pleasantly light and amusing style of writing and you will enjoy dipping into his books if the study of words has begun to interest you.

The Students' Companion, by W. D. Best, contains useful lists of proverbs, similes, abbreviations and sections on general knowledge and civics.

Dictionary of Abbreviations and Symbols, by E. F. Allen, and *A Dictionary of Abbreviations*, by E. Partridge, provide fuller lists of abbreviations than the general reference books.

SHORTHAND, TYPEWRITING AND OFFICE PRACTICE

Pitman's English/Shorthand Dictionary, should be considered as an essential part of the equipment of a shorthand-typist. The book is a combined shorthand and English dictionary.

With each word is listed its meaning and shorthand outline. In one respect it is more useful than an ordinary dictionary: as each word has a different shorthand outline, the derivatives as well as the root words are listed in alphabetical order. For example, if you cannot remember whether the word 'benefited' has one or two t's, an ordinary dictionary gives no assistance. In a shorthand dictionary, however, 'benefited' is listed after 'benefit' because the shorthand outline is different.

The Dictionary of Typewriting, by M. Crooks and F. Dawson, is the standard work of reference on typewriting. Every branch of the subject is covered. The information is arranged alphabetically and there are articles on such matters as duplication, display, legal work, forms of address, typewriter maintenance and stationery.

The Shorthand Typist's Pocket Book, by Carlton Wallace, contains articles on general office work, writing good English, Postal Services, Travel, Money, Shipping and many other topics connected with the work of a shorthand-typist.

Essential Secretarial Studies by Stanwell and Shaw (Edward Arnold) is a source of everyday information needed by all secretaries. There are sections dealing with Dictation, Typewriting and Transcription, Telephone Techniques, Mail Handling, Reprography, Reception Duties, Storage and Retrieval of Information, Planning Journeys, Committee Procedure, Finance and Statistics, Management Techniques, Personnel, a useful section on Secretarial Work Planning and ten Appendices listing Useful Terms, Abbreviations etc.

The Secretary's Handbook, by S. A. Taintor and K. M. Monro is an American book providing complete information on any writing problem from the smallest detail of punctuation to the most complicated document. The usage recommended is American, but the information in the sections on Capitalisation, Figures, Invitations, Report Writing, the Writing of Minutes, and Making an Index would be useful to many secretaries.

The Typist's Desk Book, by M. Berry; *The Real Personal Secretary*, by F. Addington Symonds; and *Strictly for Secretaries*, by H. and J. Whitcomb, are three more books which shorthand-typists and secretaries should have at hand.

POSTAL REGULATIONS, TELEPHONE SERVICES AND TRAVEL INFORMATION

Post Office Guide, published by H.M. Stationery Office,

contains complete information on all postal regulations for inland and overseas post, the Telex service, telegram and telephone services and charges, the savings and investments facilities provided by the Post Office, licences, pensions and allowances.

Telephone directories for the subscriber's area are provided by the local telephone manager's office. The London directories (four parts, A–D, E–K, L–R and S–Z) cover only the London postal areas. Directories covering another part of the country may be obtained on application to the Post Office. Foreign telephone directories are also available.

The Classified Trades (*Yellow Page*) *Directory* printed on yellow paper with a pink index. The 'Yellow Pages' may be bound into the ordinary alphabetical directory and called a combined directory.

Hotels and Restaurants in Britain (the official guide of the British Travel and Holidays Association), published annually, contains touring notes and maps of tourist areas, particulars of hotels and restaurants in London and throughout the country.

Kelly's Directories are published for counties and important towns in the country. The directories give the names of streets and nominal occupiers of each house, flat or business office. The streets are arranged in alphabetical order. Trades, professions and private residents are also listed.

The ABC Railway Guide is published monthly and lists all train services from and to London, alphabetically, according to destination. The following information about each town is also included: county, distance from London, population, early closing day and hotels. Additional information about hotels in the form of advertisements is given in the first section of the book.

The ABC World Airways Guide, also published monthly, contains complete timetables for all regular air services throughout the world. Details of passenger fares and cargo rates, airline ticket offices and travel agents, international travel requirements, passports, visas and health regulations are also included.

The ABC Shipping Guide, published bi-monthly, gives information regarding shipping lines and ports, sailing dates and fares.

The handbooks published by the Automobile Association

and the Royal Automobile Club contain road maps, itineraries, mileage charts and details of hotels and garages.

The A–Z Street Guides contain maps showing each street and indicate the direction of the house numbering. An alphabetical index at the end of the book gives the page number and map reference for each street.

GENERAL REFERENCE BOOKS

Pears Cyclopaedia, published annually, is divided into sections under three main headings: The Wider World (events, prominent people, local and central government, law, international organisations); Everyday Information (dictionary, foreign phrases, business dictionary and legal notes); and Home and Personal (medical dictionary, first aid hints, cookery, gardening, sports, domestic pets).

Whitaker's Almanack, published annually, contains statistics and information on every country in the world, e.g. names of government officials, imports and exports, revenue, population, language, production and industry. It also includes astronomical and religious calendars, meteorological records for the United Kingdom for the preceding year, and population tables. There are also sections on the following subjects: the Monarchy; the Peerage; members of the House of Commons; General Election results, addresses of Government offices and names of senior officials; the Law Courts, the Police and the Armed Forces; education; prominent events of the preceding year; principal towns and cities; principal daily newspapers; National insurance and Assistance; the National Health Service; societies and institutions; trade unions; insurance; building societies; income tax; a summary of important sports results for the preceding year; postal information.

The Statesman's Year-Book, published annually, is divided into four parts. Part I contains statistical tables for commodities (cotton, sugar, etc.), and information about international organisations (UNO, NATO, OEEC, etc). Part II covers the countries of the British Commonwealth. Part III covers the territories comprising the United States of America; and Part IV deals with all other countries. In Parts II, III and IV information is listed under the following headings: type of government; area and population; education; justice; finance; defence; production; commerce; communications; money and banking; weights and measures; diplomatic representatives; names of books of reference which may be consulted for further information.

BOAC Travellers Digest, published by BOAC, is a helpful book for businessmen who are travelling. There are sections for most countries which include a concise description of the country and useful facts, such as the currency and public holidays.

Another useful book for travellers is *Bank and Public Holidays throughout the World*, published annually by Morgan Guaranty Trust Company.

PEOPLE

The following books provide a variety of information about prominent people:

Debrett's Peerage and Titles of Courtesy
Who's Who
Who Was Who (prominent people who have died)
International Who's Who
Who's Who in America
Directory of Directors
Crockford's Clerical Directory
Medical Directory
Dentists' Register
Register of Nurses
Law List
Army List (*Air Force and Navy Lists*)

SPECIALISED REFERENCE BOOKS

In addition to the books we have already mentioned, there are many specialised reference books. The titles of the books indicate the types of offices in which they would be used:

Stock Exchange Year Book
Bankers' Almanack and Year Book
Insurance Blue Book
Municipal Year Book
Annual Abstract of Statistics
Hansard (official report of proceedings in Parliament)
Black's Medical Dictionary
Chambers's Technical Dictionary
Dictionary of Legal Terms

Facts and How to Find Them, by W. Bagley, is another book which lists sources of reference and information.

EXERCISES

1. Explain the meaning of the following words and phrases:
   (a) English usage,
   (b) synonyms,
   (c) antonyms,
   (d) derivation,
   (e) the peerage,
   (f) proverbs,
   (g) similes,
   (h) visas,
   (i) meteorological records.

2. Refer to the *ABC Railway Guide* for the following information:
   (a) the first-class return fare to Manchester,
   (b) the county in which Skipton is situated,
   (c) the population of Canterbury,
   (d) early-closing day in Guildford,
   (e) a train which arrives at Birmingham at approx. 13.00,
   (f) the arrival station in Birmingham of the train,
   (g) the departure station in London of the train,
   (h) sleeping car services from London to Penzance,
   (i) a hotel in Hull near the railway station,
   (j) the daily departure times from Dover of the Ostend ferry.

3. Refer to one of the books on English usage, or a dictionary, for the following information:
   (a) the difference between 'stationary' and 'stationery',
   (b) if 'grey' may also be spelt 'gray',
   (c) the plural of 'wharf',
   (d) an example of a sobriquet,
   (e) an example of a genteelism,
   (f) the pronunciation and meaning of 'diphthong',
   (g) a word designated as colloquial in the dictionary,
   (h) the meaning of the prefix 'super'.

4. Refer to *The Students' Companion* and find the following information:
   (*a*) the number of Lords Spiritual who may sit in the House of Lords,
   (*b*) one word for 'an expert at story telling',
   (*c*) one word for 'an instrument for detecting earthquakes',
   (*d*) complete the proverb 'To err is human; to ....',
   (*e*) the meaning of M.R.C.P.,
   (*f*) the name for a native of Sri Lanka (Ceylon).

5. Refer to *Hotels and Restaurants in Britain* and find the following information:
   (*a*) ancient buildings in Norwich of interest to a visitor,
   (*b*) the distance by road from Kendal to Penrith,
   (*c*) when the Tower of London was built, when it may be visited and the admission fee,
   (*d*) the facilities available at the Victoria Hotel, Sidmouth,
   (*e*) the cost for a single room and breakfast at the Royal Hotel, Crewe,
   (*f*) the most direct route by road from Reading to Sheffield,
   (*g*) the situation of the Courtauld Institute Galleries, and the pictures on view,
   (*h*) the address of the Tourist Information Centre in London.

6. Refer to *The Typist's Desk Book* for the following information:
   (*a*) if 'dining room' should be hyphenated,
   (*b*) the past tense of 'occur',
   (*c*) the pronunciation of 'Cholmondeley',
   (*d*) the meaning of (printers' correction sign) #,
   (*e*) the salutation (first words) of a letter to a Duchess,
   (*f*) display of an Agenda,
   (*g*) how a diaeresis should be typed.

7. Refer to *The Shorthand Typist's Pocket Book* for the following information:
   (*a*) the various kinds of cheques,
   (*b*) when a cheque is out-of-date,
   (*c*) passport regulations,
   (*d*) what is meant by a quorum,

(*e*) when numbers should be expressed in words,

(*f*) the meaning of B.S.T.

8. Refer to *The Automobile Association Members' Handbook* for the following information:

(*a*) the purpose of A.A. roadside telephone boxes,

(*b*) car ferry services to the Isle of Wight,

(*c*) the distance by road from Edinburgh to Manchester,

(*d*) early closing day in Ventnor, I.O.W.,

(*e*) the telephone number of the Crown Hotel, Ringwood,

(*f*) weekly terms at the Palm Court Hotel, Torquay.

9. Refer to *The Statesman's Year-Book* and find the following information:

(*a*) the name of the British Ambassador in Austria,

(*b*) the national flag of Norway,

(*c*) the headquarters and director of UNICEF,

(*d*) the member countries of NATO,

(*e*) the functions of the World Health Organisation,

(*f*) the wheat production in U.S.S.R. in 1959–60.

10. Refer to *Whitaker's Almanack* and find the following information:

(*a*) opening times of the Science Museum,

(*b*) the Secretary of the Table Tennis Association,

(*c*) the name of the Cultural Attaché at the French Embassy in London,

(*d*) the name of the Lord Mayor of Sheffield,

(*e*) situation of Dickens' House, opening times and admission fee,

(*f*) the Chairman of the British Travel and Holidays Association.

11. Refer to a shorthand-typewriting reference book for the following information:

(*a*) examples of tail pieces,

(*b*) methods of typing leader dots,

(*c*) the Dvorak keyboard,

(*d*) where the word 'Personal' should be typed on an envelope,

(*e*) the layout for typing a radio script,

(*f*) examples of longhand abbreviations,

(*g*) hints on deciphering manuscript,

(*h*) the meaning of the term 'dead key',

(*i*) superior characters,

(*j*) the meaning of c.i.f.

12. Refer to *Kelly's Post Office London Directory* and find the following information:

    (*a*) the name of the Press Secretary to the Queen,

    (*b*) the name of the Secretary of State for Employment,

    (*c*) the name of the Brazilian Ambassador in London,

    (*d*) whether there is a British Consul in Casablanca,

    (*e*) the nearest Underground Station to 34 Oxford Street,

    (*f*) the situation of Ovington Square.

13. In which books of reference would you look for the following information?

    (*a*) Details of the family history of a Duke;

    (*b*) The cost of sending a letter by Air Mail to India;

    (*c*) The address of a bishop;

    (*d*) The name of a 'Three Star' Hotel in Canterbury;

    (*e*) A list of the Shipping Agents in Liverpool together with their telephone numbers.

14. Name five reference books which you would expect to find in any office and briefly outline the uses of any two of them.

(RSA, OP, I)

British industry and commerce are in the process of adopting the metric system. The target date is 1975 but the process of change will be a gradual one, not a total changeover on a certain day like the adoption of decimal currency.

The Metrication Board is responsible for making the metric system of units widely known. The responsibility for authorising the units to be used in the United Kingdom rests with the Department of Trade and Industry advised by the Advisory Committee on Legal Units of Measurement. The British Standards Institution is responsible for defining the application and use of metric units in industry.

The metric system was founded during the French Revolution and gained rapid acceptance in Europe during the nineteenth century; it has now been adopted for general use by most countries, the notable exceptions being the United Kingdom, some Commonwealth countries and the United States of America.

The Metre Convention, an international treaty signed by seventeen countries including the USA in 1875 and by the UK in 1884, established and defined the values of units to be used. The Convention set up a number of permanent bodies of which the CGPM (Conférence Général des Poids et Mesures—General Conference of Weights and Measures) is the most important. Its members are appointed by the governments of the participating countries. The Department of Trade and Industry is responsible for United Kingdom representation on CGPM.

Two other international organisations are concerned with metric units, the International Organisation of Legal Metrology and the International Organisation for Standardisation (ISO—Internationale Système Organisation).

The work of these bodies has culminated in the establishment of the International System of Units (Système International d'Unités), known by the abbreviation SI in most languages, and formally adopted in 1960.

ISO is responsible for the development of international industrial and commercial standards in almost every field of technology. It is supported by 55 nations including the United Kingdom and the United States of America. The members of ISO are the national standards organisations. Their main task is to work out technical agreements which are published as ISO Recommendations. The United Kingdom member of ISO is the British Standards Institution.

353

THE INTERNATIONAL SYSTEM OF UNITS

The International System (SI) is built up from three kinds of units: base units; derived units; and supplementary units.

A. Base Units

There are at present six base units:

Physical Quantity	Unit	Symbol
length	metre	m
mass	kilogramme	kg
time	second	s
electric current	ampere	A
thermodynamic temperature	kelvin	K
luminous intensity	candela	cd

A seventh base unit, the mole (symbol: mol), for amount of substance, has been recommended by the International Committee on Weights and Measures for adoption at the next CGPM General Conference in October 1971.

B. Derived Units

These units, used for measuring other physical quantities, are derived from the base units by multiplication or division, without the introduction of numerical factors other than unity. Some examples are:

Physical Quantity	Derived Unit	Symbol
area	square metre	m²
volume	cubic metre	m³
speed	metre per second	m/s
acceleration	metre per second squared	m/s²
density	kilogramme per cubic metre	kg/m³

Committee on Weights and Measures, but they have not yet been adopted by CGPM. Another unit for pressure, the bar (10^5 N/m²) is used in some countries, including the United Kingdom. The millibar is used generally for the measurement of atmospheric pressure.

C. Supplementary Units

There are in addition to the base units and the derived units two supplementary units.

Physical Quantity	Unit	Symbol
plane angle	radian	rad
solid angle	steradian	sr

D. Prefixes

An essential feature of SI is the systematic use of prefixes to designate decimal multiples and decimal fractions of the base units and the derived units. The most commonly used of these SI prefixes are:

Prefix	Factor	Symbol
mega	One million times (10^6)	M
kilo	One thousand times (10^3)	k
hecto	One hundred times (10^2)	h
deca	Ten times (10)	da
deci	One tenth of (10^{-1})	d
centi	One hundredth of (10^{-2})	c
milli	One thousandth of (10^{-3})	m
micro	One millionth of (10^{-6})	µ

Some units so formed have long-established special names, such as:

Physical Quantity	Special Name	Definition	Symbol
length	micron	10^{-6} m	µm
area	hectare	hm²=10^4 m²	ha
volume	litre	dm³=10^{-3} m³	l
mass	tonne	Mg=10^3 kg	t
pressure	millibar	10^2 N/m²	mbar

Some of the derived units have special names and symbols, for example:

Physical Quantity	Derived Unit	Definition	Symbol
force	newton	kg m/s²	N
work, energy, quantity of heat	joule	N m=kg m²/s²	J
power	watt	J/s=kg m²/s³	W
electric potential, potential difference, tension, electromotive force	volt	W/A=kg m²/s³ A	V
electric charge	coulomb	A s	C
electric capacitance	farad	A s/V=A² s⁴/kg m²	F
electric resistance	ohm	V/A=kg m²/s³ A²	Ω
frequency	hertz	1/s	Hz

For pressure and stress, the derived unit is the newton per square metre. The special name, pascal, and symbol Pa (N/m²=kg/m s²), have been recommended for the derived unit of pressure and stress by the International

The litre is at present defined in the United Kingdom law on the basis of the 1901 CGPM definition and is therefore strictly equivalent to 1·000028 dm³. The need to amend the present definition to accord with SI is under consideration.

E. Some Non-SI Units

Some units, not belonging to the International System, are well established internationally and will remain in use along with SI units. Among these are:

Physical Quantity	Unit	Symbol
plane angle	degree	°
time	minute	min
	hour	h
	day	d
	month	–
	year	–
length	international nautical mile (1 852 m)	n mile
speed	kilometre per hour	km/h
	knot (international nautical mile per hour)	kn
energy	kilowatt hour	kW h
temperature	degree Celsius	°C

SOME EVERYDAY UNITS

The units which have been chosen for everyday use include a few which are not strictly part of SI but which are nevertheless established internationally. The following table sets out some everyday units and relates them to SI base units.

Physical Quantity	SI Base Units	Everyday Unit	Symbol	Definition
length	metre	milli-metre	mm	one thousandth of a metre (10^{-3} m)
		centi-metre	cm	one hundredth of a metre (10^{-2} m)
		metre	m	
		kilo-metre	km	one thousand metres (10^3 m)
		inter-national nautical mile	n mile	1 852 metres
area		square metre	m²	
		hectare	ha	ten thousand square metres (10^4 m²)
volume and capacity*		cubic centimetre	cm³	one millionth of a cubic metre (10^{-6} m³)
		cubic metre	m³	
		milli-litre	ml	one millionth of a cubic metre or one thousandth of a litre (10^{-6} m³ or cm³)

Physical Quantity	SI Base Units	Everyday Unit	Symbol	Definition
electric current	ampere	ampere	A	
power	kilo-gramme metre second	watt	W	kg m²/s³
		kilowatt	kW	one thousand watts (10^3 W)
energy‡		kilowatt hour	kW h	
		megajoule	MJ	one million joules (10^6 J)
electric potential difference	kilo-gramme metre second ampere	volt	V	W/A
electric resistance		ohm	Ω	V/A
frequency	second	hertz	Hz	1/s
temperature	kelvin	degree Celsius§	°C	°C=K

Quantity	SI unit	Unit	Symbol	
		litre	l	one thousandth of a cubic metre (10⁻³ m³) or 1 cubic decimetre (dm³)
weight†	kilo-gramme	gramme	g	one thousandth of a kilogramme (10⁻³ kg)
		kilo-gramme	kg	
		tonne	tonne	one thousand kilogrammes (10³ kg or Mg)
time	second	second	s	
		minute	min	
		hour	h	
		day	d	
		month	—	
		year	—	
speed	metre second	metre per second	m/s	
		kilometre per hour	km/h	
		International knot	kn	International nautical mile per hour or 1 852 metres in 3 600 seconds or 0·514444 m/s

Notes to Table

*Although the cubic centimetre and the millilitre are identical and interchangeable, it is common practice to use the cubic centimetre and the cubic metre for measuring the volume of solids, but the millilitre and the litre for measuring the volume of liquids and the capacity of containers for liquids. The accepted abbreviation for litre is 'l' which can be confused in typescript with the figure 'one'. It may therefore be advisable not to abbreviate 'litre'.

†Strictly the gramme, kilogramme and tonne are units of mass. For most people and for ordinary trading purposes the word weight has the same meaning as mass. The SI symbol for 'tonne' is 't' but, to avoid confusion with the commonly used abbreviation 't' for the imperial ton, it is advisable for the present not to abbreviate 'tonne'.

‡ The strict SI unit of energy is the joule (J=kg m²/s²). The kilowatt hour is equal to 3·6 MJ. The joule is already used extensively in scientific work and will be increasingly used in technology. The joule will become an everyday unit when, as already recommended, it becomes established in dietetics in place of the calorie (4·1868 J).

§ The degree Celsius is a unit of temperature interval identical with the kelvin. When a temperature is expressed as so many degrees Celsius the corresponding thermodynamic temperature is obtained by adding 273·15 kelvins. Thus a statement that water freezes at 0°C means that water freezes at 273·15 K. The degree Celsius is at present known in Britain as the degree Centigrade. The term 'Centigrade' is, however, used in some other countries to denote fractions of a right angle, and, to avoid confusion, it has been agreed internationally that, for the measurement of temperature, the name 'degree Centigrade' shall be replaced by 'degree Celsius'.

Notes

1. In many countries the comma (,) is employed where in the UK a decimal ('full') point is used, either on the line or slightly above it. In the UK a comma is often used to separate the digits of large numbers into groups of three, e.g. 1,456,789. To avoid confusion in international documents the digits of large numbers are often separated by small gaps into groups of three starting from the decimal point, e.g. 1 456 789. Greater detail can be found in BS 1957:1953, 'The presentation of numerical values'.

2. The spellings of the units of length (*metre*) and mass (*kilogramme*) have been adopted in the UK as they are the same as those used by the CGPM. In North America the spellings are *meter* and *kilogram*.

3. One advantage of SI is that it is simple and consistent. The names of multiples and submultiples of the base units are formed by the use of prefixes which have the same form and meaning irrespective of the unit to which they are applied, e.g.

$$1 \text{ kilometre (km)} = 1000 \text{ metres}$$
$$1 \text{ millimetre (mm)} = 0{\cdot}001 \text{ metre}$$

Here are the names of the prefixes with some examples:

Prefix	Symbol		Factor by which the unit is multiplied	Example
tera	T	10^{12} =	1 000 000 000 000	
giga	G	10^{9} =	1 000 000 000	gigahertz (GHz)
mega	M	10^{6} =	1 000 000	megawatt (MW)
kilo	k	10^{3} =	1 000	kilometre (km)
hecto	h	10^{2} =	100	
deca	da	10^{1} =	10	
deci	d	10^{-1} =	0·1	
centi	c	10^{-2} =	0·01	
milli	m	10^{-3} =	0·001	milligramme (mg)
micro	μ	10^{-6} =	0·000 001	microsecond (μs)
nano	n	10^{-9} =	0·000 000 001	nanometre (nm)
pico	p	10^{-12} =	0·000 000 000 001	picofarad (pF)
femto	f	10^{-15} =	0·000 000 000 000 001	
atto	a	10^{-18} =	0·000 000 000 000 000 001	

4. Rules for writing and typing in SI are being produced by leading national organisations.* We are at present in a period of

* *Handbook for the Typing Services, 2—Metrication for Typists*, Central Electricity Generating Board, 1971.
Writing and Typing Metric Units, The Gas Council, 1971.
Advantages of the Metric System, HMSO.

transition but there would appear to be general agreement on the following recommendations:

(a) As the comma is used in some countries as a decimal point, commas should not be used to mark thousands.

(b) Numbers up to four figures can be blocked, e.g.

| 1752 | 0·1752 | 10·1752 |

(c) Numbers of five figures or more may be blocked in threes, e.g.

| 123 456·0 | 0·123 456 |

(d) The decimal point may be central when handwritten or when a typewriter has a central point key, but otherwise will be typed on the line, using a full stop, e.g.

| 12·34 | 12.34 |

(e) No full stops are put after the symbols except at the end of a sentence, and none between them, e.g.

mm *not* mm. *and not* m.m.

(f) Symbols are the same in the singular as in the plural except for *tonne* and *litre* which become *tonnes* and *litres*.

(g) For quantities less than one, always place a zero in front of the decimal point, e.g.

| 0·123 | 0·0123 |

METRICATION IN BUSINESS EQUIPMENT*

1. In a number of manufacturing areas whilst it will not be difficult to adopt metric terminology (i.e. to quote sizes, weights, etc., in metric units) it will not be possible for some years to redesign products on a metric basis (that is, to manufacture designs based on metric units as opposed to simply quoting the equivalent metric units for imperial based designs).

2. Data Processing Equipment: The most common media on to which data is encoded for processing are paper tape, magnetic tape and punched cards. These will not be changed by metrication; they have internationally inch-based dimensions.

3. Continuous Stationery for computer print-out is inch-based and will remain so, i.e. 8 in and 12 in form depths and 0·5 in sprocket spacing. Continuous stationery printers will continue to use 10 characters and 6 lines to the inch.

4. Computer print-out: There has recently been international agreement that character sets for optical character recognition

* *Metrication in Business Equipment*, a beta 'Guide to Users' publication. Business Equipment Trade Association.

(OCR) and magnetic ink character recognition (MICR) will be standardised at 10 characters to the inch.

5. Most British reprographic machines (spirit, stencil and offset-litho duplicators) are capable of using paper sizes up to 14 in × 9 in. They can, therefore, accommodate A4 without adjustment.

6. Printing: There is no international standardisation for typographic measurement. The ISO A paper sizes offer little choice for paper sizes for booklets, etc. and present feeling is that the British Standards Institute will recommend the retention of some crown sizes together with A4 and A5. (Further information—various booklets on metrication and the printing industry have been produced by the British Federation of Master Printers.)

7. Typewriters: The standard carriage width of 11 in easily accommodates A4. Longer carriage machines, 18 in wide and over, will be suitable for papers up to A3 lengthways (16·54 in). The use of six lines to the inch for vertical spacing and 10 or 12 characters to the inch horizontally (see BS 2481) has been internationally accepted for all office machines and computer print-out.

8. Paper substance: Paper weight (formerly called 'substance' now to be called 'grammage') will be measured in grammes per square metre (g/m^2) instead of pounds per ream.

9. Paper and envelope sizes are listed in Chapter 3 (a) Typewriters.

10. Filing equipment, cabinets, folders, files and record cards: the majority of filing cabinets and folders, etc., are foolscap and can therefore accommodate the A4 sizes without difficulty.

APPENDIX II

BRITISH COUNTIES AND THEIR COUNTY TOWNS

	County	*Administrative Headquarters*
ENGLAND	Avon	Bristol
	Bedford	Bedford
	Berkshire	Reading
	Buckinghamshire	Aylesbury
	Cambridgeshire	Cambridge
	Cheshire	Chester
	Cleveland	Middlesborough
	Cornwall	Truro
	Cumbria	Carlisle
	Derbyshire	Matlock
	Devonshire	Exeter
	Dorset	Dorchester
	Durham	Durham
	Essex	Chelmsford
	Gloucester	Gloucester
	Greater Manchester	Manchester
	Hampshire	Winchester
	Hereford and Worcester	Worcester
	Hertford	Hertford
	Humberside	Kingston-upon-Hull
	Kent	Maidstone
	Lancashire	Preston
	Leicestershire	Leicester
	Lincoln	Lincoln
	Greater London	County Hall, SE1
	Merseyside	Liverpool
	Norfolk	Norwich
	Northampton	Northampton
	Northumberland	Newcastle-upon-Tyne
	Nottinghamshire	Nottingham
	Oxfordshire	Oxford
	Salop	Shrewsbury
	Somerset	Taunton
	Staffordshire	Stafford
	Suffolk	Ipswich
	Surrey	Kingston-upon-Thames
	Sussex, East	Lewes
	Sussex, West	Chichester

	County	*Administrative Headquarters*
ENGLAND—cont.	Tyne and Wear	Newcastle-upon-Tyne
	Warwick	Warwick
	West Midlands	Birmingham
	Wight, Isle of	Newport
	Wiltshire	Trowbridge
	Yorkshire, North	Northallerton
	Yorkshire, South	Barnsley
	Yorkshire, West	Wakefield
WALES	Clwyd	Mold
	Dyfed	Carmarthen
	Gwent	Gwent
	Gwynedd	Caernarvon
	Mid Glamorgan	Cardiff
	Powys	Llandrindod Wells
	South Glamorgan	Cardiff
	West Glamorgan	Swansea
SCOTLAND	Aberdeen	Aberdeen
	Angus	Forfar
	Argyll	Lochgilphead
	Ayr	Ayr
	Banff	Banff
	Berwick	Duns
	Bute	Rothesay
	Caithness	Wick
	Clackmannanshire	Alloa
	Dumfries	Dumfries
	Dunbarton	Dumbarton
	East Lothian	Haddington
	Fife	Cupar
	Inverness	Inverness
	Kincardine	Stonehaven

362

	County	*Administrative Headquarters*
SCOTLAND—cont.	Kinross	Kinross
	Kirkcudbright	Kirkcudbright
	Lanark	Hamilton
	Midlothian	Edinburgh
	Moray	Elgin
	Nairn	Nairn
	Orkney	Kirkwall
	Peebles	Peebles
	Perth	Perth
	Renfrew	Paisley
	Ross and Cromarty	Dingwall
	Roxburgh	Newton St. Boswells
	Selkirk	Selkirk
	Stirling	Stirling
	Sutherland	Golspie
	West Lothian	Linlithgow
	Wigtown	Stranraer
	Zetland	Lerwick
NORTHERN IRELAND	Antrim	Belfast
	Armagh	Armagh
	Down	Downpatrick
	Fermanagh	Enniskillen
	Londonderry	Londonderry
	Tyrone	Omagh

PRINCIPAL COUNTRIES OF THE WORLD— THEIR CAPITALS AND CURRENCY

Country	Capital	Currency
Albania	Tirana	Lek
Australia	Canberra	Dollar
Austria	Vienna	Schilling
Belgium	Brussels	Franc
Brazil	Brasilia	Cruzeiro
Bulgaria	Sofia	Leva
Canada	Ottawa	Dollar
China	Peking	Yuan
Cuba	Havana	Peso
Czechoslovakia	Prague	Koruna
Denmark	Copenhagen	Krone
Egypt	Cairo	Pound
Finland	Helsinki	Markka
France	Paris	Franc
Germany	Bonn	D/Mark
Ghana	Accra	Cedi
Greece	Athens	Drachma
Hungary	Budapest	Florint
India	Delhi	Rupee
Italy	Rome	Lira
Jamaica	Trinidad	Pound
Japan	Tokyo	Yen
Jordan	Amman	Dinar
Kuwait	Abadan	Dinar
Lebanon	Beirut	Pound (Livre)
Netherlands	The Hague	Guilder
New Zealand	Wellington	Dollar
Nigeria	Lagos	Naira
Norway	Oslo	Kroner
Poland	Warsaw	Zloty
Portugal	Lisbon	Escudos
Rumania	Bucharest	Leu
Sierra Leone	Freetown	Leone
Spain	Madrid	Peseta
Sweden	Stockholm	Kronor
Switzerland	Bern	Franc
U.S.A.	Washington	Dollar
U.S.S.R.	Moscow	Rouble
Yugoslavia	Belgrade	Dinar

OFFICE PRACTICE AND SECRETARIAL DUTIES
TUESDAY, 17th JUNE, 1975—9.15 a.m. to 11.15 a.m.

Examiner: C. R. IBBERSON, ESQ., M.Inst.A.M., M.Inst.M.
A.M.B.I.M.

INSTRUCTIONS TO CANDIDATES

Answer **any five** *questions. All questions carry equal marks.*

1. Describe FOUR methods of classifying filing, giving an example of the typical use of each method.

2. Write a few sentences to describe each of the following bank services:—

(a) Cash dispensers
(b) Travellers Cheques
(c) Bank Giro
(d) Bridging loan
(e) Current account

3. There have been a number of complaints recently about letters to your company which have apparently gone astray. Set out in detail a plan to ensure that the post is handled correctly and safely from the time of its delivery first thing in the morning until it reaches the correct destination, paying particular attention to the letters containing remittances or samples.

4. A part of your duties is the control and analysis of the use of petty cash. Using the following information which has been obtained from the completed petty cash vouchers, draw up an imprest petty cash book and calculate the imprest required at 1st June 1975.

Date	Details	Amount
MAY		£ p
1st	Typing paper	0·33
2nd	Office cleaning	0·50
4th	Postage stamps	1·92
8th	Travelling expenses	0·20
8th	Ball of string	0·12
15th	Bus fares	0·10
18th	Typewriter ribbon	0·65
19th	Office cleaning	0·50
24th	Postage on parcel	1·75
24th	Pencils	0·24
24th	Travelling expenses	0·20
27th	Tea and sugar	0·90
29th	Window cleaning	1·15

The balance c/d on 30th April 1975 was £0·94 and the cash received on the 1st May was £9·06.

5. *(a)* Write descriptive notes on the different types of addressing machine which may be used in an office.

   (b) List four uses of addressing machines other than the addressing of envelopes.

6. It has been the practice in your office for all duplicating to be taken to a local firm operating a duplicating service. The charges for this work are quite high and your firm must provide the paper and a master copy ready for use.

Your office manager decides to investigate the possibility of buying some type of duplicating machine for your office use and asks you to recommend which type that should be.

What points would you consider prior to making your recommendations?

7. The management of your company are proposing to introduce a system of flexible working hours for office staff. What is the purpose of such a system and how would you expect it to operate?

8. There are five Directors in your company, each with his own Private Secretary. In an effort to make more effective use of time, it has been suggested that a dictating system be installed for the use of the five Directors.

The two systems which have been suggested are:—

(a) A multi-bank system or

(b) A tandem system

Explain the differences between the two systems and say which system you feel would be more suitable under the circumstances, giving reasons for your decision.

9. Each year far too many people are injured at work in accidents which might have been avoided had reasonable care been taken. What, in your opinion, are the main causes of accidents in the office and what recommendations would you make to improve office safety?

EAST MIDLAND REGIONAL EXAMINATIONS BOARD 44

Certificate of Secondary Education

1975

OFFICE PRACTICE

WEDNESDAY, 23rd APRIL, 1975—A.M.   2 Hours

Candidates will be allowed 10 minutes to read through the paper before the commencement of the examination

A	
B	
2	
Total	

PART I

SECTION A

Answer ALL questions in this section

1. Write out in full the following abbreviations:

   (a) P.T.O. ....

   (b) i.e. ....

   (c) Bros ....

   (d) a/c ....

2. (a) A master sheet has to be prepared when using a .... duplicator.

   (b) When only a few copies of a typed document are required, ... may be used.

3. (a) Envelopes which have transparent panels on the front are called .... envelopes.

   (b) The charge for a telegram is calculated on the number of ....

4. (a) If you wish to make sure documents arrive safely through the post, you would use the ....

      .... service.

   (b) A .... is completed in order to assist the tracing of a postal order if it is lost.

5. (a) In order to obtain a bank overdraft a person must have a .... account.

   (b) A bank account which allows two persons to use it is known as a .... account.

1

[P.T.O.

SECTION B

Answer TEN questions ONLY from this section.

1. Name **two** ways in which the prevention of fraud is assisted by the use of cheque protection and signing machines:

(a) ....

(b) ....

2. (a) The petty cash system, whereby after some expenditure has been made the original balance is restored from time to time, is called the .... system.

(b) Receipts for payments by petty cash are given on ....

3. Name two basic filing methods:

(a) ....

(b) ....

4. Name two uses for a pro-forma invoice:

(a) ....

(b) ....

5. (a) A .... is used when a file may be placed under more than one heading.

(b) When using numerical filing, a .... must be consulted to locate a required file.

6. (a) Name the telephone service used to obtain a telephone number unknown to you. ....

....

(b) Name the Post Office service used to send an envelope containing bank notes ....

....

7. (a) What words are written on an envelope addressed c/o a Head Post Office to indicate that the addressee is going to call for it? ....

(b) Name the Post Office service which enables payments to be made by Standing Order. ....

....

8. (a) In order to convert a crossed cheque into an open cheque it is necessary to write in the crossing the following words ....

(b) A cheque on which the drawer inserts a date some time in the future is called ....

2

368

9. (a) Name one item of equipment which can be used in dealing with incoming mail. ....

(b) Name one item of equipment which can be used in dealing with outgoing mail. ....

10. (a) To find out the fullest information about a Member of Parliament you would consult..

....

(b) To find out the times of trains and fares from Nottingham to London you would consult ....

....

11. Name two members of staff likely to be working in the Accounts Department of a business firm:

(a) ....

(b) ....

12. Give abbreviations for the following:

(a) Cash on delivery..

(b) Carried forward..

13. State two situations as a result of which a credit note would be sent:

(a) ....

(b) ....

14. (a) What inducement is offered by a seller to a buyer to encourage him to pay promptly?..................................

....

(b) What is the name of the discount allowed by a wholesaler to a retailer which can be varied to avoid frequent reprinting of catalogues?..

15. Name two conditions under which the Post Office will allow franking machines to be used:

(a) ....

(b) ....

[P.T.O.

PART II

Answer **FOUR** questions **ONLY** from this part

1. Explain what you would do (*a*) to keep your typewriter in good order and (*b*) to keep the duplicating room and duplicator clean, tidy and in good order.

2. Your employer has asked you to set out the main features to be taken into account when setting up a new filing system. Give the main points to which you would draw his attention.

3. State ten of the main features of the Post Office Giro Service.

4. In connection with the telephone service explain the following:

(*a*) Transferred Charge Call Service.

(*b*) Telephone Credit Card.

(*c*) Fixed time call.

(*d*) An A.D.C. call.

5. After the morning post has been opened, the following items are brought to you for attention. State what action you would take in each case:

(*a*) A remittance advice note stating that a cheque for £65 is enclosed, but it is for £56 only.

(*b*) A registered envelope containing bank notes issued by Banks in Scotland.

(*c*) A Post Office Giro transfer form for £50 from a customer in settlement of an account.

(*d*) A new copy of the Post Office Guide.

(*e*) Three Coding Notices from H.M. Inspector of Taxes relating to new members of staff.

6. Name and describe five methods of paying through the post.

7. Select five general reference books, excluding telephone directories, for use in an office. Give reasons for your choice.

8. List and describe five documents which may be used in connection with a transaction involving the buying and selling of goods.

4

OFFICE PRACTICE

Monday, 19th May, 1975

2.00 — 4.15 pm

Working time	**2.00 — 4.00 pm**
Extra time if required	**4.00 — 4.15 pm**

Candidates are advised to spend 30 minutes in answering all the questions in Part 1 and 90 minutes in answering five questions from Part 2.

PART 1

Attempt ALL the questions in this part.
Write each answer in the space provided after each question.

1. What kind of typewriter is normally used:
   (*a*) at home ....
   (*b*) in an office ....
   (*c*) in an office where different type sizes are required in the preparation of material? ....

2. Name TWO ways in which an airletter form differs from an airmail letter.
   (*a*) ....
   (*b*) ....

3. Name the two International sizes of paper most widely used in business offices.
   (*a*) ....
   (*b*) ....

4. (*a*) A telephone call to another number on the same exchange is known as a
   ....
   (*b*) A telephone call to a number on another exchange is known as a
   ....

5. Write a sentence to explain the use of the following:
   (*a*) "Personal" (or person to person) telephone call
   ....
   ....
   (*b*) Transferred Charge or Reversed Charge Call
   ....
   ....

371

6. Name the documents which would be used in the following circumstances:

(*a*) To record acknowledgement by the seller of faulty goods returned to him.

....

(*b*) To record the sale of goods.

....

(*c*) To let a customer know that goods have been sent to him.

....

7. The discount which is deducted from the catalogue price of goods in transaction between wholesaler and retailer is known as

....

8. The discount which encourages the retailer to make prompt payment for goods delivered is known as

....

9. Name TWO types of entry which a Secretary may make in the Office Diary.

(*a*) ....

(*b*) ....

10. Give the meaning of the following abbreviations:

(*a*) E. & O.E. ....

(*b*) H.M.S.O. ....

(*c*) R/D ....

(*d*) V.A.T. ....

11. Name the process whereby a large document can be recorded and the record stored in a very small space.

....

12. Name the system of filing where files are arranged according to the name of the firm.

....

13. State what is necessary in the Numerical system of filing to enable the filing clerk to find the number of a customer's file.

....

14. How would you correct a mistake on a spirit stencil?

....

15. Name TWO types of account which may be opened at any one of the Clearing Banks.

(*a*) ....

(*b*) ....

16. How is money withdrawn from a current account?

....

17. Give the name of the document sent regularly by banks to show a customer the current state of his account.

....

18. If it is essential to have proof that the item has been posted and received, name the Post Office service which would be used:

(*a*) when sending a packet containing important documents

....

(*b*) when sending a parcel which contains a valuable article.

....

19. What is the name of the department which deals with the following:

(*a*) welfare ....

(*b*) invoicing ....

(*c*) ordering of goods ....

(*d*) handling of money? ....

20. How many sheets of paper are there in:

(*a*) a quire ....

(*b*) a ream? ....

21. Name the document which is issued by a secretary to give notice of a meeting and the programme for the meeting.

....

22. What is the name of the record of the meeting which will be prepared by the secretary?

....

Acknowledgements

We wish to thank the following for permission to reproduce copyright photographs

Adrema Ltd (124)
Ansafone Ltd (191, 193)
Barclays Bank Ltd (229)
Better Typing Attachments Ltd (70)
Block & Anderson (92, 124 top)
British Rail (14)
British Stationery & Office Equip Assoc (77, 78, 79, 84, 290)
C W Cave & Co Ltd (302)
Controller of Her Majesty's Stationery Office (315, 316, 354, 355)
Copyholders Ltd (68)
Data Efficiency Ltd (292)
Dexion Group of Companies (16)
Friden (60, 61)
Gestetner (88, 90, 97, 101)
Hermes (53, 58)
ICL (113 top, 114, 117)
IBM (62, 63, 65, 113 bottom)
Inland Revenue (319)

Kodak Ltd (284, 286)
Kores Manufacturing Co Ltd (158)
3M (289)
Midland Bank Ltd (255)
Nashua Copycat (135)
NCR Co Ltd (108, 111)
Noeline Kelly (75, 290)
Palantype Organisation (122)
Philips (30, 121)
Pitney-Bowes Ltd (106 top)
Post Office (17, 178, 180, 181, 187, 196, 197)
Rank Xerox Ltd (94–96, 194)
Rex-Rotary (89, 103)
Roneo Ltd (104)
Royal Automobile Club (245)
Southern Communications Ltd (120 top)
Twinlock Ltd (168)
Typit (71)
Ultronic Data Systems Ltd (64)

We also wish to thank Caribonum Ltd, Better Typing Attachments Ltd, Lamson Industries Ltd, Wiggins Teape Ltd, 3M, Rank Xerox Ltd, Roneo Ltd, The Palantype Organisation, the Bank of Education, and the National Westminster, Barclays, Lloyds, and the Midland banks for their help and advice.

We are indebted to the Royal Society of Arts for their permission to use questions from recent examination papers and to the London Chamber of Commerce, and the East & West Midlands examining bodies for permission to reproduce past examination papers.

Index

376